ADV

FOGLE is the author of three books and has presented numerous television programmes, including the BBC's *Animal Park*, *Countryfile* and *Extreme Dreams*. Ben's sporting achievements include completing the gruelling 160-mile 'Marathon des Sables' through the Sahara desert, and rowing across the Atlantic with double Olympic Gold medallist **JAMES CRACKNELL**, OBE. Since completing the Atlantic race, James has continued to write regular features for the *Daily Telegraph* and completed an epic 1,400-mile triathlon for charity, rowing from Dover to France, cycling from there to Tarifa in Spain and finally swimming the Straits of Gibraltar to Morocco. James is also a director of Threshold Sports, a successful sports consultancy and events company.

RACE TO THE POLE

JAMES CRACKNELL
AND BEN FOGLE

PAN BOOKS

First published 2009 by Macmillan

First published in paperback 2010 by Pan Books
an imprint of Pan Macmillan, a division of Macmillan Publishers Limited
Pan Macmillan, 20 New Wharf Road, London N1 9RR
Basingstoke and Oxford
Associated companies throughout the world
www.panmacmillan.com

ISBN 978-0-330-51290-9

Visit www.panmacmillan.com to read more about all our books
and to buy them. You will also find features, author interviews and
news of any author events, and you can sign up for e-newsletters
so that you're always first to hear about our new releases.

BEN

To my wife Marina, for everything we've been through

JAMES

To families that support each other's dreams,
and especially my own family: Bev, Croyde and Kiki,
I love you all so much

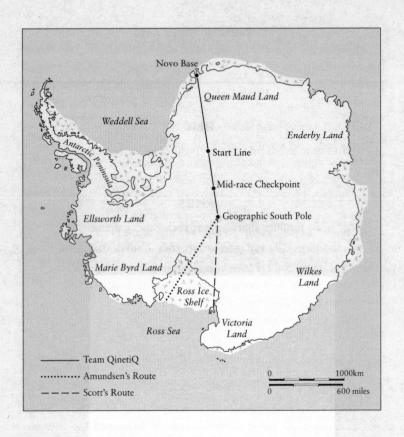

Novo Base

Queen Maud Land

Weddell Sea

Enderby Land

Antarctic Peninsula

Start Line

Mid-race Checkpoint

Ellsworth Land

Geographic South Pole

Marie Byrd Land

Wilkes
Land

Ross Ice
Shelf

Victoria
Land

Ross Sea

—————— Team QinetiQ

··············· Amundsen's Route

— — — — Scott's Route

0   1000km

0   600 miles

PROLOGUE

BEN A fierce wind scoured our faces, and ice snapped at our heels. The inside of my nose had frozen and icicles were beginning to form on my eyelashes. The cold cut through to the core, and my bones ached from the chill.

On we trudged. I'd long lost all feeling in my fingers, and my toes felt like ice cubes. I shook my arms furiously in an effort to get the blood flowing again. Every breath stung as the freezing air burnt my throat, while the moisture from my exhalations formed ice crystals on my unshaven chin. I bowed my head into the wind, gritted my teeth and pushed on, straining into my harness.

It was minus 40 degrees Celsius, a temperature at which, even in polar clothing, the body is pushed to its limit. I knew that my fingertips had dropped below freezing; the moisture in the skin had frozen and if I didn't do something about it soon, I would be in danger of losing them to frostbite. Even my eyelids were beginning to stick together in the bitter conditions.

I looked across at James. His hair was tangled with ice, his balaclava was covered in a thick layer of frost and his legs were buckling with fatigue. We had been going for twelve hours and it was time to admit defeat, get inside and warm up.

Minutes later, we clambered into the tent and collapsed with exhaustion. Unzipping the door with my frozen hands had been like buttoning a shirt with an oven glove. The thin fabric gave us some protection from the wind chill, but even inside, as I struggled to light the stove, it was still minus 25.

The lighter had frozen. I fumbled with a box of matches, but the stove was too cold to ignite. I started to feel the pressure of the situation. We had to get the stove alight, or we'd freeze. We were hungry and dehydrated, but above all we needed heat.

Not a moment too soon, the match flared into life. I held it to the shallow pool of fuel on the freezing metal and there was a small puff, as a green flame engulfed the petrol. Slowly the flame grew into a flickering orange and then a thunderous blue as the metal sighed with relief.

Lying on my back as the freezing air was replaced by a warm glow, I peeled the balaclava from my face and removed the gloves from my icy, white fingers.

Needing water, and food, we scooped some snow into the small pan and placed it above the flame. The pan had a voracious appetite for snow as it disappeared in a plume of steam. I longed for the warmth of my sleeping bag and the escapism of dreams.

I was worried about my fingers, though. They had been numb for too long. If I didn't warm them up fast, would I lose them? I shook them violently, but they remained frozen like a claw. I squeezed them back into the thin contact gloves, then the outer gloves, and the thick mitts. I pulled my hat low over my ears and pulled the damp balaclava back across my face.

I crawled across the tent towards the exit and once again wrestled with the door's zip. Snow whirled into the tent as I stooped out into the cold.

I looked back at the tent and saw the small blue flame and James's silhouette against the tent's fabric. I needed to find some help. I needed to save my fingers. I trudged off into the cold.

I lifted my hand to the metal bar, looped my arm and tugged with my elbow. At last the huge steel frame began to move, and I was overcome by a dazzle of bright light. 'This is it,' I thought, as I moved towards the light.

I hauled with my arm against the wind and the metal clunked behind me. Silence. The wind disappeared and I was overcome with a warm glow. I lifted my goggles and stripped the balaclava from my face. Half a dozen faces stared at me from behind their control screens. A scientist rushed over and began stripping the small metal thermometer probes from my fingertips. 'We need to warm your fingers,' she said, fussing round me, 'they're down below zero degrees.'

I looked through the thick window at our tent, snapping in the artificial wind created by two huge, industrial fans. In a giant freezer in Oxfordshire we had had our first taste of freezing polar conditions. I began to wonder what we'd let ourselves in for.

*

JAMES 'What are you doing now?'

That was my dreaded dinner-party question when I stopped rowing after the 2004 Athens Olympics. I had found it incredibly difficult to answer then, not because I wasn't doing anything but because – in my mind at least – nothing sounded as worthwhile as the Olympics. After rowing across the Atlantic with Ben the question had changed slightly.

'What are you doing next?'

I didn't feel under any external pressure to do something for the sake of it but I knew I wanted to do something similar again. It wasn't just the journey and the physical and mental challenges that naturally came with it; I enjoyed the planning itself, the development and the training. I missed preparing for a long-term goal and the pressure that comes with having to perform.

But though I wanted to get stuck into another big challenge there were a number of things I had to consider, the first being my family life. The Atlantic rowing race had nearly destroyed my marriage to Bev, and, for me, nothing is worth risking that. It had been a problem of communication rather than an impasse, however; I'd avoided talking about rowing across the Atlantic with Bev until the last possible moment, and not surprisingly she didn't feel included in the decision-making process. I'd spent a lot of the previous year away training for the Olympics and I hadn't explained why I'd wanted to do the row – I wasn't even sure myself. So for Bev, when she thought we might start having a normal family life and share the responsibilities more evenly, I instead told her I was rowing across the Atlantic. As diplomatic skills go it was more Genghis Khan than Gandhi, so not surprisingly it caused some tension. The press exaggerated her displeasure at my forthcoming voyage, printing articles that were hard for both of us to read. Such was the media assumption that our marriage was over that, while I was crossing the Atlantic, there were photographers outside our house trying to get a picture of Bev having an affair. If I was to go away again for a long period of time I had to make sure I discussed it properly with her.

I also had to consider where my career was heading. It's difficult starting a career from scratch. I'd retired from rowing at thirty-two and, unfortunately, market forces meant that rowing didn't pay enough for me not to work again. I needed not only to get a job but also to find a whole new career. I was lucky to still have plenty of opportunities because of my success at the Olympics, and a few new ones after the interest surrounding our forty-nine days at sea, but I still hadn't settled into a 'proper' career. Could I afford to take a such a big chunk of time away again?

The last point was an interesting one. Besides which, would I want to do something else with Ben again? Despite having very different personalities and goals for the Atlantic row we'd managed to find a way of working well together. Reaching that point involved a lot of frustration, tears and arguments but by the time we stepped off the boat we'd forged a close friendship; I was even best man at his wedding. Did we want to risk that friendship on another trip, and more particularly, given my competitive instincts, a race? When we rowed across the Atlantic there was no friendship to lose, but now there was. At the very least, if we did anything in the future we had to agree to commit to some serious long-term preparation.

I first heard about a race to the South Pole from a journalist, and it got me excited in a way that other events hadn't. Since Norwegian explorer Roald Amundsen famously beat Captain Scott to be the first man to reach the bottom of the world in 1911, many others had mounted expeditions there, either alone or as part of a team; but the Amundsen Omega 3 South Pole Race would be the first time in a hundred years that teams would actually *race* one another to the Pole, pulling their provisions behind them as the early pioneers had done. Like many people I'd read about Amundsen's achievement, which was overshadowed by the tragedy that befell Scott and his team on their return journey, but my imagination wasn't capable of empathizing with what I was reading. I had no idea what it would actually feel like to be skiing in a whiteout at minus 50 – though it sounded horrendous. I had no skills to be able to cope with that. I wanted to go there and experience a place so few people have been to; but not being an explorer the options in that region are limited.

There were several options. I could go as part of a guided expedition – something I didn't want to do. Or I could acquire the necessary experience and go there as an unsupported team (there was no way I was going to do it on my own), which would involve a lot of training expeditions to reach the level where it's safe to be totally isolated out there. Having always done events where there is a competitive element I wasn't sure I'd find a trek sufficiently motivating – but racing to the South Pole sounded brilliant. It offered the chance to be isolated and self-sufficient out on the ice, manhauling a sledge to the Pole in a competitive environment where you will be punished for making mistakes, though with a safety net in case something disastrous went wrong. I wanted to do it. Whether Ben was up for it I wasn't sure, but we had promised each other not to sign up for another long adventure without talking it through with the other first.

BEN Life had been good since rowing the Atlantic with James. I had got married, inherited another dog, bought a new house and work had been good to me. What more could you ask for?

I had started a new series for the BBC called *Extreme Dreams* in which I took members of the public on life-changing challenges around the world. I had led teams through the jungles of Papua New Guinea and Guyana, up the mountains of Kilimanjaro in Tanzania and Roraima in Venezuela and across the Sahara and Atacama deserts.

I had loved the expeditions, but I wanted a real challenge – one I could sink my teeth into and, above all, one that would really test me to my limits. Unlike James I *was* looking for adventure. I wanted to taste that adrenalin and excitement. I wanted something with claws and teeth that would shake up my comfy life and remind me how lucky I was.

James and I had become good friends. We had travelled the world giving talks about our exploits and in the intervening years I had begun to understand him. In many ways I had misunderstood him on the Atlantic. He is a complex character with an ability to over-analyse things, but he can also be incredibly thoughtful. One example will suffice: during our Atlantic row, we had run out of drinking water. It was Christmas Day and we had promised to raise a glass of water to one another every Christmas in homage to that dark moment of our voyage together. The following year, he sent me a Christmas present. It was an enormous box wrapped in sparkly paper. Inside, he had carefully placed a bottle of water with a red bow.

James had a present of a different kind when he asked me to meet him in a Starbucks just off Portland Place, in London.

'Have you heard about the South Pole Race?' asked James.

A smile streaked across my face and my eyes sparkled.

JAMES   I outlined the reasons I wanted to do the race, and Ben was up for it too, so the plan was hatched.

The race was 800 kilometres across the plains of Antarctica, divided into two 400-kilometre sections with a compulsory twenty-four-hour stay at a checkpoint. We'd be skiing and pulling everything we needed on our pulks (sledges), and even before the race started there would be a twelve-day acclimatization trek towards the start line. We would make our way with the other teams up through the mountains and on to the vast plateau, which would give us time to fine tune the skills we'd have practised throughout the year – skiing, camping, navigation, cold tolerance and temperature regulation – as well as allowing us to acclimatize to the low temperatures and altitude: the plateau we would be racing across was at a punishing 9,000 feet above sea level.

BEN I'm not sure why we met in Starbucks. James hates coffee, and I hate Starbucks. I wish I could say that we shook on our dashing plan in the Royal Geographical Society, or better still the Reform Club. I can't imagine Phileas Fogg departing on a round-the-world adventure from a coffee shop.

JAMES On 17 September I paid the £650 race deposit and we were committed. We now just needed to find another £41,350 each that we didn't have, and a third person for our team.

The race rules (at that point) stated that teams must be made up of three people, with one member having polar experience. Ben managed to scrape in under the radar by having been to Spitsbergen, a Norwegian territory in the Artic Circle, with the BBC for his *Extreme Dreams* programme – not quite the polar experience the race organizers had in mind, but it ticked the official box. That was great news for us since we no longer had to look for someone with polar experience, which widened the search somewhat, but it still wouldn't be easy. Ben and I already had a relationship after our row across the Atlantic, making it hard for someone else to come in, especially as they would be joining us on this trip, rather than the team being formed together. We'd find somebody, though, no problem. And if our three-way relationship disproved all the stereotypes about it being the worst number of people to have in a team, and if we managed to cope with the oppressive environment and the relentless hours of skiing, the crippling cold and the risk of frostbite and only very infrequently daydream about burying an ice axe in each other's head – well, then we would have a chance of reaching the South Pole.

PART ONE

HEADING SOUTH

1

NORTH BY SOUTH-WEST

JAMES   Three is an awful number to have in a team. The old adage 'two's company, three's a crowd' wasn't made up just because it sounded good, and any child who has two siblings will tell you that one always gets left out.

What is the best way to select a team? When I was involved with British rowing the team selection had always been very simple and totally objective. Over an eight-month period we would be tested and re-tested on the water and in the gym. By the time crews were chosen for the championships, there was no doubt who deserved a seat in the boat. If there were personality clashes they were frustrating, but they didn't affect the team's overall performance. No matter how much you loved or loathed your crewmates everybody had exactly the same goal: to win – and that masks a whole load of issues.

Teaming up with Ben to row across the Atlantic had been totally different. It went something like this:

Ben said, 'I'm rowing across the Atlantic next year, do you want to do it with me?' I thought about the question for a second, then asked, 'Can you row?'

'Er, no.' At least he was honest, I thought, and it helped form my next answer.

'No thanks.'

A month or so later, having decided that I wanted to do the race after realizing I was lacking a long-term goal in my life for the first time in over a decade, I got in touch. 'Are you still up for the row?' I asked.

'I've paid the entry fee and ordered a boat,' he replied.

Positive, I thought. 'Can you row?'

'Not yet,' he said, in the most enthusiastic and positive way I've ever heard anybody deliver bad news.

'If you're up for it, I am; let's give it a go,' I said, and that was the selection process. No physical tests, no personality profiling to see if we were compatible.

Rowing across an ocean had been hard, but the South Pole race was going to create stress at a whole new level. On the Atlantic Ben and I had taken turns at the set of oars and pushed ourselves hard, but in Antarctica we would have to move at the same speed, hour after hour – up to eighteen hours a day for anything up to a month. Keeping pace with each other with such little sleep was going to create massive tension, and only a good team would survive that environment.

If that wasn't enough, we were looking for quite a specific character, someone who complemented both our personalities. Too competitive, and Ben would feel bullied into adopting an aggressive race strategy; too passive and I'd be pulling my hair out in frustration.

In the end we decided that we would look at fit, motivated people in the public eye who would want to do the race because of the challenge, and not to be famous. Ben thought Prince William would be a great choice, but getting hold of him was out of my sphere of influence, despite having met his grandma just after the Olympics. Gordon Ramsay was a keen distance runner and interested in principle, but was committed to filming in the States, so that left the guy at the top of my shortlist of one: the actor Jonny Lee Miller, a very private guy who runs marathons for fun. If he was interested, it would be for the right reasons.

Ben got hold of his email address and dropped him a line introducing us and seeing if he was up for racing to the South Pole with us. A week later I got an excited call from Ben, saying he'd got a reply. Jonny's email started off with the words 'This is the best email I've ever had . . .' Coming from a man who was once married to Angelina Jolie I somehow doubted that, but I took it as a good sign.

*

I couldn't believe our luck: from a starting list of three people, we might have found our teammate. We told Jonny that we had found a sponsor, and that a documentary of the trip to Antarctica would be made, and he was up for the challenge, though with a caveat: if a show he was working on in the States was recommissioned, he wouldn't be able to make the race in January 2009. That seemed a long way off though, so we agreed to meet before heading out to Norway for our first polar training session.

I think that Jonny felt a little jumped on by the presence of BBC cameras at our first meeting, but otherwise it went well. Jonny was clearly a nice guy and had an intense, focused edge to him that I really liked. Norway was going to be an important week – we'd get to see what the race really entailed, be taught the basic skills we'd need to survive and see if we could operate as a team. It would also give us a taste of what was to come, and I couldn't help thinking that the race director, Tony Martin, was in some ways giving all of the teams a chance to drop out, if the going got too tough.

*

Wandering around Departures at Heathrow, I tried to spot other competitors, which to my mind meant looking for anyone looking vaguely healthy with a rucksack. Unfortunately, of the 200 or so people boarding the flight I estimated that 180 had a rucksack and a fleece, so I decided to wait until we touched down in Norway and boarded the coach heading to Dombås, our destination in the north of the country.

As we headed north, deep snow started appearing on the fields by the side of the road. Sitting on that coach with Jonny in front, Ben behind and snow all around, the race felt real for the first time.

BEN For the first few days at the army barracks we listened to lectures on crevasses and nutrition, clothing and emergency protocol, and had our first fiddly experiences with putting up a tent, and lighting stoves.

Finally we moved from the classroom to the outdoors and it was time to put on some skis. James and I had both been cross-country skiing once before, but for Jonny it was his first time. We strapped the skis to our feet and took our first tentative steps into the Nordic snow. At this point I should remind you that we were the least experienced of the whole group. Just about everyone in the other teams had been to the North Pole and had spent a great deal of time on skis.

All eyes were on us as we edged our way across the car park, arms flailing for balance, legs struggling for grip. One by one we collapsed in a pile as we slipped on the icy surface. We didn't stand a chance of reaching the Pole. We couldn't even ski across a Norwegian car park.

The session was a steep learning curve with more than its fair share of bruising. I lost track of the number of times we fell, but it must have been in the hundreds. Jonny remained remarkably calm in the face of farce. He struggled, and eventually persevered. The focus on his face was incredible and both James and I were impressed by his drive and determination. He was like a sponge, soaking up everything we were being taught.

JAMES Having mastered cross-country skiing it was back to the base to pack for a four-day mini-expedition in the mountains where both the Norwegian army and our Royal Marines do their arctic training. It was our first experience of what would become a theme of the year: packing up food for a camping trip or expedition. Armed with food, a tent, sleeping bags, roll mats, stoves and pans, we were issued with our sledges, and the metal tracers that connected them to our harnesses.

For novice skiers the pulk is brilliant, as it acts as a stabilizer and a brake . . . until you come to any kind of downward gradient, as we found out several times, the pulk propelling us down the hill and resulting in a series of comedy wipe-outs. We had a lot of work to do.

Learning the skills we'd need in Antarctica was obviously important, but we could do that in our own time; far more important for now was the chance to get to know Jonny before he went home to Los Angeles.

I could see Jonny's excitement at getting stuck into the detail of what the race entailed – I doubt anybody's ever paid as much attention to a snow wall around a tent before – but he clearly wasn't enjoying the constant presence of cameras documenting our first steps in polar travel.

BEN I always knew the filming might be an issue with Jonny. I knew he was private man who didn't like the press, but I had hoped that we'd get by somehow. The director of the documentary of our race was a brilliant man called Alexis Girardet, whom I had first met on BBC's *Animal Park* seven years ago. We had clicked and he had gone on to direct and produce *Through Hell and High Water*, the film about James and I rowing across the Atlantic. Along with cameraman Keith Schofield and 'the two Austrians', soundman Roly and camera assistant Georg, they made for a lovely team – handy, because we would be spending much of the next year with them.

Unfortunately, my fears were realized: where Jonny had thrived with the tuition, he felt pressurized by the camera lens. As Alexis quite rightly pointed out, a good documentary explores and follows 'everything', but Jonny was clearly a little uncomfortable being filmed all day, every day.

JAMES On the positive side, we were at least seeing how the team coped with pressure, but more than anything we faced in Norway, the tension over the filming made me wonder whether Jonny, Ben and I could work together. As we stood around in minus 20 degrees giving interviews, it certainly made us ratty with each other. Jonny didn't hold back in letting Alexis know how he felt about the intrusion of the cameras – a man after my own heart in that respect – but even with feelings aired and the situation clarified, it wasn't an easy atmosphere, just a nervous ceasefire. The cameras weren't going to stop filming and Jonny wasn't suddenly going to love having them around.

When the cameras weren't there, though, we had a great time; hardly surprising as we were getting to be kids again, camping, mucking around in the snow, skiing at midnight and jumping into freezing lakes. We started to work pretty well as a team. The group was set a navigation exercise, using a GPS to reach ten checkpoints. The points were numbered one to ten but as Jonny quickly worked out, there was no rule that said you had to visit them in numerical order . . . The Norwegian men's team were by far the quickest skiers in the group, but we'd visited every point and pitched our tent before they arrived. Clearly, speed of thought would turn out to be just as important as the ability to ski – though unfortunately the Norwegian female team had both and were already in their tent by the time we arrived.

*

Despite our minor victory in the navigation stakes, the assessment camp in Norway highlighted a few areas where we were less than proficient. Let me rephrase that: it bought home to us that if we were dumped in Antarctica with all the required equipment, the chances of us surviving would be slim and the chances of us actually getting to the South Pole would be none.

We couldn't cross-country ski, roll mats had blown away when we were pitching the tent, we were about as good at regulating our temperature as an old stately home in the country, and when it came to lighting the stove Neanderthal man with a couple of sticks would have cooked, eaten and been busy drawing on the side of the tent before we'd boiled some water.

As for our team, a last night of beers in Dombås without the cameras did as much to bring us together as a week in the tent. The filming issue was still a worry, but we would just have to spend more time together and get over it. There was only one thing for it: Ben and I had to go to Los Angeles. Well, that's not strictly true; Jonny could have come to London, but LA in March got my vote.

BEN   The flight was filled with typical LA types, but one pretty woman caught our eye. It was only after the pilot asked James and I to sign a bottle of whisky for him, that she ventured over.

'Are you Ben?' she asked in an American accent. 'I think you're going to the South Pole with a friend of mine.' It was the actress Natasha Henstridge, who just happened to be starring alongside Jonny in *Eli Stone,* the TV series that, if it was recommissioned, would break up our team. 'Jonny's totally psyched about your trip,' she added, 'I was there when he got your email, he was jumping up and down.' Suddenly things were looking more promising.

We touched down late at night and the next day we headed to Hollywood to catch up with Jonny. He and his girlfriend Michelle lived in a pretty part of LA, just a stone's throw from Hollywood Boulevard. We had met Michelle and Jonny for dinner in London, where we had presented him with a team 'emergency' watch. James and I had worn them on the Atlantic and it struck me as a welcoming gesture, not least because of its potential to cost me a great deal of money. The emergency watch was developed for pilots, with its tiny emergency radio transmitter called an EPIRB. Pull the button in a genuine emergency and a helicopter will rescue you. Pull the button when drunk in the pub, and the helicopter will come with a £20,000 fine. It was certainly a brave gesture on my part to give a near-stranger such a watch, since I had taken responsibility for the cost if he ever pulled the button.

JAMES   My hunch was proved to be correct: Los Angeles is preferable to London or northern Norway in March, and we arrived to find beautiful sunshine.

The weather reference above may have tipped off the observant reader that we weren't going to be cross-country skiing. We'd decided instead to go rock climbing in the Joshua Tree National Park, to polish up our rope skills for the crevasses of the Antarctic.

We picked up Jonny at his flat in downtown LA and headed east. It was great to see him after only having had a couple of

conversations and a few emails since Norway but the three of us
seemed to pick up where we left off. We travelled together in one
car with Alexis and the camera in the one behind, and the atmosphere was relaxed; but when Alexis came into our car to get some
shots of us travelling, things definitely changed.

The difference may have been exaggerated by the fact I was
looking for it, but Jonny definitely got quieter and Ben louder as he
seemed to switch into TV presenter mode.

As we left the main road and the classic landscape of the
National Park came into view I was determined to stop looking at
how we were all interacting and just enjoy being in a place of such
rugged beauty. When I say 'classic landscape' my knowledge of the
park starts and ends with the 1987 U2 *The Joshua Tree* album. I
was hoping to get a photo by the tree that adorned the front cover
but as the park is 789,745 acres and the tree apparently died in
2000, there wasn't much chance of that happening. Rock climbing
and team bonding it was, then.

We headed into the park early the next morning, with boulders
the size of blocks of flats springing out of the dusty ground, and set
about learning to free climb. It was great fun. If you can't enjoy the
sun beating down from a bright blue sky in a stunning location
whilst doing something exciting for the first time, it's probably time
to check out of this world for good. The climbing itself was good
for reminding us of the knots we learnt in Norway, but more
importantly we really seemed to be bonding as a team. The slightly
forced atmosphere of the day before had disappeared along with
our inhibitions as we helped each other up the cliff or caught each
other with the safety rope if anyone fell.

An hour later, the old doubts were back. Alexis wanted to do
an interview about how the day had gone, which raised similar
issues to Norway. We'd been filmed throughout the day and it
hadn't been a problem, but Jonny didn't agree with having an interview. 'How can it be an observational documentary if we're doing
sit-down interviews?' he said. It was very hard to argue with his
logic and resulted in a lot of me staring at my feet and shuffling

about until the camera was set up. The mood had changed and the reality was that we would be doing interviews in Antarctica. Could the team take this atmosphere every time we did one?

I tried telling myself that each time it would get easier and have less of an impact, but deep down I felt it wasn't going to work. What made it worse was having had such a great day together the effect of the camera was highlighted by the fact that as soon as it was away the atmosphere lifted again.

BEN My mother, the actress Julia Foster, once highlighted to me the difference between my job and hers. The role of a presenter is to be yourself, to use your own character and personality to purvey information to an audience, whereas an actor must always be someone else, hidden behind the mask of another character. This is one of the reasons presenters tend to be more outgoing and sure of themselves, while many actors are rather more reserved and shy. I really warmed to Jonny as we climbed and ran and laughed together, and I think that I began to understand him a little more. I was impressed by how he had shunned the celebrity limelight for a happy, quiet life in a leafy suburb of Hollywood. Sure, he's friends with some of the most famous people in the world, and through *Trainspotting* was part of a film that changed British cinema for ever, but you'd never know it. He's fantastically discreet and unassuming.

*

It was our penultimate night in California. We had returned from the desert and Jonny wanted to show us LA's nightlife.

We began innocently enough in a little sushi restaurant where we sat at a table next to Vince Vaughn. It was only on our tenth shot of tequila that James and I finally realized Jonny *was* our man. We had been deliberating for weeks and now, watching Jonny squirt a lemon in his eye, we both realized it was our destiny. We were meant to be a team and Jonny was coming to the South Pole.

JAMES Out of the three of us Ben didn't seem to be getting on with the tequila quite as well as we were. He disappeared for a while and the next thing we knew a bouncer was approaching us, dragging something by the scruff of the neck. 'Is this anything to do with you?' he asked, depositing a rather deflated Fogle at our feet. Ben had been in the toilet, and apparently the poor lighting made it difficult to see which way the cubicle door opened. Convinced he was locked in, he started climbing over the door . . . at which point the bouncer walked in and with his finger pushed the door, which swung in with Ben on top of it. Where was Alexis with the camera when you needed him? Ejected from the nightclub, we walked out into the warm air on Hollywood Boulevard and I took Ben back to the hotel.

The trip had been worth it. The steps we'd taken as a team gave me reason to believe that we could develop a relationship that would work, and that we could cope with the constant filming. All we needed now was the green light from Jonny's filming commitments with *Eli Stone*, and we were there.

BEN We returned to the UK confident that Jonny was the right choice, and above all Alexis had made significant inroads in gaining his confidence in front of the camera. It was March 2008 and we were back on track. Our next team-training outing was the London Marathon just three weeks later, and things were really looking good for our team, and for the race.

It was early June when we got the news.

'It's Jonny,' announced the distant voice. He was in Cape Town starring in a new Channel Four film about apartheid. '*Eli Stone*'s been recommissioned,' he said. There was a long pause. My heart sank. 'That's great news,' I lied through gritted teeth. It wasn't great news, it was terrible news. I felt sick as the South Pole dream disappeared in a mist of disappointment. We had invested so much time and emotion in it and now, suddenly, with less than six months to go, it looked like we were back to square one.

JAMES　 I was genuinely very happy for Jonny. More than a team-mate, he had become a friend, and this was brilliant for his career. But there was no way of getting away from the fact that three had become two, and Ben and I still couldn't ski. It was back to the drawing board.

2

PLAINE-MORTE

BEN 'You've got malaria,' announced the doctor with certainty after taking one look at me in the waiting room of the London School of Hygiene and Tropical Medicine. After almost eighteen months of preparation for the race to the Pole I had recently returned from eight weeks' filming in South America, and I hadn't felt well for a while. Nausea, fatigue, the sweats, a permanent headache – it all pointed to malaria, a disease that kills millions every year, and which I was very proud to have avoided in over twenty years of extensive travelling in malarial zones.

The doctor examined me more closely, and took a blood sample. My lymph nodes were all swollen and my skin jaundiced. 'Any lesions?' he asked. I pointed to a small, unusual spot on my arm. 'It's nothing,' he said.

Incredibly, the results for malaria came back negative, and I was discharged with a diagnosis of extreme exhaustion and an unidentified tropical lurgy. I needed to rest.

I called James and cancelled our training camp in the Brecon Beacons. We had fast-tracked the selection process for a replacement for Jonny, and planned to spend a week trekking in the Welsh mountains with our brand-new teammate, Ed Coats; but the doctors had warned me that the week would seriously affect my recovery time and that I risked becoming even more ill if I didn't rest. With only a matter of weeks to go before we left for the Pole this was a worry, but I was fitter than I'd been for a long time. If I could just shake off whatever I'd caught in Peru, I should be back in training soon enough.

I'd been working for months without a holiday and my wife, Marina, organized a surprise weekend break on the Amalfi coast in an effort to get me to rest. There was still so much planning to do back at home, but there was nothing for it but to lie in bed for three days, listening to the ebb and flow of the Mediterranean sea.

JAMES   While Fogle relaxed with his Peruvian man flu, I was hauling ass up various peaks in the Brecon Beacons with Ed. Ben's tiredness didn't worry me, but his mental state did. According to Marina, Ben had come back from training in Devon saying he didn't want to go to the Pole any more. He is prone to the odd dramatic statement and I had no problem with that, but we all needed to knuckle down for the next few months. My trip to the Brecons with Ed took on a whole new meaning. It might just be the two of us going to Antarctica.

BEN   I felt like a new man on my return from Italy, began working out once again and agreed to race the Royal Parks Half Marathon with Eddie the following week. The headaches and nausea had disappeared, and although the mysterious spot on my arm had blistered and was beginning to feel rather sore, I was the picture of health. I completed the half marathon in 1 hour 35 minutes – a personal best by ten minutes – and was back on track. There was time to prepare for our first serious taste of everything the Antarctic might throw at us: in this case a training camp in Switzerland.

JAMES   We had settled on the dates for a snowy camp back in July 2008. When I say we, it was Ben's wife Marina, Ed and me. Ben was away on his South American jaunt, and Marina was the gatekeeper to his diary. Unfortunately, she's more of a Winston Churchill than a Neville Chamberlain when negotiating for dates in Ben's diary, but eventually 'peace in our time' was reached and dates were nailed in.

Next came the venue. What did we want to get out of the

camp? This would be our best, and final, chance to hone the skills we had acquired since we had signed up for the race. Should we concentrate on getting some miles under our belts on the skis? Sledge-pulling technique? Navigation? Or make it a full-blown practice expedition? Recreating any of these was going to be difficult in October in the Northern Hemisphere, with little daylight and no snow – the polar opposite (I know, poor pun) to the conditions we'd be facing in Antarctica.

A shortlist of options was drawn up: Norway – not enough snow, expensive, limited light; Greenland – long travel time, the wrong type of snow (too wet, apparently), expensive and again limited daylight. At a loss I thought of Bernie Shrosbree, former Royal Marine, Special Boat Service (SBS) commando, British Triathlete and Great Britain Biathlete (cross-country skiing and shooting).

I first met Bernie in Lanzarote at Club La Santa (a training venue, not a nightclub) in 2000, where the British rowing team had a training camp and Bernie was training Formula One drivers Jenson Button and Mark Webber. Bernie is an easy guy to hit it off with and one of those annoying blokes who's not only done everything you have done (and a hell of a lot more), but more quickly to boot. Two years later, when the rowing team went on a cross-country skiing trip, Bernie was our coach. It was an almost impossible task – we were just glad to be out of the boat for a few weeks and were more interested in racing each other than learning more than just the rudiments of technique. In fact the one person who put Abraham Lincoln's famous line 'If I had six hours to chop down a tree, I'd spend three sharpening the axe' into practice was gliding past us at the end of the camp, despite being the slowest skier at the start – much to Bernie's delight. Bernie is all about getting the technique right.

With Bernie's Arctic warfare experience, racing mind and attention to detail, he was the perfect person to help us out. I had phoned him in late July 2008. I was calling from a campervan on the dockside at Calais with my son Croyde hanging out of the window shouting 'Bonjour, quel âge avez-vous?' at anyone walking back to their car, and proudly offering them 'a piece of pain'. So pleased was he that a little bit of French had managed to wrestle its way into his vocabulary that it was difficult to hear the speaker at the other end of the phone.

A long dialling tone told me Bernie wasn't in the UK. A few rings later: 'Who is it?' answered a panting Bernie down the phone.

'Bernie, it's James, can you talk or is it a bad time?' I asked, more than slightly put off by the heavy breathing at the other end.

'I'm halfway up Alpe d'Huez, call you back at the top.' That was that, not even a goodbye. The situation summed up Bernie perfectly: not only was he cycling up one of the most brutal mountain climbs in the Alps, but felt able to take a call at the same time.

Thirty minutes later the phone rang, and an annoyingly fresh voice chirped out from the earpiece.

'Lovely view at the top, mate, what are you up to?'

I explained the situation.

'I know just the place; let me make a few calls.' And that was that.

I dragged my little French linguist back inside the campervan, apologized to the adjacent car for being offered the full range of bread and dairy products from our fridge, and boarded the ferry back to the UK. I was only home for a day before heading off to Beijing for the Olympics and I wanted to make sure that I had the venue for this snowy camp sorted. I felt it was going to be the most important week in our whole preparation for the Antarctic.

Unfortunately, this premonition turned out to be true. Since Ben had missed both a tyre-pulling session in Croyde Bay and the camping trip to the Brecon Beacons this was the first time all three of us were going to spend a night under canvas together, with less than eight weeks until we left for Antarctica. To think that when I organized the trip it was just the skiing and pulk-pulling I was worried about!

Bernie and I had spoken about what we wanted to get out of the trip. There were a number of areas I thought we needed to focus on, and so having Bernie with us on the trip was going to be invaluable. As we'd discovered in Norway, some of the other teams in the race were Scandinavian and we'd never hope to match them on skis, but I wanted us to come out of our trip with Bernie being able to move efficiently both in terms of energy conservation and injury prevention.

If we could be efficient within our skill range and even develop some glide, then we'd have taken a massive step forward. As I've said, Bernie is relentless on technique and he was going to be vital in making sure we improved in this area. I also wanted us to nail our tent routine – both the way we erected the tent and our efficiency within it. Finally, we needed to try to get used to hours of skiing without much rest. Having no experience in this I'd spoken to polar explorers, who were typically on the move for about eight hours at a time before resting up. People who race in these environments would expect to be skiing for twice as long in a stretch, but with a similar amount of rest. This massive difference in volume of skiing is down to the length of expedition, with explorers typically being on the move for seventy-five or more days whereas we would be racing for around thirty. Theoretically, we could ski for longer, and get away with less rest.

'Right, leave that with me,' was Bernie's slightly worrying response.

BEN I was dreading our training camp. Marina and I had just found out, to our delight, that she was pregnant, and suddenly here I was, having to leave the country again. I knew we needed to test ourselves, but I was worried how it would affect us in the run-up to the race – and suffice it to say, Bernie Shrosbree's reputation went before him.

James and Bernie had discussed our requirements for the week, and James had briefed him about each of us and what we needed to get out of it. I was nervous about this, given James's propensity to push everything a little too far: I was worried what sort of programme a former member of the SBS would put together for us – especially as Ed still hadn't been on a pair of cross-country skis and James and I had long forgotten the lessons we learned in Norway at the beginning of the year.

I was also concerned that James had given him the brief. James has always had an uncanny ability to push himself to the limit, and the prospect of a former member of the SBS *and* Cracknell setting the agenda for the trip could mean only one thing: Ed and I were in trouble.

'Bernie says to get as much sleep as you can before you leave, because we won't be getting any in Switzerland,' said James with a twinkle in his eye.

The three of us met at Heathrow Terminal 5 and exchanged last-minute pieces of kit. I had been put in charge of thermals, James was in charge of goggles and sunglasses and Eddie had a bulging bag of scientific kit from QinetiQ, our space-aged sponsors for the race, to monitor our progress.

JAMES   We headed for Crans-Montana, two neighbouring ski resorts in Switzerland that, according to the guidebook, 'Sit on a sun-drenched plateau high above the Rhône Valley with an impressive view of the chain of mountain peaks from the Matterhorn to Mont Blanc.' Obviously that location sounded too good to be true; we were going to be training on a 10 kilometres-square glacier sitting at 3,000 metres with the inviting name of Plaine-Morte: Death Plain – funnily enough, that translation wasn't in the guidebook.

3

CIRCUIT TRAINING

JAMES Ben might have been expecting boot camp, but Ed was by far the most positive of all of us. He couldn't wait to get up the mountain and into the action – ah, the naivety of youth!

BEN A short flight and train journey later and we were met by Bernie at the station. He was exactly as I expected: a no-nonsense, straight-down-the-line kind of guy. He drove us to a hotel at the bottom of the mountain and briefed us on the days ahead.

With the aid of a simple flip chart he explained the plan. As a gentle warm-up we would hike 1,500 metres up the mountain to the glacier, where we would then begin the training. We would start with a six-hour session, followed by a six-hour break. Then another six-hour session, and a further six-hour break. We would then be launched into an eighteen-hour cross-country session with a six-hour rest, another eighteen hours on skis, and so on.

My heart sank. I knew we needed to immerse ourselves, but eighteen hours without rest? We had often talked about our planned routine during the race, and eighteen hours had often been mooted by James as the daily target, but until now it had all been hypothetical. The reality of continuing on an eighteen-hour cycle with just three hours' sleep in between suddenly seemed impossible. Bernie's eyes sparkled at the sight of us shuffling uneasily at the unfolding plan. He had scored a psychological bull's-eye with all of us. We were scared. Really scared.

JAMES If we got through all that, it was up to us what schedule we set ourselves for the last three days. Having every hour of the next four days laid out came as a shock; it shouldn't have, but six hours earlier we had been in the UK, and my mind was having trouble catching up with my body.

Half an hour later that didn't really matter because my body was in the same situation – not knowing what had hit it. As we left the hotel for the glacier, it was dark, raining and we were staring down the barrel of a three-hour hike up the mountain to our glacial home.

BEN Jean-Yves Rey, one of Switzerland's top cross-country skiers, joined us for dinner: 'Jonny Boy', as Bernie referred to him, was an old mate, and the two were thick as thieves.

After dinner the five of us set off up the mountain. We were walking up partly because the cable car hadn't yet opened for the season, but also because Jean-Yves only ever ran up the mountain. His record time was an hour and a half. We were carrying our heavy packs and estimated a more leisurely three hours for the ascent.

JAMES Poor old Jean-Yves wasn't really used to walking up the hill so slowly.

I used to go altitude training with the British rowing team. To have any significant benefit such training has to be done over 2,000 metres, so we would typically train somewhere between that and 2,300 metres. I'm not sure whether our training height was a scientific choice or the fact that there is a distinct lack of lakes any higher. The first day on such a training programme went something like this:

DAY 1

A.M. Walk round lake – acclimatize

P.M. 20 kilometres of endurance training

90 minutes heavy weights

We used to laugh about the impossibility of acclimatizing in a morning, despite what the coach wrote down. Now I was having a flashback, except it was worse – Bernie wanted us to acclimatize as we were walking up. In Europe the tree line (the height above which trees don't grow) is around 2,000 metres, and as the trees disappeared beneath us I knew it was going to get significantly harder from this point. Jean-Yves was champing at the bit to push on, claiming that the pace was 'Too easy!' and he was getting cold. I kindly offered him my rucksack, but my selflessness must have got lost in translation.

BEN   Up we trekked as, right on cue, the heavy cloud cover that we had seen from the hotel turned to a steady rain. The temperature began to drop as we ascended above the 2,000-metre level, and it wasn't long before the bright colours of a crisp Swiss autumn faded to the stark white of the snow line.

JAMES   As the wind got stronger and the snow harder I could see Bernie's spirits rise. 'Excellent! The weather I ordered has arrived.'

BEN   The snow was thick under foot and our hiking boots disappeared into the white powder as we descended on to the glacier. I suddenly understood why it was called Plaine-Morte. It was bleak and eerie as the wind howled around the icy bowl. It was at this point that everything began to unravel.

JAMES   Sheltering from the wind we put down our packs and searched for our warmer gloves, hat and jacket, only to be faced with same problems as the Allied troops had in Gallipoli in 1915: the guns they needed to fight their way up the beach were handily buried beneath the chests of tea. Nearly a hundred years on, my gloves were hidden underneath my food, sleeping bag and spare socks. I could see Bernie shaking his head with a mixture of sympathy and despair. In hindsight, I might have imagined the sympathy.

We hadn't even got to the training base yet and already we'd been taught valuable lessons: regulate and react quickly to changes in body temperature, and have the necessary kit within easy reach. Conditions can change in an instant at altitude.

As we continued up the glacier, I was struggling to keep up, while Ben, clearly having thrown off his bout of 'malaria', was skipping up the hill, which he graciously attributed to the time he had spent at altitude in South America over the summer. Ed was steadily stomping up, whereas I felt like the last boy to be picked for football at school – somewhat ironic, as I really was often the last to be picked; funny how life comes full circle.

It was past midnight when we arrived at our campsite and were ordered to put up our tent. This was going to be difficult in the day-light, as we had packed up the pulks to be shipped out over a week ago and weren't exactly sure where everything was – not ideal when the temperature was dropping, we were no longer moving and it was snowing.

BEN   'Don't take off your gloves, Ed,' hollered James as Eddie removed his mitts. If there was one thing we had learned in Norway, it was the importance of always ensuring a 'contact' layer between skin and objects. Without it, the skin quickly cools and eventually freezes.

'I can't feel my hands,' bellowed Eddie as James and I wrestled with the tent in the wind. 'I'm getting frost nip – I can't feel my fin-gers.'

'Put your gloves on,' we shouted.

'Warm your hands, Ed,' barked Bernie. 'Stick them under your armpits or into your groin.'

I left James with the tent and went to help Eddie.

JAMES   It's fair to say it wasn't our finest hour. The tent had been split into a couple of bags so it could be divided between packs in the Brecon Beacons, and hadn't been repacked in Antarctic 'style' where the poles are already inserted for quick erection. In fact the poles were nowhere near the tent, but that wasn't the problem – it was the lack of communication between us. Everyone was busy, but I didn't have a clue what the others were doing.

BEN   We had been on our training camp for less than four hours and already our composure as a team was falling apart. The tent was tangled and it took us more than an hour to pitch it in the howling storm. It was a disaster.

JAMES   Bernie went away to rest his neck from what must have been a Repetitive Strain Injury, as he'd been shaking his head for most of the last four hours.

On a positive note we got the stoves up and running very easily, and made a hot drink. The storm blew itself out in the early hours of the morning and despite the way we'd pitched the tent, there were no dramas during the night. I didn't need to see the tent in daylight to know that we'd pitched it on a pretty steep slope; Ben and Ed had proved that point perfectly in the night by continually rolling on to me.

BEN   We lay in silence as the wind buffeted the tent. Our attempt to pitch it had been an unmitigated disaster, and I didn't dare to imagine what the consequences might have been out in Antarctica; but we were finally here, on the long-talked-about training expedition. It was the first time the three of us had been in the tent together, and we had just faced our first team crisis together.

*

The storm had passed and we woke early to a winter wonderland. It was as if a chunk of Antarctica had been dropped into the Swiss Alps, desolate and deserted.

The plan was simple: Bernie would give us some skiing tuition with Jean-Yves throughout the morning to perfect our technique, and, in Eddie's case, teach him to ski from scratch.

The morning passed swiftly and before we knew it we were

packing up camp and setting off on our first six-hour circuit. Jean-Yves and Bernie had marked out an 11-kilometre route around the glacier that avoided the hundreds of crevasses that criss-cross the valley; the body of an Englishman remains somewhere on the plain, twenty years after he went missing, the violence of his death swapped for a slow, stately journey to the bottom of the mountain.

I had been nervous about the question of the team's pace ever since James and I both agreed to take part in the race together. On the Atlantic we had been able to row at our own speed, but out here we would have to travel at a group pace. Many people like to say you are only as fast as your slowest member; Bernie preferred to say 'You're only as fast as your team.' Given that I would be skiing with a former double gold-winning Olympic rower and Eddie, who had competed at international decathlon, there are no guesses as to who would be the tortoise of this team.

What I worried about most, however, was whether we would set a realistic pace. It was all very well going hell for leather, but we needed to keep it up for eight days in this instance, and for at least a month in the case of the race for the Pole itself. I could but hope that in such a slow grinding race, a tortoise might have just as much chance over the long haul as a thoroughbred hare.

JAMES The glacier appeared a different place in the light and the sun. It was our own private playground for a week and if we couldn't improve our standard here, then we deserved to be shot. From the look in Bernie's eyes, it was clear he felt the same way.

We harnessed ourselves to the pulks for the first time. Within a few pushes of the skis we found that skiing with a pulk removes virtually all the glide on the skis. My theory was that if we could even get one centimetre of free movement every time we pushed off, that was going to make a huge difference in Antarctica – and Bernie was going to be vital in that process. It's not just about banging your head against the wall and plodding on, but doing things in the right way.

Two hours later the sun went down and with it a lot of our

energy, though mentally I still felt pretty positive. We completed our first lap and headed off round the circuit again. Ed took his turn at the front, and the pace dropped slightly. He was obviously knackered, but I was lost in my own private world as I tried to come to terms with exercising deep into the night. I was snapped out of it by Bernie shouting: 'Stop! Stop! What's going on? Has anyone noticed the drop in pace? I'm hardly moving!'

We all had, but I wasn't aware it had been that dramatic.

'Are you all right, Ed?' I asked.

'I'm not feeling great,' he replied, 'I think I've got a bug or something, I feel a bit virally.'

I was annoyed at the disruption to the training, but our rapid ascent to altitude had clearly taken its toll on Ed. He wanted to press on, but Bernie wasn't so sure.

'Why don't you ski back to base camp and pitch the tent?' Bernie suggested.

'Why ski for another forty minutes? If Ed's ill, let's pitch the tent here and let him recover,' I reasoned.

'That's the first positive team decision you've made since you've been up here,' Bernie stated. That mildly encouraging statement was followed up by probably the most hurtful comment he could have made.

'You guys aren't ready for this. There is no way I'd be on your team. All of you get your heads down. Ben and James, up in five hours and knock on my tent when you come past base camp.'

We put the tent up in silence, and forced a shell-shocked Ed into his sleeping bag, laid low by the altitude, dehydration, exhaustion and what lay ahead of us, both here on 'Death Plain' and at the South Pole. It was clear he wanted to be left alone with his demons.

Helpful comments like 'Don't worry, mate, we'll get through it' were muttered before Ben and I got our heads down.

BEN It was humiliating and frustrating that we had just failed the second task of the training camp. It was also a blow to lose Ed so early. We still didn't know each other and this would set us back even further. We hadn't even managed six hours and we still had the prospect of an eighteen-hour shift looming. We were all quiet as we pitched that tent in the dark. We had learned from the previous night's experience however, and were able to pitch in just thirteen minutes. I lit the stoves, and we boiled up three litres of water each.

At 2.30 a.m. James and I got up, lit the stoves, made breakfast, boiled up another few litres of water each and then set off on another attempt at a six-hour circuit.

It was strangely familiar, setting off with just the two of us. I had flashbacks to the Atlantic as we skied around the course largely in silence.

I have always enjoyed working through the darkness. I find something comforting in moving while others are sleeping, thinking about Marina and the dogs all tucked up in bed. James, on the other hand, has always struggled with night-time exercise. It had been the same on the Atlantic, and he was certainly feeling it again now.

Together we got through the first six hours before returning to camp and to Eddie, who had drunk six litres of water to rehydrate his body.

JAMES We stripped off the harnesses attaching us to the pulks and collapsed into the tent; Ed had the stoves on and looked like a different person. Bernie popped his head through the door.

'Viral Eddie, how are you?' he asked with his usual gentle bed-side manner.

'I was just really dehydrated,' Ed said, adding, 'I've never been to altitude before,' by way of a caveat.

Bernie rolled his eyes. You can clearly take a man out of the Forces, but you can't take the Forces out of the man. Viral Eddie was born.

Ed wasn't the only person with problems. Apart from being physically knackered, dehydrated and hungry I was suffering from massive blisters. Ed had kindly patched them up after the first morning's skiing but now they needed further treatment. I lay down in the tent as Ed pulled off the zinc oxide tape.

'Fuuuck!' I screamed.

Ed followed that up with an 'Ahh.' A whistling intake of breath through his teeth, and then, 'Those are the worst blisters I've ever seen.'

'At least they'll take my mind off everything else,' was the most positive response I could manage. But the reality was that if they got any worse there was no way I could ski. If the scenario was repeated in Antarctica they would have to carry on without me. I'd been taught yet another lesson.

BEN   I knew we needed a short sharp shock to prepare us for the South Pole, but my worry had been that if we made it too tough, we may well question our participation in the race. After all, there was still the possibility of pulling out in the two months before the start line, here where civilization and phones were just a mountainside away; but once we got to Antarctica, our chances of pulling out would be greatly diminished by geography and logistics.

My concerns were becoming a reality as we began to crumble psychologically. Typically, James had overdone it – his feet were in tatters – but we were all struggling with the elements, the altitude and the schedule, and it took a huge amount of personal management to look after ourselves.

JAMES   I had started to think ahead to the real race, across the bottom of the world. What was I doing here? This wasn't fun. I was in my mid-thirties, I had a little boy and a pregnant wife (one of Bev's big concerns about Antarctica was that, as she delicately put it, 'You might come home with your balls in a bag!', so we hadn't wasted any time on that score) – surely I should be with them at Christmas? What was I trying to prove? And to whom?

Before I had signed up for the race I had to sit down with Bev, talk her through everything the race would involve and see what she thought. I wasn't expecting a brilliant reaction; however much she hated the thought of my rowing across the Atlantic at least I could row, whereas I had no experience of extreme cold. I'd not only be away for nearly two months in Antarctica but I'd also have to go on a number of trips throughout the year to perfect the skills we'd need down there.

I didn't need the soul searching answer I'd prepared because Bev was nothing but supportive, saying 'I know you feel the need to do these weird things and I can cope with you being away. It's good to have our own space but when you're at home you've got to be at home for both Croyde and me.'

Looking to my left in the tent at Ben, I could tell from the look on his face that he was running through a similar catalogue of worries.

BEN It was a shock to the system all right. I had flashbacks to the 'freezer' in Oxfordshire nearly a year earlier. We hadn't progressed, and I felt hopelessly out of my depth. What were we thinking?

I longed to speak to Marina. There had been longer periods of radio silence over the summer in South America when we often went for two weeks without speaking to one another, but here I found myself thinking about her all the time. I hadn't yet been able to discuss the adventure of parenthood and the joy of bringing another person into this world. I found myself skiing in a sort of daydreaming stupor.

JAMES Fortunately, kindly Uncle Bernie had the answer to our worries, by just making us walk all night.

*

BEN As a team, there was little communication. We were all run-down, and conversation was glaringly thin on the ground. In fact the only chat revolved around pace, logistics and strategy. Where was the humour and the laughter?

'Why don't we ever chat about stuff?' I asked James while Ed was off with the film crew. 'We never seem to laugh.'

'It's a training camp,' shrugged James.

The exchange seemed to sum up our differences once again.

When James went off with the film crew to be interviewed, I broached the same subject with Eddie, who was clearly quite emotional.

'You know what,' he said, 'I've taken off six months for this and I want it to be fun, but the biggest laugh I've had in the last four days is with Alexis and the film crew. I want to enjoy it,' he concluded with a tear in his eye.

We were on the same wavelength. Training camp or no training camp, this was a once-in-a-lifetime opportunity that we should have been savouring and maybe even enjoying.

'I find it hard to speak to James,' added Eddie. 'Me too,' I replied. It was strange. Since rowing the Atlantic, James had become one of my best friends and yet I still found it difficult to talk to him.

Eddie and I chatted honestly and openly for the first time. It was as if a pressure valve had opened for each of us.

'I haven't told you about my best friends, or my sisters or about how much I love Karina,' continued Eddie.

He was right. Where was the conversation? The laughter? The banter? This was an adventure of a lifetime, not an ordeal.

JAMES   For me it was a fairly cathartic TV interview. I was frustrated by our lack of readiness with eight weeks to go, but once I got it all out I realized I wasn't taking any pleasure in all the positive advances we'd made since coming up the mountain.

Leaving the interview I headed back to the tent to apologize to Ed and Ben for any frustration that might have darkened the atmosphere of the trip. They'd clearly been talking about the same subject; Ed said that he was struggling to be honest with me, partly because of my straight talking and partly because of some of the sporting success I'd had. I pointed out that he'd seen me try to put a tent up a few days ago; I wasn't someone to look up to.

This sparked the first honest debate about how our personalities affected each other within the team, and we were just getting into the bones of it when Bernie called us out for a debrief. He was characteristically frank: his biggest surprise was our lack of leadership and confidence, not just as a team, but individually.

He was probably right. There was no doubting that we all lacked confidence in this environment, and needed to bring the qualities out of ourselves that have made us successful in other areas of our lives.

BEN 'Ben,' said Bernie, 'I didn't know much about you other than what James said in his brief, but you have really impressed me.' I looked at James. How had he described me to Bernie in the first place? I wondered.

To date, I had left every training exercise we had done under a cloud and I wasn't prepared to let that happen again. We had already put in a huge amount of hard work in Switzerland and I wanted to leave on a high rather than a self-imposed low.

The debate was a turning point in the Swiss expedition. It seemed to break the talking moratorium. With renewed verve and enthusiasm we found ourselves increasing our circuits from six hours to seven hours to ten hours. It was more of a psychological barrier than a physical one.

Eddie had been having trouble with his Achilles heel and James was suffering from debilitating blisters on his feet. Eddie was unable to complete the first ten-hour session, but I noticed a different, more compassionate, James. We were really starting to come together as a team, thinking about each other, and there was a renewed sense of enthusiasm between us.

James and I completed the first ten-hour session and returned to Eddie, who had been tent-bound. We both knew how hard it must have been for him and we resolved to reassure him as much as we could. Eddie is an ox and we both knew he was capable.

As we sat munching on our rehydrated ration meals, Eddie broke down in tears. We knew he would be beating himself up about it, but it was heartbreaking to see his pain. James put an arm around him. This was why we were here. This was what the training had been all about. It had to reach this stage. We needed these tears.

*

JAMES Ben and I had a minor spat when he accused me of bullying him to ski faster, but we got through the handbags at dawn and finished the ski with a satisfied exhaustion for the first time; we'd skied for ten hours, a target worthy of a pair of polar explorers. With Ed back for the final few hours, the satisfaction when we pitched the tent that night was immense. I was sure there would be worse days in Antarctica, skiing in a whiteout or with a massive wind chill, but mentally that was as testing a ten-hour session as you could get, and we had come through it. The sun was coming up as we went to sleep.

What seemed like no time at all later, Bernie stuck his head in the door and said, 'Pack up the tent, we're going down the mountain, you've shown me enough.' Funnily enough he didn't meet with much resistance.

BEN 'What have you learned?' asked Ed as we packed up camp. I thought long and hard. Bernie had driven us to our emotional and physical limits. In just a week, he had created the artificial pressures of the South Pole, put a mirror to our faces and let us learn by our own mistakes. We had dived in at the deep end and he had let us flail and flounder until we had finally found our stroke.

He had exploited our individual weaknesses but above all he had ensured we worked together as a team. For the first time in over a year I finally felt prepared. The menacing cloud that seemed to shadow our every training session had disappeared, leaving a bright sparkling sun.

I thought about Ed's question. There was one thing.

'I've learned that I *really* hate the cold.'

JAMES During the mental struggles we were going through, Ben had said, 'When we leave here we'll forget all the bad parts and just remember the fun bits.' I wasn't convinced my memory was that selective, but I remember talking to Ben a couple of weeks after we'd finished rowing across the Atlantic, and even then he'd said, 'I miss life on that boat.'

'You what?' I had replied, astounded. 'You were the most negative person on board, you hated it! What do you mean?'

'It really wasn't that bad,' he shrugged.

I was about to get a massive sense of déjà vu. The doors to the cable car slid shut and we were fired out of the station, swinging motionless for a second over the glacier.

Ben turned and broke out into a big, beaming smile. 'That was brilliant,' he said, 'I really enjoyed it!'

4

EATEN UP INSIDE WITH WORRY

BEN Switzerland had been a key moment in our training. It was the first time that Ed, James and I felt like something approaching a proper team. We came back from the Alps much more confident in our equipment and, even more importantly, confident in our ability to cope.

'Trust in yourselves,' were Bernie's parting words – words that would haunt and inspire us in equal measure over the coming months.

The small lesion on my arm had failed to heal and had become a niggling worry at the back of my mind. I headed back to the School of Tropical Medicine, where the doctors gave me a local anaesthetic and took a biopsy sample from my arm. It would take ten days for the results to come through, as the biopsy had to be analysed at a specialized lab in Geneva. I should have dropped it off on my way back from the Swiss Alps.

With just a few weeks to go before our flight to South Africa, from where we would depart for Antarctica, James, Ed and I had only managed one tyre-pulling session, the age-old training method of polar explorers the world over. We planned to spend three days at James's holiday home at Croyde Bay in Devon, dragging tyres along the beach for added friction, but the previous session had ended early due to my suspected malaria. I was still feeling under the weather, but had been energized by our Swiss experience. For once, I was actually looking forward to a few days' training with the boys.

Eddie was still new to the team at that point, and with James and I using our contacts to organize everything, I could sympathize with Eddie for feeling a bit like a spare wheel. It was clear that we'd left out a key stage of polar preparation, one glaring omission in all our training and planning thus far: we still hadn't got drunk together. Until now, all phone calls, meetings and training sessions had been to do with the South Pole and we needed to let our hair down, relax, and above all make Eddie feel like an equal partner in our adventure.

The dates coincided with my birthday, and so we planned to get ourselves completely, dribblingly drunk. I initiated a 'no South Pole talk' policy, and anyone caught talking shop would be penalized with a shot of tequila. James passed out in a local's house and I ended up with a tattoo on my shoulder, for which my wife will never forgive me; but we had fun and it suddenly seemed the barriers were coming down. We had patched up any differences, and any metaphorical cuts and bruises in our team's outlook had begun to heal.

But Eddie was still having problems with his heel – which left just James and me to haul tyres up and down Saunton Sands in Devon. It was a disappointment that, once again, there were just two of us. The progress we had made in Switzerland was unravelling before our eyes; and things were about to go from bad to worse.

'Mate, that looks wrong,' winced James, looking at my arm. The lesion had continued to grow. It was now rather deep, less like a wound and more like a, well, like a hole. James was right, something was very wrong. A course of antibiotics had failed to heal it, and it was growing by the day. I was still waiting for the results of the biopsy and time was running out. I called Marina, who still hadn't forgiven me for my new tattoo, and begged her to help speed up my diagnosis. I'm not sure what she did, but by six o'clock that evening I was sitting in the private clinic of a Harley Street doctor who had my results. Once again we were forced to curtail one of our training sessions as I drove up to London to find out what was wrong with me.

'I'm afraid it's not good news,' announced the doctor with start-ling honesty. 'The tests have come back positive for Leishmaniasis Viannia.' My heart sank and I felt sick. Leishmaniasis, I knew, was a particularly unpleasant flesh-eating bug transmitted by the bite of sandflies. That small, innocent spot on my arm is the same that kills tens of thousands of people in South America and Africa every year.

'Viannia is a particularly nasty strain that affects the facial tissue and can lead to facial mutilation,' he continued. It was like a nightmare. Things had just gone from bad to much, much worse.

The treatment, he explained, would involve a three-week, high-intensity course of drugs that would be administered intravenously each day. 'I need to warn you that the drug is highly toxic and can have significant side effects,' he explained as he handed me a bottle of a drug whose label carried the word 'Poison' scrawled above a skull and crossbones. Sadly, I'm not making this up.

'Can I still go to the South Pole?' I spluttered. It seems strange now that even when faced with physical deformity and a month of chemotherapy, my abiding worry was still the race. The South Pole had got under my skin and even a flesh-eating disease wasn't about to stop me. Or so I thought.

The doctor explained that the drug's side effects included severe muscle pain and nausea, but above all it can interfere with the heart. I would be bed-bound and unable to train for the duration of the treatment. Worse still, most people took a month to recover from the intense treatment. The South Pole was disappearing before my eyes.

JAMES Following some frank exchanges earlier in the year, when we had done the London Marathon together, Ben had committed to both the training and the time we needed to put into the Antarctic race. He had put more into the preparation for this race than any-thing in his life, and he had been absolutely flying on the ten-hour ski, so to be struck down with Leishmaniasis was a dreadful blow. Ben said he felt terrible, unable to do anything but sit around the house and wonder if he'd recover in time. For the first time, he understood what it must have been like for me to get ill the day before I was supposed to race at the Olympics, and have to pull out.

BEN   It was mid-November, and there were just five weeks to go until departure. Time was running out and I was yet to begin treatment. The drug had to be administered by a qualified nurse under strict supervision in hospital, which meant waiting for a bed to become available. Even then there was no guarantee how I would react to the drug, or if indeed it would work. Untreated, Leishmaniasis kills thousands around the world each year, and yet little is understood about the disease. It used to be mistaken for leprosy, as it disfigures the body in a particularly nasty way. The drug of choice hasn't changed much in the last fifty years and is a highly toxic mix of chemicals that essentially constitute a form of chemotherapy. Quite apart from the smaller side effects – nausea, headaches, muscle pain and loss of appetite – I had been warned that patients sometimes lose the ability to walk and many end up hospitalized for the duration of their treatment. I wouldn't be able to exercise either, as there was a very real risk of a heart attack since the drug also affects the rhythm of the heart.

The bottom line was that even if the drug worked, my chances of getting to the start line were 70:30 against.

A bed was found and with now only four weeks to go before we were due to leave for South Africa, I headed to University College Hospital for my first course of treatment. I should at this stage explain that I have had a remarkably healthy life, only ever going to hospital as a visitor. Now, however, just before the greatest adventure of my life, I was a patient. I took the lift to the eighth floor, the Infectious Diseases ward, and prepared myself for the worst.

The doctors took me to a small room with a bed. I was hooked up to an electrocardiogram and had blood taken. They took my pulse and assessed the levels of oxygen in my blood, before a nurse fitted a tube called a 'canula' into my arm that would need to be replaced every three days. I have never liked needles and felt the blood rush from my head as the thin pipe was inserted into my vein.

People came and went as I lay on the bed in the stark, white room. My head was swimming. 'If you react negatively to the treatment, we'll have to stop it immediately,' warned the doctor. It was like a game of Russian roulette where all the chambers contained a different bullet. If the treatment failed, my life would be at risk; but if the treatment worked . . . well, I would be free to go to Antarctica – free to risk my life.

My cocktail of poison was wheeled in on a trolley. I sat in a chair as they hooked the pipes to the canula in my arm. 'Are you ready?' the medical staff asked solemnly. I sat back in the chair, closed my eyes and nodded. 'It's started,' said the nurse. 'Here's the emergency button. I'll be back in ten minutes,' and with that, I was on my own. Just me and my poison. I watched the bag above me as the clear liquid dripped. Small droplets fell into the pipe, made their way down the tube and into my body. I imagined a little skull and crossbones on every drop, and began to repeat a kind of mantra, under my breath: 'I will be strong, I will be strong.' I had to react well to the treatment for the sake of Marina and our new baby, quite apart from any dreams of still making the trip to Antarctica. If they had to stop the treatment for whatever reason, I would run out of time. Even if all went to plan, I would have only a few days to recover before heading south, and would have missed weeks of valuable physical training. It was easy to forget that we weren't going on a skiing holiday; we would need to be pulling big weights across 500 miles of snow and ice, for up to eighteen hours a day.

I sat in the chair, dazzled by the white strip lighting. I couldn't help worrying about all the people depending on me. What would happen to James and Ed if I couldn't go? My head started spinning. 'I will be strong,' I repeated again and again. The blood began to drain from my head and I started sweating profusely. In minutes my shirt was drenched and my mouth tasted of metal. The room started spinning as I repeated my mantra over and over again. A black dot appeared as my vision began to disappear. 'Shit,' I muttered as I pushed the panic button and my South Pole dream vanished with my consciousness as I slumped in my chair.

'Ben! Ben . . .' I heard the nurse shouting as I regained consciousness. I had fainted. The nurse stopped the IV and I vomited in the sink. 'That's it,' I thought to myself. I lay on the bed and fought back tears. It wasn't supposed to end like this. The trip hadn't even begun.

The doctors rushed back into the room and my ECGs, pulse and blood oxgygen levels were taken once more. 'Don't worry,' smiled one of the doctors, 'it's quite common the first time. We'll try again and see what happens.' Once more, I was hooked up to the IV drip and the nurse restarted the infusion. I closed my eyes and crossed my fingers.

'It's done,' smiled the nurse as she unhooked the machine and bandaged the canula to my arm. An hour had passed and the doctors were happy with my reaction. I felt dehydrated and dizzy as I hailed a cab on Tottenham Court Road and headed home. I was relieved I had got through the first treatment, but I still had to return every day for the next three weeks and even then, there was no certainty it would work. The South Pole still hung in the balance.

The story had somehow leaked out and hit the press. 'Ben dangerously ill with flesh-eating bug' screamed the headlines, before I had had time to warn everyone – and the shit hit the fan.

JAMES I had heard that a picture of Ben receiving treatment had been put out by his publicist, and I got a message that he was going to leave the UK a few days early to go to Cape Town for recuperation. That meant he'd miss attending an event for Sparks, the charity we were raising money for, and one for QinetiQ.

I called Ben to see what was happening as I was driving to QinetiQ's cold chamber to meet Ed. Marina answered the phone and we ended up getting into an argument about them going to South Africa early and how important it was for Ben's recuperation. 'Four extra days in South Africa aren't going to make any difference and if he needs to recuperate that badly should he be going at all?' I asked, probably too aggressively.

'It's better than staying here; we haven't been out the house for three weeks!' Marina shouted back.

'We've got commitments here to sponsors,' I said.

'They'll understand, he's been so ill,' she fired back.

Ben could hear the argument going on and grabbed the phone from Marina. I could hear them shouting at the other end of the phone – I was impressed that I could start off an argument between a couple from the other end of the line.

BEN   I couldn't believe what I was hearing. I had just fought through weeks of painful treatment. I hadn't been able to answer my phone for fear of speaking to a journalist and further upsetting QinetiQ and the BBC, and now I was being berated for suggesting four days in Cape Town with my pregnant wife before the race! It seemed unfair for a start, but it didn't even make sense: every polar explorer I had met had advised doing nothing but rest and eating for the final three weeks and here I was being denied the final four days with my wife.

JAMES   'Hey, James, I won't go to South Africa early,' Ben stated dramatically, sounding absolutely awful.

'We can talk about it, there's no need to be so dramatic,' I said. I've had a day of messages, you going early, and that picture being placed in the paper which caused a few problems,' I said, trying to sound calm.

'That picture was not placed, I can't believe you'd say that! How can I help it if someone takes my picture!' Ben roared down the phone.

'Someone told me it was, I'm sorry if it wasn't but the line "a friend revealed" made it look that way,' I said, regretting that I hadn't asked him about it first. Either way, I believed Ben and was instantly sorry.

'We need to sort this out,' he said. 'I'm coming down to QinetiQ.'

BEN   QinetiQ and the BBC had asked me to put out a press release to relieve the pressure from the growing media interest. I had bent over backwards to tow the party lines and it annoyed me that I was the one suffering. Why was James berating me for releasing information at the request of our sponsor? It was so unfair. James had been incredibly supportive, and I knew he was frustrated, but I felt let down and wanted to talk about it face to face.

JAMES   'Mate, don't bother, we're about to go into the sleep lab, we'll talk about it when I get out,' I said, trying to calm him down.

'You and Ed have made the decision to go without me,' Ben said suddenly. 'I can't believe it, I feel like this and you've already decided.'

'We haven't spoken about you,' I said. 'As far as I'm concerned, you're coming until I hear otherwise,' I continued in the most relaxed voice I could muster. 'Look I'll speak when I get out of the freezer, everything will be clear then, after you've seen the doctor.'

*

BEN   We had had our first major disagreement and we hadn't even reached the ice. I felt terrible. I was torn between my team and my wife. Marina had been a pillar of strength during my treatment, but I felt guilty. She was pregnant after all, and I was supposed to be fussing over her, not the other way round.

It was awful lying at home, watching Ed and James emerge from the deep freeze live on breakfast television. I was meant to be there. It was all wrong and above all it felt unfair. I have never dedicated so much time and effort to one cause, and this was my reward. It was a very dark period in my life.

I made my daily vigil to UCH, where I would spend several hours receiving my infusion. Without the hard physical training I had become used to, I began to lose weight. My muscles ached constantly and as my immune system was weakened, I developed pneumonia. Before long I was confined to bed. Gaunt and feeling depressed, I lay at home watching daytime telly, and I rang James to tell him that I wanted him and Ed to go without me if my condition worsened. My chances of going were better but still slim, according to the doctors: 60:40 against.

Days turned into weeks and December was almost upon us. I had just a few days of treatment left, but even then I would have to be given the all clear that the Leishmaniasis had been purged from my body. If I somehow managed to get over that hurdle, the BBC, our sponsors QinetiQ, the South Pole Race organizers and even the Foreign Office were all demanding doctors' letters and second opinions on my health.

With just a week to go before my planned departure to South Africa, I went in for my final infusion of poison. A blood sample had been taken the previous day that would establish the presence of any pathogens in my body. In short, I would learn whether the course of drugs had worked or not. I looked and felt like a frail old man as I made my journey to UCH. I found it painful to walk and was still suffering the residual effects of the pneumonia. But I had my fingers crossed all the way across London.

I stared at the bag of fluid as it emptied its last drips into my arm and the painful canula was finally removed. I lay on the bed staring at the white ceiling, as I had done for several weeks now. I sometimes used to imagine I was in Antarctica, the white floor, walls and ceiling being the snow and ice of the faraway continent I so longed for. I have never wanted something so much in all my life.

The doctors entered the room. Their stern faces gave nothing away. My dreams hung in the balance. 'Please, please, please,' I repeated over and over in my mind. If the treatment had failed, I would need to continue the course for a further six weeks. Six weeks. It was agonizing and I wasn't sure which was worse – not being able to go to Antarctica, or a month and half more of this hell. I wasn't sure my body could take it. I held my breath as she opened my file.

'Your treatment has been successful,' she announced, matter of factly.

'And what about the race?' I implored. 'Can I still go?'

'Apart from the fact that your fitness has dropped, we see no reason why you can't go,' she replied.

'I could kiss you!' I beamed. She blushed and suddenly the world seemed bright again. I skipped out of the hospital. Re-energized, even my aching bones and muscles seemed to be feeling better. All I had to do now was pass all the doctors' medicals and the race was back on. The flame had been reignited and I felt on top of the world.

5

HEADING SOUTH

Tuesday 16 to Thursday 18 December 2008

JAMES   The last time I was in Cape Town I had green hair. I was there for a training camp, and had spent three weeks cycling around the stunning, hilly coastal roads of the Cape. I didn't get much of a chance to enjoy the bars and restaurants that were springing up on the waterfront as South Africa's post-apartheid tourist industry boomed. I spent most of the time either in the saddle, the gym or stuck in a hotel – cue boredom and green hair.

Twelve years on and apart from having learned that green hair is not a good look, especially on a thirty-six-year-old, not that much had changed as I landed in Cape Town. I was still there for sporting reasons, although the six hours' training a day I did then would be a short stint compared to what I was facing when the three of us got stuck into our daily routine down in Antarctica. The Cape Town waterfront and docks were crammed with shops, restaurants and apartments that weren't there over a decade ago, but the sense of frantic construction was still the same, as South Africa began to get ready for the 2010 FIFA World Cup.

We had landed at 7 a.m. after a twelve-hour flight, and jumped straight into a briefing about our schedule for our time in Cape Town. It was like being back on a training camp; had my life moved on at all since John Major was in power? Even though we were only going to be in South Africa for three days before heading out to Antarctica, our time was going to be split into two distinct sections: a mad rush of preparation for twenty-four hours, followed by forty-eight hours of sitting around like a man on death row with nothing to do but reflect and stew on what faced us as we waited to fly south.

Ben had flown out early with Marina, our row now forgotten. Flying out a few days early felt insignificant compared to having the team back together.

*

BEN   Marina and I were still to announce the pregnancy. I had told a small band of people, including James and Ed, who were both delighted. Marina was due her three-month scan the day before we left for South Africa and I was delirious with excitement. I was finally going to see my child. I couldn't wait to tell the world.

Once again I found myself in a Harley Street clinic. My wound was still covered with a big bandage, and my arms were pockmarked from the endless needles and canulas. This time, however, was different. I was beaming with excitement as the doctor began the scan.

Moving from one side to the other, again and again she circled Marina's tummy, pressing harder each time. The screen emitted a blur of images I couldn't decipher. She shook her head and continued. Something was wrong.

'I'm afraid it's not good news,' she said. 'There's no heartbeat. I'm sorry.' As simple as that.

I looked at Marina, her smile fading. I stared at her as her eyes lost their sparkle. Marina is one of the strongest, most stoical people I know, and I shall never forget those moments; she was stronger and braver than a lion. The doctor explained that Marina had miscarried and that the foetus was still in her womb. She was still carrying our dead child, and yet Marina remained calm and pragmatic.

A tear fell from my cheek. It was so unfair, after all we had been through. We didn't deserve this, but above all Marina didn't deserve this. My heart ached and I felt numb. We were led into a small private room; Marina would need an operation to remove the foetus. We sat in the room and Marina called her gynaecologist. 'I lost the baby,' she explained and burst into tears. We wept together.

We had planned a small dinner for a dozen close friends that evening. We had planned to tell them all our exciting news. 'Let's cancel tonight,' I said as we drove home.

'No,' Marina replied, 'tonight, I want to be surrounded by my friends.' Marina has never ceased to amaze me with her strength, and I fell in love with her even more that evening.

*

We had just two days before we were due to fly to Cape Town. Marina's operation was carried out the following day, while I packed my pulk and my kit. I don't think I'll ever really forgive myself for not being there when she needed me most, but it was then or never. Her mother, Monika, spent the day with her and I collected them in a car filled with my South Pole kit. It seemed wrong. Everything was conspiring against us and the doubts returned.

I was due on BBC *Breakfast* news early the following morning to talk about my recovery. It was agony. I was trying to put on a positive face about my recovery but inside I was crying.

I got back home at 7 a.m. and Marina was up. We sat and we cried together. I can't explain why, but they weren't tears of grief for a lost child, but tears of sadness for Marina. Of course there was grief for our loss, but it was the loss of something we never really had. It was the loss of our dreams, of our future plans. We had carried those dreams for three months and suddenly they had been shattered.

'Do you think I should still go?' I asked. She held my face in her hands. 'I want you to go,' she whispered. 'We'll get over this and we'll start again when you're back.' With those few words, Marina changed my life. She was right. There was no point wallowing in grief and sadness, and if we could overcome this, we could do anything. We still had the rest of our lives together.

The hardest part of a miscarriage is telling those who knew about the pregnancy. Even now, it feels as if there is a stigma attached to it, and many women feel almost guilty. I would argue that miscarriage is nature's way of saying 'it wasn't meant to be', but it doesn't make it any easier when you have to call your mother-in-law and your mother to let them know the sad news.

Just twelve hours after Marina's operation we were on a flight to Cape Town.

JAMES All the arguments about our relative departure dates were rendered meaningless and put into perspective. I felt awful for Ben. Leaving your wife after she's just suffered a miscarriage must exponentially increase the feelings of selfishness at being away for such a long period of time. Marina was amazing, both in the way she coped with the situation – saying that 'We've been so lucky in our lives and if we can't handle this, something that happens to so many people then we aren't very strong. It simply wasn't meant to be,' – and in the way she filled Ben with the confidence to go. The last few days for them in Cape Town were invaluable. Nothing that Antarctica had to offer would be as bad as what they were going through now.

6

WHAT WOULD AMUNDSEN DO?

JAMES We still had so much to do before we could fly south, and our thoughts were focused on a frantic day ahead. Our equipment was being sent freight from the UK, and had to be at the airport warehouse two days before flying. Getting the equipment ready wasn't the problem – I'd packed and repacked that at home as I tried to work out how many hats and gloves I was likely to lose on the journey. How often would I change my base layer? How big a tube of toothpaste did I need for eight weeks? How many pairs of socks? I thought I was taking a risk with the small amount of kit I was taking. Then I remembered I was packing my pulk on 14 December, the date that Amundsen had got to the Pole in 1911. How many spare socks would he have taken? I looked at my pulk and took a few things out, with a nod to the great man.

So with personal kit and the equipment pretty much packed, we were left with the minor task of sorting out the food. Because the race organizers have a duty of care for the competitors (for their own peace of mind, not to mention satisfy their insurers) they were going to provide 90 per cent of the food. That way, all the teams would be pulling the same amount in their pulks, and we would all have enough to last the entire race. The final 10 per cent was down to our personal taste – or lack of it, as will become clear.

We had pored over the data from our experiences over the previous twelve months in Norway, Switzerland and the cold chamber to come up with a menu that would strike the right balance, but with most of the food being provided by the race organizers, we were in their hands. At the briefing we were instructed to make up food for the ten-day acclimatization trek that would follow our arrival in Antarctica, and two sets of fifteen days to cover the two halves of the race itself, and told that we would find the food in our rooms.

Opening the door to that room, I had an insight into what it might be like entering the *Big Brother* house and meeting all the other housemates – a combination of excitement and fear as you find out who you are stuck with for the next couple of months. With food apparently becoming an irrationally important part of life on the ice, when we walked into our room this was what we had to take, like it or not, and it would be with us every step of the way to the Pole.

My initial reaction when greeted by a fridge full of 120 rehydrated meals, 120 rehydrated puddings, 2.5-kilo slabs of cheese, yard-long salamis and 15-kilo bags of porridge, was 'Holy shit, how can we eat all that in forty days?' And a more pressing problem: 'How are we going to break it down and repack it in just twelve hours?'

Ed and I made a start as Ben spent a final few hours with Marina before taking her to the airport. Ben was quiet when he came back and had clearly been crying, so we figured the best way to get over Marina's departure was by chopping a huge mound of cheese into bite-sized chunks. It's fair to say that it focused his mind for the next five hours.

BEN   For four days Marina and I had eaten, strolled and chatted in the South African sunshine. I felt life returning to my body and my aching muscles and joints began to bounce back from their ordeal. I had made a remarkable recovery physically, but mentally I was scarred – and scared. It was terrible waving goodbye at the airport but James was right; it was time to throw myself into the distinctly unglamorous task of attacking 15 kilos of industrial Cheddar cheese.

So there we were, cramped into a small, sweaty apartment in Cape Town. It was a blazing 90 degrees outside, there was no air conditioner and we had a thousand chunks of cheese to cut before noon the following day, when all our kit, pulks and supplies would be loaded on to the Russian Ilyushin cargo plane. I sweated, the cheese sweated, and I began to develop 'Cheddar blisters' on my hands. I don't remember Scott or Shackleton complaining about that in their polar diaries.

QinetiQ had given us some nutritional advice, and we had had several meetings with nutritionist Joanna Hall, who has overseen a number of expeditions and has given advice to both the Royal Navy and the British government. Both Joanna and QinetiQ had worked on the basis that we would need to pack a certain calorie intake per day and no more. We were confronted by a basic fact of physiology that has troubled polar explorers right back to Scott, Shackleton and Amundsen: pulling heavy loads in sub-zero temperatures, we expected to burn anything up to 9,000 calories a day, but the human body simply can't digest and absorb much more than 6,000 in a twenty-four-hour period.

JAMES　To put it another way, we could overload the pulks and exert ourselves dragging along enough food to force down 9–10,000 calories a day, but a lot of it would be passing straight through us – a double whammy, since as well as lugging all that extra weight, we would have to stop more often for 'comfort breaks' for good measure. A good movement might be the highlight of my day at home with a book and a nice warm toilet seat, but out in Antarctica a 'comfort' break is a misnomer, to say the least. As far as I was concerned, the fewer times I had to bare all in sub-zero temperatures the better. I wasn't keen on either eating or pulling anything that wasn't going to be used by the body.

BEN　We estimated that breakfast (porridge oats, milk powder and sugar) would need to be 700 calories; a rehydrated dinner, which came in foil bags that doubled as a 'bowl', would give us another 850 calories, pudding 600 and each snack bag 3,000 – but we wouldn't know if that was too much or too little until we were actually there, pulling it along behind us for up to eighteen hours every day for a month. We began to decant all the individual rehydrated meals into plastic bags, saving us several kilos in weight from excess packaging

JAMES Because of the pristine nature of Antarctica – and the lack of dustbins along the route – everything we brought in we had to take out, so packaging had to be minimal. We opened up three meals, bagged them up in one bag and added noodles for the extra calories we'd need, and repeated that forty-two times.

The same applied to drinks: we took tea, coffee, hot chocolate, soup and sports drinks – both electrolyte and protein. It was easy to work out the daily amounts for the latter, since, like them or loath them, our bodies needed them and we had to drink them. Trying to work out how much of the others was more difficult; every cup of water had to be melted from snow so a social cup of tea was out of the question. It was a case of giving your body and your mind what it needed. We had to factor in the length of time we'd be skiing each day, and worked out that even the best thermos wasn't going to keep drinks warm for twelve to sixteen hours at minus 30, so we had to work out what we'd like to drink and when, understanding that while a nice warm soup would be lovely after fifteen hours of skiing, in reality the soup would be stone cold so it would probably be better to have something that tasted vaguely OK cold.

Admittedly, cup-a-soup, coffee and tea bags aren't the heaviest goods, but our experience of pulling pulks in Switzerland showed us that every bit of weight makes a massive difference and none of us wanted to get to the finish line with a full drinks cabinet proudly sitting there. The rules of travel in Antarctica and our own respect for the environment meant we weren't going to bury anything; we had to make the choices here in Cape Town, and anything we took with us was either going to get eaten, drunk or brought back.

We stood in the room weighing up coffee, cup-a-soup powder and hot chocolate, estimating – well, guessing – what we'd feel like drinking the most when we were there and how much of it. In the end we relied on the tried and tested, highly scientific method of 'Sod it, that'll do.'

BEN What had happened to James? He was so careful about any extra weight on the boat when we were preparing to row the Atlantic, and here he was acting like Willy Wonka! Suddenly, nothing was too much or too heavy for our sledges. I wasn't about to complain, though.

Packing and unpacking, mountains of cheese, nuts and raisins swam before my eyes as Ed chopped the salami and James broke the chocolate into bite-sized chunks . . . Before we had even reached Antarctica we found ourselves in a race of a different kind, as the chocolate melted in the South African heat. It was 5 a.m. when we finally rolled into bed, in a fug of cheese and salami fumes.

JAMES Well, two of us got beds. Based on the tried and tested saying that possession is nine-tenths of the law, Ed and I had nicked the beds when Ben was at the airport. He got the sofa.

BEN Main meals and drinks sorted, the next morning we set about creating our 'snack bags', the food that would double as lunch while we skied, and last us from our morning porridge until our evening meal. Suddenly, with the pressure of time and with a mountain of food in front of us, we felt rather alone as we debated how best to pack the bags. We knew the first ten days of the acclimatization trek would be easier than the race period, so perhaps the way to go would be to pack ten small snack bags and thirty large 'monster' bags each? We had estimated that we would take around fifteen days for each leg of the race using the highly scientific method of 'complete guesswork' – two words we would become familiar with over the following weeks in Antarctica.

The organizers permitted us to supplement our mountain of staple food with a further 60 kilos of treats, so we had some more decisions to make. As we planned to spend up to eighteen hours on our skis, this was a long period that required a massive amount of food. This was also the one area in which we really lacked knowledge. In all our training sessions in Austria, Norway and Switzerland we had repeatedly failed to pack either correct food, or the correct quantities. Taste buds change in the cold, and we never seemed to get it right. Favourites back at home often become loathsome in the cold, while you begin to crave things you never knew you liked.

I knew that I liked chocolate, but 24 kilos of the stuff?

JAMES In fairness, the term 'snack bags' doesn't really do them justice; they had to supply us with enough energy for a day of gruelling physical exertion, while having a wide variety of tastes and textures to avoid boredom. Striking that balance is very tricky, and I decided to base the design of my bags around the snacking technique I've developed with years of practice and effort over Christmas. If I get the combination of sweet and savoury right – nuts, chocolate, biscuits, crisps, sweets, cake, cold meats, cheese and chutney – I can almost literally eat solidly from Christmas morning until at least the New Year. I wanted to put this hard-earned experience into practice as we worked our way to the Pole.

BEN Cape Townians had never seen anything like it as we hopped into a taxi, raced to the nearest supermarket and began to load our trolley with kilos of dried fruit, cashew nuts, Dairy Milk, biltong and sweets. It was a dentist's nightmare.

JAMES Apart from being an important source of energy, the snack bags were also an important source of motivation. My experience of endurance events has taught me the value of certain foods as mood enhancers, and we would need every bit of enhancing we could get. Nutritionally, 50 per cent of the calories in the bags needed to be provided by fat, 35–40 per cent from carbohydrate and 10–15 per cent from protein. Cheese, salami and nuts were the best sources of fat and protein, chocolate and biscuits a mixture of fat and carbohydrate, with sweets and dried fruit a source of simple sugar. Everything had to be ready to eat so that we could just dip our hand into a pouch on our harness and shove in some food whilst skiing, and that wouldn't work if we had to unwrap the chocolate bar or try to bite off a piece of minus 30 degree salami. Time to get the spreadsheets out, and start mixing cheese, chocolate and salami. It was then back to the hotel for more frantic chopping and bagging it up.

We'd planned – or at least I had vociferously stated – that we should pack the sweet and savoury into different bags, because I didn't want my chocolate to taste of salami and cheese. For this I was chastised for being fussy, but if that was my major worry out on the ice then things weren't too bad. I tried arguing that little comforts aren't necessarily a bad thing and it wasn't as if I was talking about taking a cappuccino machine with me.

BEN   It wasn't worth arguing; it was already 10 a.m. and we had just two hours to fill 120 snack bags. The science of packing disappeared with the minutes as we stuffed bags with handfuls of sweaty cheese and salami, nuts, fruit, biltong and wine gums. We created a miniature factory line, at the end of which sat bag after bag of congealed chocolate and salami. It looked distinctly unappetizing already and it hadn't even begun its journey.

Would I really eat all that, I wondered? And in that state? We didn't have time to debate. It was nearly twelve and we'd run out of time. The sledges were packed on to a flat-bed lorry and we finally had time to relax. It had been a hectic twelve hours and you could almost see the steam streaming from our competitors' rooms.

7

THE LONG GOODBYE

JAMES   We literally had nothing to do until the plane took off in just under two days' time. Admittedly, there are worse places to spend a couple of free days in December: it was 28 degrees, clear blue skies, the food and drink were cheap and the choice of restaurants with fantastic sea views plentiful. The only cloud in the sky was the dark one that seemed to be permanently sitting over my head.

   I found it hard to switch my mind off, enjoy the moment and not look too far ahead. To be honest, I've always found living in the present hard, which drives my wife mad as I'm always looking forwards and worrying or thinking about something else, unable to just relax and switch off. I'm sure this is a character trait that served me well when I was a sportsman, but right now it felt like a curse. I had major concerns about whether I could cope with Antarctica – the freezing temperatures, whiteouts and living in a tent for two months. The only way I would know for sure was when I was there – but once I was there I couldn't come back. Once I stepped on that flight there was no way out. The next plane out of Antarctica was the one we were booked on in two months' time. I struggled to relax despite the beer in my hand as I looked out over the shimmering water at the horizon. I kept thinking, 'I'm heading over 3,000 miles that way.' I couldn't get Antarctica out of my mind.

BEN   It was summer, and we wandered among the crowds along the waterfront. The hours of heat, shorts, bottled water and fresh fish were numbered. I looked at the couples who had no such deadline. They weren't worrying about frostbite and hypothermia or flesh-eating diseases and miscarriages. I felt the weight of the world on my shoulders. I still had my doubts about going. Those doubts weren't helped by the dozen or so Brits who came over and warned me not to go south on account of my recent illness. They were, of course, trying to be kind, but their words suddenly sounded ominous. I thought of Marina back in rainy, overcast England and I wished I was there.

The race organizers had arranged a 'last supper' for all the competitors that evening at Cape to Cuba, a surprisingly good restaurant on Cape Town's cool Long Street. South African drag queens performed on the stage while we ate and drank. I was there in body, not mind; like the others, my thoughts had already drifted to the snowy plateaus of Antarctica.

D-day had arrived. I had been here before. I'll never forget the day we set off across the Atlantic in our tiny rowing boat. This was déjà vu. I was nervous, excited, anxious, happy, sad, and terrified all at once. It was impossible to pin down any one particular emotion. I had waited so long for this day, and it was finally here.

'Bye, Mum,' I whispered as my voice cracked into my mobile. I didn't want her to know how scared I was. I spent most of the day alone, lost in my own bizarre world of emotional turmoil. I sat on the water's edge and called my friends and family. 'Please look after my beautiful wife,' I texted to just about everyone I could think of. I hated the thought of Marina being alone. I called my sisters, then Marina's sisters and my mother-in-law. She is the most amazing mother-in-law anyone could ever ask for. You can choose your wife, but you have no control over her family, and I never realized how lucky I was until I married into the Hunt family. Monika had shared our highs and lows, and it was Monika who helped us through our miscarriage. Finally it was time to call Marina.

Race rules stipulated very clearly, 'no outside help', and that meant no communication with the outside world. Apart from a quick 'vetted' call on Christmas Day, this would be my last contact until we finished the race. Before James and Ed arrived in South Africa, Marina had handed me a pile of envelopes tied together with one of her hairbands, one for each day. She implored me not to let James see them in case he deemed them too heavy – she knew James well, after the Atlantic race! I had decided to leave my wedding ring behind in case the metal froze to my skin in the freezing temperatures, and threaded it onto Marina's necklace for safe-keeping.

Marina and I are used to long periods apart, but we can usually communicate via a satellite phone. I have lost track of the number of times I've hung out of a tree or floated in the middle of an anaconda-infested river in the middle of the jungle to call home. Six weeks with no contact felt like a very long time. 'I'll think of you every minute of the day,' my voice trailed off as a tear trickled down my cheeks. So many tears. Marina began to cry on the other end. 'I won't be long,' I assured her. I was racked with guilt and sadness. Why was I doing this to her, to us?

'I love you,' she said, and with that Marina disappeared from my life for six weeks.

JAMES My last few days at home before flying out had been a frantic rush and it was only now that I started to really appreciate not only how long I was going to be away for, but also the lack of contact I was going to have with home. I would only be allowed to talk to Bev and Croyde once mid-race before (hopefully) I got to the Pole.

Bev and I had said goodbye in a very different way from three years earlier when I rowed across the Atlantic. Then, I hadn't really known why I was going anyway, I just felt it was something I needed to do. Having been away so much when I was competing as a rower, it felt as if I was just going away on another slightly longer training camp but for once I wasn't preparing for an Olympics, and rowing the Atlantic wasn't my job. Bev thought I would be around more once I'd stopped competing, and contacting someone in the middle of the Atlantic is not as easy as a hotel by a lake, which is where I'd been if I was away from home for the first few years of our relationship.

That miscommunication meant that I didn't understand why Bev was so against my going, and instead of trying to explain and get her to really understand I got angry and felt that she was telling me what to do. Our marriage went through a really tough patch, both before I left and when I came back. We had a young boy and were in the process of renovating a house, so disappearing across an ocean required a more thoughtful explanation. Thankfully, I've matured in the intervening three years: our marriage is stronger and Bev understands me better now. She knows why I felt the need to push myself in Antarctica – and that I wasn't blind, blasé or naive about the potential effects on our family, especially the needs of an energetic five-year-old boy who needed his dad around when Bev was heavily pregnant and so unable to take over wrestling duty.

As my departure from the UK grew closer I felt so selfish. I was finding it hard to spend as much time with Bev and Croyde as I'd planned because there was so much to do as D-day approached. The reality of how long I was going to be away, how much I'd miss Bev and Croyde, how much they'd miss me and that Bev would be nearly eight months pregnant when I got back was really hitting home. To be honest, it looks even worse on paper than it did in my head. Bev was brilliant: 'Go, enjoy it. Don't worry about us. We'll be OK. It'll be amazing.'

With nothing to do for the first time in months the thought of deserting the family and my selfishness kept coming back into my head. Time was ticking and soon I'd be calling home for the last time. I was worried about the last call; I wanted to have a nice conversation with Croyde. If he was tired or frustrated that I wasn't there it would be a horrible memory to take with me. Similarly with Bev: I didn't want to catch her in the middle of juggling five things at once.

I tried to pick a time post-school but before the nightly pre-bedtime battleground. Croyde was in a chirpy mood. He'd broken up from school and Christmas was coming – and for a five-year-old that's as good as it gets. I was determined that I wasn't going to let any sadness come across in my voice, no matter what I felt.

Our conversation took a familiar pattern: 'What have you done today?' I asked.

'Nothing,' he replied.

'Are you sure?' I pressed.

'Oh yeah, I went swimming but needed a poo, so I had to get out of the pool,' he remembered proudly. Pooing and swimming are two of his favourite activities, though thankfully not – as of yet – at the same time.

'Daddy is off to the South Pole now,' I said, starting to shift the conversation round to the final goodbye.

'You're always going to the South Pole,' Croyde replied. For the last month every time I'd gone out he'd tell me to have a good time at the South Pole.

'No, Croydie, remember, I was just getting ready, training. I'm going for real now. Can you look after Mummy for me?' I asked.

'Yes of course, no problem,' he said in his grown-up voice, followed by, 'can you bring me back a penguin and a pot of snow?'

I wasn't sure exactly how to answer that. Not only was I failing as a parent by disappearing for two months over Christmas, I wouldn't be able to come good on the presents without some miracle of refrigeration on the plane home and risking arrest for smuggling a penguin. I figured I'd front up to those challenges later and settled on 'Yeah! You bet. I love you, little guy.'

'Love you too, bye!' he shouted, clearly walking away from the phone.

'He's gone, baby, off to get his light sabre,' Bev picked up the conversation. 'Don't worry, he's doing OK.'

'How are you doing?' I asked.

'OK. It's a bit crap without you but we'll be fine,' she replied. There wasn't a hint of anything other than a bit of sadness that I wouldn't be there.

The last chat was probably easier for me than for either Ben or Ed because having Croyde meant it was almost impossible for Bev to look too far ahead. Young children live in the present – as admirably demonstrated by Croyde's continued attempts to interrupt the phone call.

The actual goodbye was coming, and like a British family having a picnic with a rainstorm approaching, we were stoically trying to ignore it. 'Baby, I'm going to have to go. We're about to head to the airport and I've got to hand my phone in,' I said.

'Ok,' she replied quietly.

'I'm going to miss you, beautiful, thanks for letting me —'

'Can you wipe my bottom?' It was Croyde, not Bev.

'I'm going to have to go, baby,' Bev said. 'Have fun, I'll speak to you soon. Have an amazing time, love you.'

That was it: a lovely conversation, a memorable goodbye and no tears from anybody. It was time to get to the airport and head south for the second time.

*

I might have been feeling more positive about being away from home for so long, but as we drove to the airport there was no denying that the nerves about Antarctica were still there, scratching away at the back of my mind. I tried telling myself that it was just adrenalin and excitement, rather than anxiety. Unfortunately, even I'm not stupid enough to trick myself that easily. Over the last month at home, I'd regularly gone onto Google Earth, typed in 'South Pole' and watched the globe rotate and rotate. The UK rolled over the top and the globe kept spinning until I was looking down on Antarctica. It highlighted not only how far it is from the UK, but how far it is from anywhere. The images weren't even taken by satellites, since their orbits don't cover the poles; the only pictures of the continent are those taken by people on various space stations. It just felt so wrong to be heading down there, and it was hard to imagine that when we stepped off the plane, the temperature would be about 60 degrees colder than when we boarded in South Africa.

At least Cape Town airport made the journey appear slightly

normal. I walked into Departures and looked up at the board: above a very tempting sign that read 'London Heathrow: 23.10', there it was: 'Antarctica 23.10'.

BEN I had been impressed with how James had approached the race. (For starters he had actually told his wife about it instead of leaving the application form on the kitchen table, as he had done before the Atlantic race.) Joking apart, where I had been shambling, erratic and laissez-faire in my approach, James had been a rock: diligent, thorough and dedicated.

I wondered whether he had thrown himself into training and preparation as a way of dealing with his fear of the Antarctic – a fear I shared – and as a way of controlling the prospect of being apart from Bev and Croyde. Croyde had grown from a baby into a small boy since the last time we had been away and I knew James was going to find it hard to be apart from his son. He loved recounting tales of Croyde's conversations and – as you will no doubt already have worked out – James finds endless delight in his son's fascination with poo.

Still dressed in shorts and T-shirts, we enjoyed our final burger, chips and beer before heading through Immigration, clutching our piles of polar gear. The grey, boxy Russian Ilyushin plane sat at the edge of the runway ahead of us, like no aircraft I had ever seen before. With wings that looked as if they'd been put on upside down, no windows and a weirdly outsized tail fin, the Ilyushin had been designed to cope with the worst that Siberian weather could throw at it, and to touch down on short, icy landing strips: an extraordinary plane for an extraordinary destination.

We climbed up the ladder and entered the vast open body of the aircraft. British Airways this was not: multinational flags were hung from the sides in an attempt to make it more cosy, but they couldn't disguise the pipes and wires running along the ceiling, or the two portaloo cabins roughly tethered at the back of the cabin. We were joined by several dozen stern-looking Russians who could have come straight out of central casting. They took their seats in silence, clutching bottles of vodka as the mighty plane prepared to take off, while the steward, a well-fed Russian in jeans, issued us with ear plugs to help protect us from the deafening noise of the aircraft.

JAMES   Looking around at our fellow passengers, it was easy to distinguish those going out there for pleasure from those travelling for research or to keep the various bases operational during the long, oppressive Antarctic winter. The latter looked as though they'd be happy working outside in minus 50 degrees wearing a T-shirt. Obviously I drew a burly Russian as my neighbour for the six-hour flight: there was a short-lived battle for supremacy of the armrest until it became clear he wasn't going to back down. I chastised myself for not putting up more resistance; surely Scott or Amundsen wouldn't have backed down so quickly? Was I in the right frame of mind? After some deep soul-searching I got a grip, and decided that my willingness to fight for an armrest shouldn't be taken as a sign of readiness for coping with Antarctica.

BEN   I dozed in and out of sleep for six hours until a message flashed up on the screen: 'Please change into polar clothing' screamed the sign in large flashing red letters. This was a first. I had been told to fasten my seatbelt hundreds of times, but I'd never been instructed to change my clothes. The cabin was a hive of activity as passengers replaced jeans and shorts with thermals and fleeces, the smell of suncream enveloping the plane as people lathered their faces with factor 50. Sunglasses were removed from cases and sandals and sneakers replaced by Baffin boots. Everyone doubled in size as they sat in their multi layers of polar clothing and we looked like a planeload of Michelin men. Hats of all colours disguised faces and it was almost impossible to tell people apart. For an hour we sweated in our thermals, soaring over the remote Southern Ocean, all thoughts on what we might find when we landed.

We were flying into Novo, a Russian base 200 kilometres from the coast of Antarctica, in Queen Maud Land. The area operated on Greenwich Mean Time and, for what it was worth, it was the middle of the Antarctic summer. It was 2 a.m. as we began our descent.

JAMES   The plane had a camera in the nose, which was great for watching the dramatic sight of the Antarctic ice shelf rising out of the sea, but less welcome as we approached the runway. Normally I will happily watch anything after the pilot of a plane has turned off the in-flight entertainment, even the lights and tarmac of an approaching runway, but it's not such a relaxing sight when the runway in question is made of iron-hard ice and the tough Russian next to you decides to break his six-hour vow of silence with the words 'Shit, bloody windy.'

PART TWO

ACCLIMATIZATION

8

NOVO

BEN The bright polar sunlight illuminated the white ice and snow below. It was like watching a movie rather than real life as the plane cruised down, down, down and I began to be able to make out the ice below on the screen and spindrifts of snow whipped up by the wind. I had never landed on an ice runway before, and since the Ilyushin lands on wheels rather than skis, I couldn't for the life of me understand how it would avoid skidding.

Bear Grylls, a friend and fellow adventurer, had been evacuated on the same plane just two days before after falling and fracturing his shoulder. That day the Ilyushin had been forced to land in bad weather and it had been a hazardous landing. I hoped ours would be safer.

The plane bounced as the wheels struck the ice. The engines raced and roared as we sped down the three-mile-long runway, the massive plane wheezing and screaming as it fought to keep its grip on the solid ice. Before I knew it we had come to a halt. Without windows we could have been in Timbuktu for all we knew, but a blast of cold air as the door opened left us in no doubt: we had arrived in Antarctica.

JAMES In fact I'd had bumpier landings at Heathrow, but I was slightly concerned by the enthusiastic bear hugs the pilots gave each other when they climbed out of the cockpit and came into the cabin. Was it a lucky landing?

BEN I had read so many books, seen hundreds of photographs and watched dozens of films on Antarctica. I had been fascinated by this vast continent ever since I was a child and yet I still didn't know what to expect. Would it be the hellish image of Scott's fateful journey, or the bountiful heaven of Attenborough's *Life in the Freezer*?

I pulled on my gloves, zipped up my jacket, put on my sunglasses and made my way to the front of the plane. The sunlight was staggering; even with my sunglasses, I felt the urge to squint. Clambering down the ladder I jumped to the ice and on to Antarctica. One small step for mankind, one giant leap for Ben Fogle. It was momentous. I was here and no one could take that away from me. All those endless days in the windowless hospital room receiving my cocktail of poison, I had dreamed of this moment and for a long time thought it would never come – and yet here I was, in Antarctica. It felt good. It felt cold.

JAMES   I made my way down the ladder and stood on the runway. White in every direction, but it didn't feel that uncomfortable. I can do this, I told myself. The reality was that we'd been given a gentle introduction to the continent: it was a breezy minus 20, but sunny. And I had only to look behind me to see the plane and, a way off, the ice that previous generations couldn't have even imagined. The nerves I'd had in Cape Town were starting to dissipate; as with anything, the fear of the unknown is often worse than the reality. Until now my only experience of Antarctica came from books where the authors seemed to highlight the worse elements of the place. The title of the book by Apsley Cherry-Garrard, a member of Scott's final expedition, is bad enough – *The Worst Journey in the World* – but the famous opening paragraph is a theme that runs through so many books about the continent: 'Polar exploration is at once the cleanest and most isolated way of having a bad time which has been devised . . . I do not believe anybody on earth has a worse time than an Emperor Penguin.'

Having read one book on Antarctica while preparing for the race, I decided I didn't want to read any others. Explorers make their living telling stories of extreme weather and hardship, and such tales are more likely to sell books than travelogues that concentrate on the nice sunny days that Antarctica sometimes throws up. Reading too many books describing hell on earth wasn't going to help me. Nor did I want to relive someone else's interpretation of the place. When I watch a film I deliberately avoid reviews so as not to form an opinion before I go.

The reality of Antarctica, as I was to find out, is that some days it is the most stunningly beautiful, sunny and hospitable of environments, despite the low temperatures; on other days it is an absolute beast and you'd pay to be anywhere else in the world – or at least I would. The Norwegians seemed to like it. The name 'Antarctica' derives from the Greek, and literally means 'opposite to the north'. In so many ways, this extraordinary continent is the, well, the polar opposite of the Arctic. Where the North Pole sits over the frozen Arctic ocean, Antarctica is a true land continent, albeit one where 98 per cent of it is buried beneath a mile of ice. Indeed it contains 90 per cent of the world's ice and fully 70 per cent of the fresh water on the planet. If the ice were to melt – as many fear it will in coming years – sea levels around the world could rise by up to 60 metres. Perhaps that gives some sense of the sheer size of the place, a third bigger than the whole of Europe. It's big, it's cold, it's icy and it's a long way from the UK.

The most common description of Antarctica you'll come across is that it is the coldest, driest, windiest and highest of all the continents. Temperatures have been recorded as low as minus 89 degrees Celsius and in some areas of blue ice there is actually negative annual precipitation due to the effects of sublimation, which actively takes moisture *out* of the ice and into the air. Coastal areas experience heavy snowfalls but the high Antarctic plateau is a frozen desert, and the whiteouts we might expect to experience would be caused by snow blown along by the wind rather than actual fresh snow. It is the height of this plateau, an average of 3,000 metres, that makes the continent the highest overall, rather than the presence of a few huge mountains. Basically then, it's not a very hospitable place, which is why nothing lives up on the plateau and all indigenous species live no more than spitting distance from the coast. If it wants to, Antarctica will chew you up and spit you out.

As I walked across the runway, it was all I could do not to jump back on the plane, hide in the portaloo and fly back to Cape Town.

Friday 19 December

BEN   I'm not sure what I was expecting, but at first sight it was fair to say that Antarctica looked flat, and white, and cold. A series of Portakabins and tents were man's only imprint on this barren place. It was only three in the morning, but the base was a hive of activity as rotund Russians hurried around on Ski-Doos and caterpillar trucks.

*

JAMES   The Russian airfield at Novo may not be as architecturally stunning as Terminal 5, and the Arrivals lounge needs some work, but we all got our luggage safely. Luckily, its most lovingly cared-for feature is the runway; the rest is made up of tents and Portakabins. When winter hits and planes can't fly, the whole settlement is moved a few kilometres away into the relative shelter of the hills, to prevent it from being completely buried by snow.

Novo sits on the north-eastern coast of Antarctica and acts as both entry point and hub for other countries' stations in Dronning Maud Land, including Norway (who lay claim to the whole of Dronning Maud Land), Germany, South Africa, India, Belgium, Japan, Sweden and Finland. It was to be our base for the next three days while we sorted ourselves out.

BEN   We were directed to a large red mess tent about 500 metres from the plane and wandered over in silence, each of us lost in his own thoughts.

The mess tent contained half a dozen plastic tables and chairs and a television playing Russian soap operas. Indian scientists mingled with Norwegian engineers and Russian pilots while an enormous chef, Lynard, cooked up a vat of what looked like beetroot and bacon-fat soup.

JAMES Lynard might have looked more Vin Diesel than Jamie Oliver, but over the following six weeks his rustic offerings acquired three Michelin stars and in my mind I couldn't wait to get back. Does funny things to you, Antarctica.

BEN In one corner sat an impossibly cool group of German climbers dressed from head to toe in designer Adidas. Long-haired and bearded, they had spent two months climbing and base jumping Antarctica's highest peaks, including the famous 'Wolf Fang'.

Kit had been a major issue. Although most had been supplied as 'standard'by Tony, there was still an element of choice and I had spent months sourcing gloves, balaclavas and fleeces from across the world in an effort to find the perfect combination. In the end though, a scientific freezer in Dorset was never going to be a substitute for the raw reality of Antarctica. In the end, our kit was simple: we each had a windproof Gore-tex jacket and trousers, one fleece, two pairs of thermals, two pairs of socks and pants and a big duvet/duffle jacket for the extreme cold. The problem was that all the kit was identical. To distinguish between James's pants, or Ed's jacket, I had found some spools of luminous ribbon. James was neon pink, Ed was baby blue and I was electric yellow.

We spent several hours cutting and looping lengths of the silk ribbon into our clothing. On our outer wear, the ribbon doubled as a 'pull' aid on all zips, allowing easy access even while wearing thick gloves. Given that each race jacket had eight zips, we looked like Christmas trees. I looked at us draped in bright ribbon, and at our German counterparts in their wrap-around sunglasses and snowboarding jackets. The ribbon had to go.

At this point I should probably tell you a little about our competition. There were six teams in total, far fewer than the twenty teams that originally signed up. As the world's economy nosedived, so did the number of teams. Sponsorship dried up and many people had to pull out for lack of funding.

Of the six Norwegians we had originally trained with in Norway earlier in the year, just one team of two remained, Rune Malterud and Stian Aker. Archetypal Scandinavians with their fair hair and light skin, the two former soldiers were well at home on the snow. Expert skiers, they had not only trained in Arctic warfare, but had served in Afghanistan and Iraq. Their team, Missing Link, would represent Norway's Antarctic heritage and they had captured the nation's imagination, becoming celebrities in their own right back in Norway. They had trained every day for a year, pulling tyres through the summer and cross-country skiing throughout the winter.

Team South Pole Flag included Mark Pollock, who was aiming to become the first blind man to trek to the South Pole. His team was led by polar expert Inge Solheim. Inge was part of the victorious Norwegian team in the BBC series *Blizzard* and had spent months in the North and South Poles. As well as racing he would lead all the teams in the acclimatization trek as we traversed the hazardous crevasse fields that criss-crossed the mountain range. Mark was also accompanied by Dubliner Simon O'Donnell, a friend from university who also happened to be a rugby coach. Mark may have been at a disadvantage because of his blindness, but he had already run the North Pole and Everest marathons and the Gobi desert challenge. A motivational speaker, he was also an accomplished adventurer out to prove that you needn't be restricted by sight. Team South Pole Flag were there to race, no question about it, and we all agreed that with their high levels of fitness and Inge's experience of the conditions, they were the dark horses of the event.

Team Danske Bank included Christian Hillkirk, a forty-something banker who was born in Norway but had cross-country skied for Great Britain; and 'the Two Garys', a former marine called Gary Bullen and Gary Marshall, both of whom had previously raced to the North Pole. It was clear that they'd thought hard about their kit (and had made several adaptations that James especially was very jealous of), and were as at home on the snow as on a pavement. They had skied circles around us during our Norwegian training camp, and were serious competition.

Team Due South included one of the race's two female competitors, Rachel Andrews, a physiotherapist from Plymouth who had also competed in the North Pole Race and who proudly showed off biceps that were bigger than James's. During the Norwegian training camp she had slept out on the snow in minus 25 conditions in just a sleeping bag, while back in England she had trained in the back of a chip-shop freezer van in preparation for this race. Rachel had teamed up with Phil Hayday-Brown, a long-time North Pole racer who had decided to step up from organizing our race to take part; and Hylton James, a charming South African with a belly and a smile.

Finally there was Tess Burrows and Pete Hammond of Team Southern Lights, the grandparents of the race in every sense of the word. At sixty-six Pete was the oldest competitor and had undergone major heart surgery just six weeks before, which rather put my nasty bout of Leishmaniasis in context. He and his teammate Tess had travelled the globe with their peace messages. They had been to the North Pole, the Himalayas and the Andes, and after the South Pole planned to finish their world peace pilgrimage on Mount Kilimanjaro in Tanzania.

JAMES The teams that eventually made it onto the ice roughly fell into three groups, as far as I could see: completers, competitors and racers. Obviously everybody's primary goal was to complete the challenge and reach the South Pole – there's not much chance of winning a race if you don't finish it – but there were some seriously experienced people taking part, and it would be interesting to see who would set an early pace when the racing started.

BEN The one thing they all had in common was their drive to beat us. Correction: their drive to beat James. The effect James has on other people has never ceased to amaze me. As a world-class athlete with two Olympic gold medals he receives more than his fair share of praise and admiration, but he also has a remarkable talent for firing up people's competitive streaks. From marathons to a charity boxing match and the Atlantic rowing race, people somehow feel it is their duty to try to beat an Olympian.

I suppose a gold medal is in some ways a poisoned chalice, and I am always impressed by how James deals with it. Many sportsmen give up any form of competition after they retire for fear of failure, even ridicule, and yet James has done the opposite, swimming the Straits of Gibraltar when he can hardly swim, and, above all, teaming up with a soft TV presenter to row across the Atlantic. I respect James for his competitive composure. I also hate him for it, because I am now on the receiving end of it, by association. There suddenly appears to be a wild, totally unfounded assumption that I am some kind of sportsman. This couldn't be further from the truth and makes my wife and my sisters laugh a lot.

I was never any good at sport and probably never will be. I can't kick a football, or catch a cricket ball. I'll have a go at anything, but I don't like competition, and yet here I was again, the one to beat by association, and it made me feel uncomfortable. It added to the pressure and fuelled my unease about the race.

Looking at our rag-tag band of adventurers, thoughts turned to the first part of our adventure proper: the acclimatization trek. As a group, all the teams would be led up through the mountains and onto the vast, flat plateau where the race itself was to take place. The trek would give us the chance to acclimatize to the altitude and the low temperatures, spend a little more time crevasse training with Inge and get used to spending hour after hour on the skis. Above all, it would give us one final opportunity to drop out. The Ilyushin plane would remain on the ice runway until we left, a tantalizing reminder that we still had a chance to throw in the towel. Worryingly, I was still having doubts, and having the plane sitting there as we prepared was a terrible temptation.

9

PITCHING UP

JAMES We set about pitching the tent for the first time in earnest; training and a photo shoot for the *Radio Times* in a West London studio didn't really count. All year we'd used a Hilleberg Keron, a tunnel tent that is simple to erect, roomy inside, stable and the default tent of choice for polar regions. Our assumption had been that we'd be using this in Antarctica . . . until, a week before flying here, we were informed that everyone in the race would be using a new 'Nanook' tent. This was lighter (not a bad thing), designed especially for the race (again, not a bad thing), smaller (not a good thing) and it hadn't been tested in a polar region (definitely not a good thing).

The fabric was deliberately thin and orange so it was easy to spot from the outside, and would absorb heat from solar radiation. It let in so much light that it was like being inside a very bright orange, and the other two looked as if they'd been spending far too long on a sunbed.

The Nanook was a whole section shorter than the Hilleberg, meaning the inner tent was only about six feet four inches long. If I stretched out, my head hit one end and my feet the other, and it was impossible for the three of us to lie in a row without our shoulders touching. The advantage of the tent being so small (or as an estate agent might say, 'cosy and intimate') was that it didn't take long to get warm when the stoves were going, but the constricted vestibule was an issue. Since we planned to cook there, using it as our nominal 'kitchen', every square centimetre of space is appreciated, given that nylon tents and open fires don't get on so well. Add to that the fact that our team contained two incredibly clumsy people – Ed, the 'Tent Rhino' and me – and you have a recipe for all sorts of fun and games; think a round of Twister mixed with *Ready, Steady, Cook*.

Over the course of the race we would find that when the sun was shining it seemed almost spacious inside, but when the wind was blowing it was more like stuffing all three of us into Steve McQueen's cooler in *The Great Escape*. We put our race suits underneath our sleeping bags to save space and act as an extra layer of insulation against the snow, while goggles, gloves, hats, balaclavas and felt liners from the boots lived in a net suspended from the roof of the tent, which sagged under the weight and quickly became known as the Hanging Gardens of Babylon.

Tent up, we settled down for our first 'night' in Antarctica.

The sun was blasting through the thin orange flysheet, giving Ed and Ben a WAG-like skin tone, our shoulders were pressed together and it was like trying to sleep with all the lights on. Given that the sleeping bag was designed to cope with temperatures down to minus 45 degrees, in these relatively mild minus 20 conditions, it was poaching me.

BEN   We were here during the Antarctic summer, when average daytime temperatures in twenty-four-hour sunlight reached the dizzying heights of minus 20 rather than the impossibly cold minus 70 of a dark Antarctic winter. I had experienced long daylight hours before in northern Norway, but not to this intensity. Here the sun spins in a high arc that is barely perceptible to the human eye – a sun that blinds and burns you all day, every day, and every night to boot. Even a toilet trip in the night necessitated sunglasses and suncream.

We were all worried about sleep deprivation, especially with the sun blazing through the orange tent wall. I had reasoned that Ed would probably fare the best given his hospital shift work, but I was genuinely worried how any of us could cope on as little as three hours' sleep a night.

JAMES For all that I would be grateful to the constant sunlight for getting us through long days of skiing, it was a pain in the ass when we were in the tent. I'd decided not to bring the sleep mask from our flight down to Cape Town, figuring that if I wore it I'd disappear into such a deep sleep that waking me up would be like trying to rouse the dead. But after squinting for forty minutes, I admitted defeat and resorted to wearing my skiing goggles, much to Ben's amusement. His punishment for laughing at my Top Cat sleeping gear was to sleep with his head next to my feet, because all of us having our heads at one end clearly wasn't going to work. The lack of room meant we were nearly mouth-to-mouth, let alone shoulder to shoulder. Dental hygiene wasn't going to be at the top of our lists while consuming 6–7,000 calories of chocolate and cheese for the next three weeks, so rather than face the breath of Hades every night, it was simple common sense to sleep top-to-tail.

Before coming to Antarctica, if I'd been asked to anticipate the worst part of my day, it would have been when the alarm went off and I had to stick some part of my anatomy out of a warm sleeping bag into the freezing air of the tent. As we had found out during our training trips to MIRA, the big artificial freezer in Oxfordshire, the tent was warm from the stoves when we slipped into our sleeping bags, but as we slept the temperature would drop rapidly. Temperatures inside and outside the tent on an Antarctic morning are worryingly similar.

Saturday 20 December

When the alarm went off the next morning I couldn't wait to get out of the bag, and out of the tent. I was too hot, and although having survived a night in the deep freeze filled me with confidence for the race ahead, I needed fresh air and some personal space.

We believed we were ready when the pulks were loaded in Cape Town, but it was amazing how easily we managed to fill our three days at Novo. A lot of the fiddling and adjusting we made to the kit was because we had time on our hands, and the alternative to making changes was to sit in our tent or see how long you could bluff out meals in the mess tent before Lynard's dirty looks turned into a flying carving knife. It was nearly a year since all the teams in the race had pitched tents together in the snow in Norway. I wouldn't call it espionage as such, but we had certainly picked up some good ideas from nosing around.

Ed and I spent a good few hours making a stove board. It shouldn't have taken so long, but in true British style we expanded the task to fill the time available. Getting the stoves on as quickly as possible was going to be vital when we'd been skiing for hours, tired, cold and in need of a hot drink and food. It was important to use time efficiently: we wouldn't be stopping for long and each minute spent setting up the stoves or cooking was a minute less sleeping time. I wouldn't rank coordination in the top three or even the top five of my finest qualities, so unpacking and setting up fiddly stoves exhausted and with cold hands, a raging thirst and grumpy with hunger wasn't going to be a smooth process. By securing the stoves to the wooden board we'd at least have something to rest them on as we cooked, save time and make life a lot easier. It was a case of devising a system that also protected them when we were skiing because the stoves were our life support system – without them there was no way we could survive. Indirectly they were our source of food and water, not to mention heat.

Ed and I developed an ingenious way to attach them by combining the best design elements other teams had employed. It turned out it was better not to be totally prepared after all because we wouldn't have come up with such a good system in isolation. But a perceived lack of preparation of a different kind was what kicked off an argument between Ed and me.

BEN   James, Ed and I had all spent more than a week together and there had been remarkably little friction between us. Nonetheless, hours of 'team dynamics' sessions at QinetiQ's headquarters in

Farnborough had revealed some fundamental differences between us.

James and I had a history of adventuring together, had shared many tough experiences and had an established friendship. I had spent nearly three years growing a Cracknell-resistant skin, and though occasionally he still breached my defences, I had learned to understand him. Ed on the other hand was the new boy on the block and I was concerned about how he'd cope with James's personality. Ed, too, was continually worried that he wasn't an equal partner in the team.

It was difficult to assuage these worries, and to my mind the many hours of debate had simply exacerbated the problem by highlighting it. I was always paranoid and made a concerted effort to ask Ed questions before James, and we always ensured Ed was between us during photographs and interviews; but shortly before we left the UK, during one of the last team dynamic sessions, Ed revealed he still felt ostracized from the team.

One thing QinetiQ's psychologists established was that both Ed and I erred on the sensitive side of the spectrum and were more likely to be hurt and offended, while James was at the 'straight-talking' end and more likely to be the offender. It was an explosive mix and I worried how we would cope together in the emotionally intense wasteland of Antarctica.

To date, though, we had remained remarkably well behaved. We had also been blessed with bright sunshine and a relatively balmy minus 15–20, but we had been warned that the weather was due to change. 'Nothing will be as bad as the cold chamber,' shrugged Ed innocently, referring to his forty-eight hours in QinetiQ's cold lab with James. It was a throwaway comment, but James wasn't about to let it pass unchallenged.

JAMES The surprise wasn't that an argument happened – I do have the unique ability to start a quarrel in an empty room – but that it happened when we weren't under pressure.

Ed was sorting out the solar panel he was going to use to charge his iPod. Obviously I had no problem with that, but I'd watched him become slightly obsessed with it and was concerned with the importance he was placing on having music. Ed had had a brutal couple of days in the cold chamber, perhaps because he had gone in there under-prepared both practically and mentally. That's probably being a bit harsh, as I'd had a similar experience at MIRA with Ben almost exactly a year earlier and we both struggled in exactly the same way. Being locked in a freezer at minus 40 degrees with nothing but a couple of treadmills and a tent is hard physically, but worse mentally. It totally numbed our senses; there was nothing to look at, it felt claustrophobic and the minutes ticked by unbelievably slowly. I'd come prepared with music to dissipate the pain of boredom; Ed hadn't, and so he'd struggled. We were set a brutal regime with over thirty-five hours on the treadmills and just a few hours' sleep. Ed kept drifting off whilst walking and I tried to keep him talking whenever I saw he was wobbling.

After his experience in the chamber, music seemed to have become the key to overcome boredom, but in truth that wouldn't be enough. I knew we had to talk about whether we were all psychologically ready for the race ahead, since skiing for the number of hours we were talking about day after day was going to be brutal and we had to be prepared for some horrible times. How to kick off the discussions was another matter.

Ideally it wouldn't have happened the way it did – it certainly wasn't the way we'd spoken about raising sensitive issues in our team dynamic sessions at QinetiQ. I was watching Ed fuss over his charging mechanism again: he is one of life's worriers, and I don't mean that in a disparaging way; it's just that he wants to get everything right. But compared with Ben and me Ed is certainly more of a worrier.

We had to go and set up our skis and I made a comment that charging iPods wasn't the most important thing we had to do. Ed reacted angrily: 'You accused me of not being ready when we went into the chamber.' After exiting the chamber we had had a debrief and I'd said he hadn't given enough thought to what it was going to be like inside and how to get through it. That was a month ago and he hadn't said anything at the time or since, but it was clearly still an issue. 'I do something about it and you have a go at me.'

'I wasn't having a go at you; I've just seen you fussing with that panel ever since we've been here. None of us can rely on music to get us through this,' I replied, determined to keep the discussion in the present.

'I'm not going to rely on it. It's not going to be as bad as the chamber. I won't be staring at a wall covered with black plastic,' he stated.

Now I was worried. 'It's not going to be as bad as the chamber? Are you serious? The chamber was only forty-eight hours. No matter how bad an experience is, if it is only forty-eight hours long you can always see the end. There is no way we are going to be able to see the end of this.' Ed hadn't got his head around it.

'I didn't mean it like that,' he protested, 'you've taken it out of context.'

'There was no context, no reason to say it unless that's what you think. Sure, I agree, we're not going to be inside staring at a plastic wall, but we might be skiing in a whiteout for days at a time. We only walked for about ten hours in a session at QinetiQ, whereas we'll be skiing for a lot longer here day after day.' I was on a roll now. 'I don't want to have an argument about this and we've got the whole acclimatization trek to get our heads ready for what is coming our way, but I don't want you to feel like Ben and I felt for the first week when we rowed across the Atlantic.' Alexis had been sorting out his camera equipment nearby, had heard the first salvos of an argument and was now filming us. I thought about stopping but it was too important an issue not to have it out, camera or no camera.

'It was awful. I wouldn't wish that week on anybody, not being able to get my head around what we had started and unable men- tally to get into the routine that would have seen us through,' I said as reasonably as I could.

Ben had arrived halfway through my speech and worked out what the argument was about. It was the first stressful situation where the outcome could be two people agreeing, leaving the third feeling isolated. Being slightly more tactful than me, Ben explained how he felt in the first week of our Atlantic race, but Ed wasn't going to just back down.

'You've just picked up on one point and slammed me for it when it wasn't what I meant. I know I need to make sure I'm ready and I will,' Ed said.

'I'm not having a go, mate, but we have to prepare ourselves for the absolute worst possible situation and if it's not that bad then that's brilliant, but if it is worse than we thought then we will find ourselves in a whole world of hurt,' I replied.

'Not everybody motivates themselves that way,' he protested.

'I appreciate that, but thinking it won't be as bad as the chamber could leave you in a lot of trouble out there,' I said, pointing at the white horizon. 'I know you'll get yourself right before the start, it's just that I couldn't hear you say what you said and not say something.'

'I understand and I'll be ready,' he replied.

'If you've got any other issues or problems lingering we've got to talk about them now otherwise they'll destroy us out there.' I gestured dramatically to the horizon again.

BEN I caught the tail end of Ed and James's domestic. James had a point, but he had launched a fully loaded attack on a poor unsuspecting Ed. I agreed in part with what James was saying, but I also wanted to hug Ed and say 'Welcome to the world of Mr Cracknell!' Not for the first time, I felt divided in my allegiance to my two teammates.

JAMES We smoothed over the awkward atmosphere at the end of the conversation by having a man hug with lots of backslapping, but whether the tension had been put behind us or just into hibernation remained to be seen.

The team that never was: climbing with Jonny Lee Miller in Joshua Tree National Park, California.

Bathtime, polar style. Training in Norway included jumping into a frozen river fully clothed, with skis.

Ben, James and rubber duck undergo a hypothermia test at Portsmouth University.

All tied up: crevasse training on an Austrian glacier.

Sadly for Ed, this isn't steam; it's early-morning mist rising off a frozen lake in Austria.

The Norwegians would be quaking in their ski boots if they could see our slick technique around Eton's Dorney Lake . . . probably.

Ben in the middle of a flat-out 'VO$_2$ max' fitness test at QinetiQ.

'Tiny Tyres' is put through his paces on Saunton Sands, north Devon.

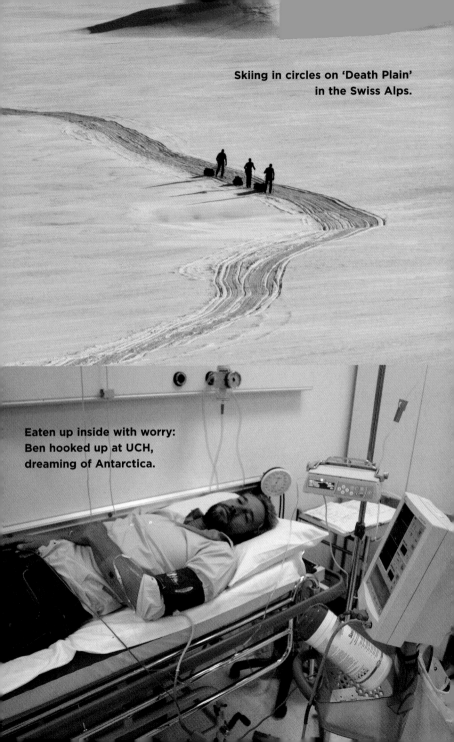

Skiing in circles on 'Death Plain'
in the Swiss Alps.

Eaten up inside with worry:
Ben hooked up at UCH,
dreaming of Antarctica.

Ed and James struggle on in the 'freezer' at minus 40.

The three orange amigos. Life in the tent was cramped and smelly, but at least we weren't skiing.

Soldiering on: our first whiteout, skiing as a group during the acclimatization trek.

10

LIFE IN THE FREEZER

JAMES To be fair to Ed, I had rather blocked out just how horrible that cold chamber could be. The harsh reality of what we had signed up for was first revealed in a twenty-four-hour stint in a wind tunnel at MIRA in October 2007, long before Ed joined the team. MIRA was a place more used to testing the latest cars to their limits before they hit the roads. It's a secretive establishment; when you arrive, any cameras are handed over along with promises that you won't report on anything you've seen inside the complex. That wasn't really likely as Ben and I were going to be locked into a freezing wind tunnel for twenty-four hours. We weren't there to make notes on the cornering ability of the latest Land Rover.

The man who was going to be the race doctor down in Antarctica had come along to keep an eye on us. He introduced himself as Weasel – a nickname I'd have thought most people wouldn't have been as proud of as he was. Weasel had come to make sure we were OK in the chamber, and give us our first introduction to polar conditions. He brought a whole heap of polar kit, the fit of which would have had a Savile Row tailor slashing his wrists. Beggars can't be choosers though, and without them I'd have been in there in just jeans and a jumper.

The chamber was frozen down to a brassy minus 40 degrees, based on the scientific reason that the Centigrade and Fahrenheit scales collide at that point, and the fact that our BBC director, Alexis, thought that allowed for no confusion to anyone watching the documentary. It sounded like a logical argument until we poked our heads into the chamber and felt what that was like. The instant freezing of my nasal hairs and a coughing fit induced by a 60-degree drop in air temperature left me thinking that surely a little bit of confusion wasn't that bad.

Wires to monitor our fingers, toes and noses were taped on by QinetiQ scientists, whom we would see a lot more of when the company became our sponsors for the race. Our skin temperature was going to be monitored and if it dropped too low, we'd be warned and possibly pulled out of the chamber. Wired, dressed and ready we went in.

BEN 'I can't do this for two months,' screeched a voice in my head as we entered the chamber. It quite literally took my breath away. I had never experienced cold like it. My skin stung and my throat ached with each breath.

I watched as James's whole body seemed to slump, hunching his shoulders against the shock of the cold. It was awful. Bleak, miserable, terrible. I could go on, but I don't want to depress you. This might have been a place for frozen peas and ice cream, but it wasn't for me.

I had serious doubts about whether I would last the course of a day, let alone the race to the South Pole.

JAMES I was there in body, but my mind had yet to join in. I'd known how many hours we were going to spend in the chamber and what the temperature would be, but those were just numbers: twenty-four and minus 40. I could say them over and over again, but they didn't mean anything. Lying in bed for twenty-four hours goes a lot faster than twenty-four hours in a classroom or a boat in the middle of the Atlantic, and minus 40 means nothing until you've experienced it. Now I'd felt the temperature, I realized it was going to be a very long twenty-four hours.

We were at the very start of our South Pole campaign. I had zero experience of these temperatures and had been flung in at the deep end. In the still air minus 40 (nasal hair aside) was bearable, but the wind changed the situation entirely. Upon entering we had to pitch the tent we were going to spend the night in. I couldn't remember the last time I'd put up a tent and when I had it wasn't one like this. As we got the tent out of the bag the jokers in the control room turned the big fans on, and not only did the temperature drop but the snow in the chamber started flying around and my goggles froze. Laurel and Hardy had just entered the building: it was a disaster. Thirty minutes, a lot of swearing and some very cold fingers later, the tent was up.

Two skiing machines were now ready for our pleasure as yet another frustration of Antarctic life came hammering into view – temperature management. At first it was a joy to be pounding away on the machines. I could feel the warmth flowing through my body followed by the first beads of sweat on my forehead – which is about as welcome as a wasp in your motorbike helmet. I opened up the flaps in the borrowed suit to let some cool air in, but I was past my sweat threshold and it was pouring down my face and instantly freezing in my facemask. I stopped for a drink and the sweat turned to ice. I spent the next seven hours alternating between sweating and shivering.

Ben went out to warm his fingers up; I didn't want to leave, as I knew I wouldn't have come back in again. I kept trying to remind myself why I'd signed up for the race, a question for which, despite the huge amount of thinking time, I couldn't come up with a good answer. 'I really love a challenge!' wasn't cutting it.

BEN What were we doing here?

I felt humiliated at being called out by the scientists. I felt as if I had already failed and it certainly didn't help my fragile state of mind. I returned to the horror chamber and continued to pound away at the treadmill. It wasn't long before I lost all feeling in my fingers again, and then I started to shiver.

I didn't want to give up again, though. I was determined to impress James. I bit my lip and soldiered on.

JAMES You can tell when Ben is not quite right, as he goes quiet.

As nice as the silence might be, it acts as a warning sign, especially when combined with some uncoordinated swaying whilst exercising. Eight hours of tedious exercise on the ski machine, trying to maintain a constant body temperature in polar gear that didn't quite fit, had taken its toll. Unlike down in Antarctica, however, the tent was already handily pitched following our battle with the wind machine earlier.

There was no way Ben was going to stop unless he collapsed or someone told him to. This was fine and honourable behaviour in a safe environment, but not the type of behaviour recommended in Antarctica for dummies. If anybody gets himself into a situation where they can't function properly then the whole team is in trouble, and it was of paramount importance to be honest about how you were feeling. So showing uncharacteristic common sense (the chamber must have adversely affected me as well) I told Ben he should go into the tent, get the stove on, make a hot drink and warm up. My suggestion was not motivated by totally unselfish reasons; it hadn't escaped my notice that by the time I'd finished on the treadmill the tent should be nice and warm, with a hot drink waiting for me. Ah, the Royal Tent.

From the skiing machine I could see the bright glow through the flysheet as Ben struck a match, followed by some frustrated muttering. Rather than allow the flames of the stove to lick the inside of the tent, Weasel had obviously had enough of watching a grown man struggle, and came in to help.

I abandoned my perch on the skiing machine and came down to see how it was done. 'The key is warming the fuel cup so that the fuel lights easily,' Weasel informed us, casually striking a match.

As much as I wanted to get warm, I was pleased that Weasel's casual confidence with the stove met with the same results as Ben's attempts. 'It hasn't been lit for seven months,' he muttered as he struck another match. Guy Fawkes, though, would have been proud with his second attempt.

Ice melted, water boiled and food dehydrated, it was time to get a few hours' sleep. Whilst we were asleep in the chamber our core body temperature had to be monitored. This could be done in two ways, either by inserting a small wire where the sun doesn't shine, or by the QinetiQ physiologists coming into the tent so that the small thermometer that we swallowed could be read by a machine. There were obvious disadvantages to the former but we would not be disturbed, whereas the latter meant the heat we'd put into the tent would be let out when our temperature was measured.

A tent full of minus 40 degree air, or a wire up your bottom. I think the person who first uttered the words 'It's a lose-lose situation' must have been in a similar predicament. Ben fancied the cold air rather than the wire, which kind of left me no choice, as I'd get the cold air anyway when the tent opened for Ben's temperature to be checked, so the wire would have been there purely for pleasure. Given a free choice I may well have opted for the warm tent, whereas Ben I think would rather have frozen to death. What's the saying about those who protest too much?

BEN For that matter, what is it about sportsmen and bottoms? I have managed to avoid rectal probes all my life and I wasn't about to give in to one now. We were covered in sensors, and sleep seemed unlikely anyway. What difference would it make to have a probe held to your stomach every few hours?

JAMES Sleeping at minus 40 wasn't too bad once I had snuggled right down into my sleeping bag, leaving only a small gap around my mouth so I could still breathe while not exhaling the moisture in my breath into the sleeping bag. A bad habit to get into, as over time it would freeze inside the down layer and the bag would not be as warm, besides being heavier to haul across the ice. It was getting out of the bag I had a problem with; my watch alarm rang, hanging from the roof of the tent. I wrestled my arm out of the bag, grabbed the watch, and pulled my arm back in as quickly as I could. 'Sod that,' I thought, 'Ben can light the stoves.'

I looked across at him; he was still cocooned in his bag pretending that he hadn't heard the alarm. I'd made the schoolboy mistake of turning the alarm off, so it was my responsibility to get the stoves going. I saw that he'd matched my schoolboy mistake by leaving his full pee bottle outside his sleeping bag and was going to be greeted by a litre of frozen urine when he woke up. At least it cheered me up when I was lighting the stove – that was until he woke up and then shoved his pee bottle in the saucepan, which gave the tent a smell similar to the gents' toilet at half-time during a football match.

After breakfast we had to pack up, take down the tent and get on the treadmills to simulate the routine we'd go through in the morning in Antarctica. As I'd predicted, that particular morning was a windy whiteout, dropping the temperature by 10 degrees as they turned the fans on again.

'This is no way to live!' I shouted at Ben. He nodded his eyes as if to say 'What have we signed up for?' This was truly horrible.

When they opened the big roller doors at the end of the chamber the minus 45 degree air met with the plus 15 degree air outside and produced the most amazing cloud. We emerged through it looking like utter heroes, but feeling the exact opposite. If the South Pole Race entry form had been put in front of me I wouldn't have signed it, but unfortunately it was too late. I'd signed and paid the deposit already – big mistake.

BEN If we thought MIRA was bad enough, then life was about to get a whole lot worse.

Portsmouth University, my alma mater, had agreed to demonstrate the effects of hypothermia on the human body, using us as guinea pigs. How on earth anyone got me to agree to this one is a mystery. I had only recently been carted off in an ambulance after developing hypothermia while taking part in the World Tin Bath Racing Championships off the Isle of Man, and I wasn't particularly keen to experience it again. Somehow however, I answered in my typically cavalier manner.

JAMES 'Brilliant, we'll do that!' said Ben, so we were signed up.

He lived to regret that decision because after Professor Michael Tipton had given us a briefing, which involved showing us a tank of very cold-looking water and saying we'd be in there until our core temperature dropped to 34.5 degrees, he handed us an internal thermometer.

BEN   Did I mention I have never had a rectal probe?

JAMES   'When you say internal, do you mean up the bottom?' Ben asked.

'Why, do you fancy swallowing all this, wire as well?' I joked, holding up the coil of flex that ended in the anal probe.

The professor smiled and gave us a tube of KY Jelly and we headed off to the cubicles. No matter how little I wanted a plastic flex up my bum it was made easier by how much Ben detested the idea. It's true there is always someone worse off than you. A voice came over the top of the next cubicle.

'How far do we push it in?' Ben shouted.

'Just up until the tide mark I think,' I said, straight faced.

'Aargh! They've used them before?' He sounded disgusted.

We wandered back to the tank room, complete with our plastic tails. We had to have a quick medical and ECG to make sure we didn't have any heart problems; as I suspected, the ECG picked up the ectopic beat in my trace, which is basically a disturbance of the electrical conduction system of the heart, causing additional beats. For people with a serious problem suddenly immersing them in cold water could cause a cardiac arrest, but my irregular beat is not uncommon in endurance athletes who have spent years building up the strength of their heart. After all, the heart is one big muscle. If the trace is exercise-induced then it will settle down when the person starts exercising. So, as Ben was lowered into the tank, I got to cycle on an exercise bike until my trace normalized.

BEN   First in, first out, I reasoned. I wandered over to the pool trailing my wires and clambered to the side of the 'jacuzzi'. Half a dozen scientists and some members of the local press had assembled to watch. I hate the cold, but I hate cold water even more. I can't stand swimming in cold lakes or a cold ocean, and avoid it at all costs. If I had been able to produce a sick note at this moment in time, I would have done so.

'Fuuuuuuuuuuuuuuuuuuuckohmygodohmygod. My. God. It's. Coooold. Hooow. Long. Doooo. I. Haavvve. Tooo. Stay. Innnn,' I stammered.

'About half an hour,' smiled the scientist. He had to be joking. Half an hour? I wasn't sure I'd last half a minute! My legs were like frozen drumsticks as I lowered myself into the bubbling water, my mouth ajar with shock.

James looked concerned. A camera bulb flashed.

JAMES   Unfortunately, my heart trace went into a healthy pattern just as Ben started screaming and hyperventilating as he went into the water.

Bugger, I had no excuse not to go in now.

For the previous two weeks I'd had cold showers to get ready for this, and having fallen into enough cold rivers and lakes in my time I knew it wasn't going to be a barrel of laughs. I gingerly climbed in and could feel the shock of the cold water making my chest want to breathe faster and faster. I concentrated on controlling my breathing and not screaming. It felt as if my skin was being attacked by thousands of tiny little pins. 'You feel that pricking?' The professor asked.

'Yeah, what is it?' I asked.

'That will last for about three minutes and then you'll feel better for about a quarter of an hour. Then the fun will start,' he said. I didn't like the sound of that.

Having gone in fifteen minutes before me, Ben was already shivering; great, I had that to look forward to. 'Can't I just watch Ben and see the stages he goes through? It seems silly two of us getting cold?' I asked the professor with a smile. He just smiled back.

My core body temperature had dropped very quickly and even

though I'd been in a lot less time than Ben we were nearly at the same temperature and I hadn't started shivering. This began when my core temperature dipped below 35 degrees, and it carried on sliding down. When it reached 34.5 I had to type a text message on a mobile phone to show how much our coordination had dropped in a short space of time – I'm not sure that showed them much though, because my coordination is appalling in any temperature. I was then taken out since the health and safety limit had been reached.

BEN   I couldn't believe it. James actually got out before me. What was that all about? I had been in for fifteen minutes longer already, and I was freezing my increasingly smaller nuts off. 'Come on, body temperature,' I pleaded with myself, 'DROP!'

JAMES   Apparently I hadn't started shivering because my body was used to the cold, thanks to my showering regime, and hadn't felt the need to signal to my muscles to rapidly contract in order to keep warm. The body conserves its energy until it really needs it, so as a result my core temperature had dropped very fast. Ben's body felt cold soon after getting in and so his body did everything it could to warm itself up, which was why his core temperature had remained nice and high and kept him in there for over an hour.

'I'm off for a nice hot bath. You want me to run you one?' I asked. He flicked me a 'V' sign. 'No? OK, see you in a bit.'

The lesson I took away from that was the body can get used to the cold, and it was up to me to make sure that it did.

BEN   My lesson was simpler: Don't say 'yes' to everything. And start taking cold showers

*

JAMES   Almost exactly a year later I had the chance to see how much improvement I'd made in that area as we had another session in a freezer. This time it was at QinetiQ's climatic chamber at

Boscombe Down, and this time I was with Ed because Ben was still undergoing treatment for Leishmaniasis.

QinetiQ had planned a fun forty-eight hours for us, although it was actually seventy-two because we had to report to Farnborough twenty-four hours beforehand and were kept from sleeping so that we went into the chamber exhausted, making for a more accurate simulation. They didn't need the sleep lab – I was exhausted already. I'd been rushing around for the last week trying to work my way through the list of things we had to do before leaving the following week, and we still didn't know whether our team was going to consist of two or three people.

I'd had a stressful day before I checked into the sleep lab, rowing with Ben about the picture of his receiving treatment in the paper, and when I arrived at the sleep lab Ed was already laying out the equipment to be packed into our pulks.

The thick doors closed behind us exactly at 7 a.m., and we wouldn't come out for forty-eight hours unless there was a problem.

As soon as we'd entered my nasal hairs froze and the memory of the chamber at MIRA a year earlier was playing in my head as though my mind had instantly selected that DVD and put it on. The difference was, I knew I could cope with it now whereas last time it had got on top of me. The kit I had on fitted, and since our training camp in Switzerland I believed I'd finally got my head around this trip. The next forty-eight hours were going to put my new-found confidence to the test.

I'd told Ed how Ben and I had struggled in these conditions and that we both needed to prepare for forty-eight hours of hell – and that's what we got. The advantage with it only being forty-eight hours was that we could see to the other side, no matter how bad it got, but our hell had been very well planned by QinetiQ: we had to cover 63 miles over three shifts of about ten hours on the tread-mills, walking with weights attached to our harnesses via a pulley system. It was going to be boring and cold, and we had to try and switch the brain off. The first session passed relatively easily, a combination of novelty value and our determination to rise to the challenges QinetiQ were throwing at us. We put the tent up and tucked into a warm meal and were about to get into our sleeping bags when the tent opened and a roll of gaffer tape together with a smashed-up bucket was passed in.

Simon Wickes, who had worked with us on our physiological preparation, said, 'Simulated repairs, mend the bucket.'

'Thanks very much,' I replied. We spent the next thirty minutes trying to make the bucket vaguely watertight and put it back outside the tent. Only two and a half hours' sleep later we were back on the treadmills again. So far the temperature hadn't been a problem, but as I started to feel more tired, I also felt colder.

Simon came in with a sign that read 'You've come across an area of rough terrain. You can either carry on straight or divert east to flatter ground, but add 10 kilometres to your journey.'

'What do you want to do, Ed?' I asked.

'Not fussed,' he replied. 'You?'

'Go straight, mate, always go straight,' I said. Ed shrugged his shoulders and I told Simon we'd head on. He nodded and then added some extra weight to the pulleys and increased the incline on the treadmills, smiled, waved and walked out. Great.

We had to work harder because the speed had remained the same, which meant we were both getting hot and our goggles were starting to steam up. We weren't going to be hot for long.

Simon came in with another sign when we had around three hours of the session left. This time it read 'You've left the sastrugi field, but the wind has picked up to 30 mph. Do you want to keep walking?'

Again I asked Ed: 'Mate, do you want to put the tent up and wait it out, or keep pushing on?'

'Keep going, we can put the tent up in wind up to at least 35 mph,' he reasoned.

Simon nodded, gave us another cheeky grin and wheeled in two massive fans. I dug out my Gore-tex gorilla mask in preparation for some serious wind chill and Ed did the same. We checked each other's faces for any exposed skin and got ready. At least I wasn't going to be hot for a while.

Though it was miserable, we were coping. Effectively wearing a Gore-tex condom from head to foot wasn't particularly comfortable, but it was doing its job and keeping the wind out. Simon came in with another board. 'What now?' I muttered under my breath.

It read: 'The wind has increased to 35 mph. Do you want to keep walking?' I looked at Ed and shrugged my shoulders, as did he.

I had to shout over the wind and through the Gore-tex to be heard, a problem we would encounter in Antarctica. 'I'm OK. You want to carry on?' Ed gave a weary thumbs up and we carried on as the temperature dropped below minus 40. I felt as comfortable as you can in that environment, but I was feeling increasingly knackered. We finished the second stint in 35 mph winds and had to put the tent up in these conditions, which required us to be steady and methodical when all we wanted to do was get straight in there and grab some kip.

Ed was struggling to eat. He had sore teeth, probably caused by the intense cold, and so had eaten hardly any of his snack bag – this, combined with the lack of sleep, must have made him feel terrible. We both dropped off almost immediately.

I woke up with the sensation that I was being pushed down the tent, and I remember thinking that Ed must have rolled over on top of me. I was about to shout at him when I felt a force being pressed down on me and realized it was the roof of the tent: it had collapsed.

'Ed!' I shouted. 'They've let the tent down on us.'

'Uh! What?' he said.

'The tent's collapsed, I'm going outside to have a look,' I told him.

'You want me to come?' He sounded hopeful for a no.

'No, mate, I'll go and take a look and yell if I need you,' I said. The tent had been let down and covered in snow; I couldn't re-erect it on my own.

'Ed mate,' I called, 'two-man job I'm afraid.' I looked at my watch; we'd been asleep for an hour.

More joys followed over the course of forty-eight hours, and we ended the session exhausted, suffering more with fatigue, hacking coughs and an inability to concentrate on anything other than the cold. Our spirits rocketed when we got news from the outside world that Ben had been told that the treatment had worked on the Leishmaniasis. Now all he had to do was rest up and he should be on the plane with us – well, a few days before!

I've never been so glad to get out of a room in my life. BBC *Breakfast* had come down to interview us as we came out and Ben was watching on TV at home. He said he was shocked at the state of us after only two days. I'd had a total of about five hours' sleep in the last four days, and it showed: during the team dynamics briefing that followed, I had to be woken up.

But despite our both picking up a nasty case of one of the most aggressive illnesses around – man flu – we'd survived the ordeal, and from my perspective the fact that the temperature wasn't the problem was brilliant. All we now had to work out was how to stay awake, force ourselves to push on, keep concentrating and make sure we got enough food inside us to keep the energy levels up. Easy.

11

RUNNING REPAIRS

BEN Back on the ice, the six teams prepared to set off on the acclimatization trek, along with the Norwegian film crew (Martin and Petr), the BBC film crew (Alexis, Keith, Georg and Roland) the Icelandic truck drivers (Gigli and Kora), the race doctors (Ian and Deidre) and the South Pole Race organizers, Tony, Sarah and Kenny.

While we would cover the acclimatization trek and race on skis, the rest of the crew would follow in specially adapted vehicles shipped from Iceland. Four Toyota Hilux vehicles that resembled American monster trucks had been designed to withstand the extreme conditions of Antarctica, complete with roll bars in case they fell into a crevasse.

I had been anxious about the vehicles from the start. Antarctica and the South Pole rightly elicits huge emotion in many people, some of whom argue that the world's last great wilderness should be left untouched. The presence of four vehicless was bound to court controversy. However, those four vehicles constituted the cleanest transport available to the support team in Antarctica. Massively more efficient than highly polluting aeroplanes, Ski-Doos and caterpillar trucks, they would remain on the ice long after the race to ferry Russian scientists and engineers around Queen Maud Land.

To date, scientists and explorers have always relied on the tiny Basler planes, which act like Antarctic buses in the vast wilderness. The success of the support vehicles would offer a genuinely greener alternative means of moving scientists around the ice.

There are those who feel the untouched beauty of the place should remain just that, and that no one should visit Antarctica. The very nature of an expedition, even a human-powered one like ours, often necessitates various modes of transport to get in and out of remote regions. I would be lying if we claimed to be a 'green' expedition, but we tried to reduce our carbon footprint as much as possible and hoped that by highlighting the beauty of Antarctica, we might inspire another generation to continue to protect it.

Saturday 20 December

JAMES There wasn't that much to do before setting off, but somehow we managed to expertly drag it out for the whole day. We had to get our skis ready, which involved attaching the bindings and gluing skins on the bottom. Listening to the Norwegian members of the expedition, it became clear that attaching the skins and preparing the bases was something of an art form, having a huge effect on the balance of grip and glide in the skis. I think it's fair to say that we were on the agricultural end of the fitting market, but we figured that when one of your major concerns is remaining upright, perfectly calibrated skis would be wasted on us.

Traditionally, seal skins would have been used, but we had what is probably best described as an artificial one-way carpet. The hand glides across it when you stroke it in one direction and in the other gives traction – exactly the same as if you stroked a seal, whose fur points towards the tail to reduce friction when it swims. It is the combination of traction and glide that make seal skins (or man-made versions of them) perfect for cross-country skiing. The material would grip the snow when we pushed down to propel ourselves forward, and as we pushed off our weight would be transferred from one foot to the other, gliding foot. 'Push down, glide, push-glide push glide' – well, that was the theory. In reality it was more 'shuffle-shuffle – oh shit don't fall! – shuffle-shuffle'.

Having attached the skins to the skis, it was time to come to terms with their other, rather disconcerting feature: the design of an eerie man's face staring up at us. Inge, the Norwegian polar expert, was slightly offended when I asked who the bloke was on our skis; it turned out to be Fridjof Nansen, the Norwegian explorer, zoologist, oceanographer, pioneer of neuron theory, humanitarian, League of Nations High Commissioner and Nobel Prize winner. One of life's passengers, then . . . Not surprisingly he is thought of as a saint in Norway and had an inspirational, almost paternal relationship with the new legion of explorers who followed him: Amundsen, Shackleton, Peary, Scott and Byrd.

I didn't know all this until I returned to England, after the race. Strapping on those skis under a cold Antarctic sky, all I knew about the man whose face I'd be staring at for hour after hour was that he was a Norwegian explorer who had slept with Scott's wife while he was on his fateful expedition to the South Pole. I'm not sure how that fitted in with the paternal/inspirational role that he's reported to have had with Scott, but Inge took great delight in relaying that story to me as if to say 'We [Norway] discovered the Pole first and whilst your heroic loser arrived there to find a Norwegian flag, his wife was in bed with Nansen.'

I was going to come to know that face every bit as well as Kathleen Scott by the end of the trip, and would very possibly arrive at the Pole to see a Norwegian flag. Isn't it strange the way history repeats itself? I was just glad that Bev didn't know many Norwegians, and that we had left each other on good terms.

I had a more pressing issue than the alleged infidelity of Mrs Scott, however, and that was my boots. Ever since pulling them on in the Ilyushin, I tried to convince myself that my aggressive reshaping process back in England, where I had heated them up and expertly battered them around, had given me the extra room my feet needed. But after nearly two days of wearing them, it was obvious there was no way I would be able to ski in them for hours on end. Recriminations against the organizers for supplying the boots a week before leaving (and for Norwegians for not having size 13 feet) were of no use now; it was obvious I had to do something drastic. I spoke to Inge about it. He put his 'I'm stuck in the middle of nowhere with no tools, how would I solve this?' face on, despite the fact that we were actually in a well-equipped base with plenty of tools. Evidently he preferred being in the former situation than the latter when it comes to sorting out a problem, however, and his face brightened as he came to a conclusion: we had to cut the boots open. I was out of ideas and Inge knows what he's doing, so I went along with his suggestion; we cut vertically down through the toe cap and pulled it apart. I now had plenty of room in the toe, but the boots resembled sandals, with a lovely open view of the snow through the massive hole in the front of the boot

'What shall we use to cover up the hole?' Inge asked.

'I hoped you'd thought of that before you cut the hole?' I replied warily.

'Go and cut some material from your tent bag.' That was his solution? Granted, the material was windproof, but it already had a relatively important job: protecting our precious tent! I could tell Ben and Ed felt the same way when I came back to the tent and cut a square out of the tent bag, mumbling something about Inge telling me to do it and showing them the gaping holes in my boots.

My scepticism in Inge was unfounded, of course, as he set to work and showed that with huge amounts of glue and some Dr Frankenstein sewing, it was possible to become a master cobbler. The only immediate downside to the 'improvements' to the boots was that I had to let them dry for a few hours and so couldn't give the skis a test run with Ben and Ed. It had been almost a week since I had last got a good sweat on in the UK, and I was struggling to remember a longer period of time when I hadn't trained. I also wanted to reacquaint my feet with a set of skis as soon as possible. In the end the 'rest' turned out to be a blessing; Novo was surrounded by sheet ice with very little snow covering it and was an absolute 'bastard to ski on' according to the Norwegians. Ed just described it as 'horrible and impossible'. Brilliant. I was looking forward to 800 kilometres of that.

I wouldn't have long to wait before getting some practice in. Our twelve-day acclimatization trek started in the morning.

12

THE JAWS OF FENRIS

Sunday 21 December

BEN   We must have looked like quite a caravan as the nineteen competitors and support vehicles began to snake their way across the Antarctic tundra. It felt good to leave the Russian base. We would miss their stews and broths, but we were finally making headway and the sooner we got to the start line the sooner we'd get to the South Pole and home. I didn't want to wish away my experience, but my emotions were in turmoil and I still wasn't sure if I was meant to be there.

JAMES   As we set out on the acclimatization trek I couldn't help but think of the UK. Back home it was the shortest day of the year, dark and gloomy by 4 p.m. and with only the prospect of Christmas on the horizon to brighten your mood. On the other side of the world I was about to embark on the longest day of my life: I wouldn't be seeing a night sky until February. As my old rowing coach said whenever someone was struggling, 'Not every day will be sunshine', but down here on the bottom of the world, even in our darkest moments, it was funny to think that the sun would always be there.

So much for my optimism: a bad day was around the corner, with 35 mph winds and temperatures down to minus 47 predicted over the next forty-eight hours – our gentle introduction to Antarctica looked as though it was coming to an end. At least during the race we wouldn't have any forecasting. I find it better not to know what's coming, especially when there's nothing you can do about it. I told myself it would be good to get that first storm out of the way, cope with it and prove to ourselves that we could manage getting through whatever weather conditions Antarctica could throw at us. Who was I kidding? I wanted bright sunshine for the next two months, not just the next two days.

South from Novo took us across the runway but before crossing it we had to wait for the Ilyushin to take off and head back to Cape Town. It had been sitting on the runway for three days as people arrived from the surrounding bases, ready to go home for Christmas. It wouldn't be back until 30 January, when we were due to make our exit back to civilization – unless anyone in the race had a spare £250,000 rattling around in their pulk for an emergency evacuation.

BEN   There had been a buzz in the base before the Ilyushin left. This was the last opportunity to leave Antarctica. From here our acclimatization trek would take us up into the mountains, and out on to the high, flat plateau where the real race would take place.

I watched as the plane taxied down the runway. I could hear the deafening roar of its engines as it rumbled down the ice before soaring into the clear blue sky. All around me people stood alone lost in their own thoughts as the plane disappeared towards Cape Town and civilization. This was the point at which 'Antarctic fever' usually sets in; the point at which isolation becomes a reality and escape is impossible. It affects different people in different ways and, according to local folklore, some people go mad.

I felt a twang in my stomach but it felt good waving goodbye. No more temptation. No more second thoughts. No more opportunity for doubt. It was just us and a great white sea of nothingness.

*

JAMES   Once the drone of the engines had disappeared we were left with the sound of Antarctica: silence. Throughout the trip the quiet was something I never totally got used to – or failed to appreciate. Living in London (especially under Heathrow's flight path) there is always background noise, and it's not until it's stripped away that you realize how intrusive it is.

We'd spoken about enjoying this part of the trip, making the most of the spectacular scenery as we made our way over the crevasse fields and up through the mountains. We knew that once we started racing there wasn't going to be the time, inclination or energy to soak up the sights, and up on the plateau it was going to be, as Lord Melchett put it in *Blackadder Goes Forth* when looking at the wrong side of a map, 'a barren, featureless desert out there.'

Apart from the physiological acclimatization, this was our chance to nail the skills that would ensure we got the most benefit from every minute we weren't moving: eating and sleeping. After the first day's trek, despite there being no real time pressure, we tried to put the tent up and get the stoves on at full speed. Our communication and execution was pretty good, but it remained to be seen whether we could have done it in the same way after sixteen hours of skiing rather than a leisurely six.

*

We skied for eight hours at a steady pace in single file. Rather than staring at the pulk in front, I spent most of the day looking at the approaching mountains. Perhaps the word 'approaching' was wishful thinking on my part: that first day brought home just how big Antarctica is, since the mountains seemed just as far away when we made camp. The mountains we were heading towards were part of the Ovinfjella Massif, a series of mountain ranges separated by ice streams that flow north. The specific range we were slowly plodding towards was the Drygalski Mountains that included Fenriskjeften, which literally translated means 'Jaws of Fenris'. Fenris was the monstrous wolf of Norse mythology who was destined to eat the world, gods and all, at the end of time. Fair enough. At 2,931 metres Ulvetanna, 'Wolf Fang', is apparently a beast of a climb that challenges the world's best; even getting to it is difficult.

It certainly suits its name, granite fangs piercing the mile-thick continental ice sheet.

I wondered what the first people who saw these mountains thought. Did they realize that they were skiing over ice that was a mile thick? And that, like an iceberg, most of the mountain was buried beneath it? I concluded they must have; to make their way down to Antarctica a century ago required a special kind of person. Not so long before maps were inscribed with 'Here there be monsters' rather than 'Antarctica', so explorers with the passion and desire to discover and conquer new lands, the skills to navigate there, the determination to raise the funds for an expedition, not to mention the commitment to spend at least a year doing the trip with no guarantee they would return, meant that they were very special people. Shackleton's advert for an early transantarctic expedition sums it up fairly well: 'Men wanted for hazardous journey. Low wages, bitter cold, long hours of complete darkness. Safe return doubtful. Honour and recognition in case of success.'

Fortunately, the information collected by Shackleton and men like him meant that I didn't have to wonder what was beneath the ice. It made me realize how much of our assumed knowledge comes from people who were prepared to do extraordinary things in order to find out the reasons why that situation existed, whether it be evolution, polar conquests or space travel. Luckily society's not relying on me, as I'd still be in my hut with no windows and a square wheel waiting for the intelligent people to come up with the clever ideas.

As you can probably guess, there is a lot of thinking time when all day, every day, is spent skiing. The risk of crevasses means that it is much safer to ski in single file, but the result is a distinct lack of conversation. I'd decided not to listen to any music yet, so it didn't become something I had to have, but this meant I had to entertain myself. As I'm not somebody who can just daydream – I need to focus on something specific – I found it almost impossible not to think about the race and the teams around us.

A lot had changed since most of the group were together in Norway the previous January. The difficulty in just getting to the start line was highlighted by the fact that no team was the same as a year ago. People had struggled to get sponsorship, two guys were trying to go to both the North and South Poles in a year but hated the experience up north so pulled out, and there were fallings outs within teams, resulting in their being disbanded. The Norwegian all-women's team had pulled out, their men's team had gone from a three to a two and although we were still a three-man team it wasn't the same personnel. Others had come to Norway as individuals who had entered the race aiming to form a team with those in a similar situation; but no team that was formed there had made it to Antarctica without a change.

BEN   Apart from acclimatizing to the cold and the altitude, the reason for the group trek was to navigate our way through the hazardous mountains, home to dozens of hidden crevasses.

Crevasses occur where the ice sheet begins to push against something like a mountain, creating cracks and holes in the ice. Sometimes these are left exposed, but often they become filled with a thin layer of snow and ice, creating snow bridges. This crust, or 'lid' can be anything from a couple of metres to a couple of inches thick. Anyone who has read Joe Simpson's *Touching the Void* will know something of how terrifying the resulting game of Russian roulette can be. Crevasses have caused the deaths of thousands of unsuspecting hikers, skiers and mountaineers around the world, from Switzerland to the Antarctic.

During our training we had spent four days on a glacier in Austria learning about how to identify crevasses and, more importantly, how to escape from one. This had involved dangling precariously off a cavernous ice wall while your teammates tried to haul you up. Even in a controlled exercise this was surprisingly scary, and we had been warned crevasses would be one of our greatest dangers.

I had had many nightmares about falling into a deep fissure –

as had the race organizers and their insurers. As a result, it was decided that all the teams would navigate the dangerous crevasse fields together as a group, with Inge leading. He would teach us signs to look out for, leaving the individual teams better prepared for the race proper, across the relatively crevasse-free plateau.

To begin with, the terrain all looks the same as you ski across a snowy landscape – a little like walking across a field of grass. But after a while you begin to notice subtle differences in the texture, and even the colour, of the snow and ice.

'That is a crevasse,' announced Inge proudly, pointing at nothing in the snow. It was just a patch of white. For us there was little to define it from the rest of the landscape, but 'it has a different texture,' he continued. I stared at the invisible line, strained my eyes and even then found it difficult to spot the danger. A thin layer of snow was all that hid every polar explorer's worst nightmare. We skirted along the side of the hidden fissure and I tried to photocopy the image in my mind for future reference.

*

Inge staggered the group behind him, with the slowest skiers at the front, and the fastest at the back. Strung out like a necklace, we cut our way through rock-hard sastrugi, learning how to navigate around and over these icy knolls. To clarify, Antarctica's surface isn't as flat as you would think. The wind carves the snow and ice into a seamless, limitless sculpture of hardened ridges, like frozen waves on an enormous lake. These rolling formations are called sastrugi, and range from a few centimetres to a couple of metres high. Rather like the rippling of the sand created by the receding tide on a beach or migrating sand dunes blown by the wind, Antarctica is a gallery of snow and ice chiselled away over millions of years by that great artist, Nature.

The effect was startling. Much like watching clouds on a summer's day, this vast white canvas soon began to resolve itself into recognizable shapes as we skied. Icy crocodiles, whales and fantastic dinosaurs, even a fairly decent rendition of Munch's painting *The Scream* filled the landscape. It wasn't just me. The others saw the familiar shapes too. The slightly disturbing thing was that these imaginary creatures always appeared to have their eyes closed. They looked dead. This may sound crazy, but as my mind raced I began to imagine that this was where all the spirits of dead creatures came to rest. I should add that I hadn't even begun to dip into our supply of hallucinogenic painkillers by this stage.

The sastrugi were difficult for even the fittest, and for Mark, who is blind, this was his first experience of what lay ahead. Inge had developed a system whereby two carbon fibre poles went from the back of his pulk to hoops around Mark's wrists. The movement of these poles as Inge's pulk dipped and climbed, gave Mark a chance to 'see' the terrain through touch – or at least that was the theory.

The concentration needed must have been incredibly debilitating as he fought to maintain his balance and keep up with one of Norway's top polar travellers. It was incredible to watch, and if ever I began to struggle in the coming weeks I would think about what Mark was going through. Not once did I see him fall.

The Norwegians Rune and Stian were always at the back. A little like the two identical Belgian detectives in Tintin, they always wore the same clothes as each other, and both had long, curling blond beards. If one wore his Norwegian flag hat, then so did the other. If Rune removed his coat, then so did Stian. They always kept a little distance between themselves and us. Even when we stopped for a break, they would keep back. I never understood why, but what I took for rudeness was in fact strategy. They were observing us, analysing our technique and checking out the competition.

*

There wasn't much talking during the trek. It was difficult to communicate in single file, and I soon learned to switch off and concentrate on my skiing technique.

Every two hours we would take a break. 'Lunch break!'

hollered Inge every time, and we would pull our pulks alongside one another and munch on congealed cheese and chocolate. The breaks often seemed to last longer than the skiing sessions, which began to bother James.

I had warned him back in Cape Town that the acclimatization trek might be frustrating, as we would be handicapped by speed and ability. 'Let's just enjoy it,' I reasoned. 'This will be our opportunity to take in Antarctica before the racing begins. Our chance to relish earth's last great wilderness and enjoy each other's company.'

It didn't take long for James's frustrations to catch up with him though, and soon the sighing, tutting and arm flailing began. He tried to hide it, but for all James's attributes and skills, he's no actor.

We would ski until six or seven each evening before setting camp. There would be a flurry of activity as tents were erected and latrines dug, before everyone disappeared into their temporary homes.

JAMES   I spent most of that first day skiing behind Ben and wondered what was going through his mind. He'd had an awful last six weeks at home. As was highlighted in our row across the Atlantic – and to be honest, in virtually everything we do together – we approach things from two contrasting standpoints. I'm much more structured, while Ben is, shall we say, a little bit more random in his preparation. The contrast is accentuated when we're preparing for something a long time in the future. Having had to focus on the Olympics for most of my career, I don't have a problem with committing to a long-term goal, whereas Ben, who works in the far more short-term medium of television, operates more along the lines of the Japanese industrial system of Just-in-time Management.

However, I had to hand it to Ben: he had put in a lot of work preparing for the South Pole Race, and no one could have predicted the double whammy of a bout of Leishmaniasis and a tragic miscarriage just a few short weeks before the race. Ben's course of treatment had obviously worked, as he was skiing in front of me – physically he had bounced back incredibly quickly – but I really felt for Ben and Marina, going from the high of his recovery to such sad news in a heartbeat. Ben has a great ability not only to be positive but also to daydream, and I hoped he was putting both of those skills to good use and not dwelling too much on what had happened. It was vitally important that Ed and I support Ben on the acclimatization phase of the trip, both physically (to make sure that he didn't get to the start line exhausted) but also mentally. We had to do everything we could to keep his spirits up.

Part of that was to make sure we had fun in the tent, and it didn't get any more exciting than my nightly questionnaire. I'd drawn up a spreadsheet to try to work out what we were drinking and how much. Were we eating everything in our snack bags, and finishing meals? How many times were we pooing each day, and how much toilet roll were we using? Croyde would have been proud of me.

Though I applaud the skill of a single-sheet clean-up operation, my aim wasn't to chastise someone for using four sheets instead of two; I simply wanted to work out how much of everything we needed to take on the actual race. There was no point in taking a hundred cup-a-soups if they weren't getting drunk, or ten rolls of toilet paper if we could get by on less. If people were struggling to eat certain foods, this was a great chance to swap things around and maximize the calories they were taking in. (Although I reserved the right to tell the offending person not to be such a fussy bastard, and eat it anyway.)

Who am I kidding? Basically, I was trying to cover up a weight-culling exercise with an amusing questionnaire. To be honest, I think they saw through my cunning plan but let it slide as there wasn't much else to do in the tent.

13

WHITEOUT

Tuesday 23 December

BEN   We had been trekking for a week now as a group, and James had grown increasingly restless. He was running out of patience, and we were running out of luck. Until now, we had been blessed with fine sunny weather, but things were about to change.

The wind began as a whisper, almost imperceptible as it blew a thin layer of spindrift low across the polar tundra. By morning it was a raging gale, battering the tent and smothering our pulks in a hefty layer of snow.

The wind always sounds worse inside a tent, the thin fabric buffeted like a jelly. I lay in my sleeping bag listening to the change in the weather as the wind picked up from a dull hum to a deafening scream. 'There's no way we could venture out in this,' I thought as I lay huddled in my thick sleeping bag. I watched the tent sides flap in the wind. Occasionally the whole tent would be squashed down by the pressure of one of the big gusts. As some wag had once explained to me, the wind in Antarctica 'doesn't blow; it sucks'.

Any thoughts of a day off were soon shattered. 'We're still leaving at 10 a.m.' hollered Inge above the howling din of the wind. We ate our porridge in silence, deafened by the gale. This was ludicrous, I thought. Shouldn't we save ourselves and stay put? Blizzards and Brits have always been a fateful mix, and I wasn't sure we were ready to add to the list.

For the first time in days, I took extra care in dressing. I tucked my thermal vest firmly into my leggings and made sure all zips were firmly closed – after, all this was frostbite weather.

During my treatment for Leishmaniasis I had been referred to a Dr Van Tulleken. He had made a name for himself presenting a Channel Four series, *Medicine Men*, with his twin brother. He had also been a part of the BBC series *Blizzard*, but more significantly he had been the doctor during one of the more notorious episodes of polar racing. The start of that race to the North Pole had been hit by a massive storm, with wind chill temperatures of an unimaginable minus 70 degrees. One of the competitors, a Brit of course, had peed shortly before the start, and had inadvertently zipped and then unzipped his trouser flies. A double zip is really quite common on outdoor gear, allowing the wearer access from both ends and also acting as a back-up. In his case he had grabbed both zips with his heavy gloves and while he thought he was closing the zip, he was actually opening it. You can probably see where this is going: his family jewels were left exposed to the arctic wind. Numbed by the extreme temperature, he was unaware of what had happened until several hours later when he looked down at his blackened penis.

'Don't let this happen to you,' smirked Dr V-T as he showed me a photograph of the frostbitten willy. My zips would remain firmly closed.

Until now I had skied wearing just a woollen hat on my head, but today it was time for the full balaclava. I have never liked balaclavas as I find them too claustrophobic and restrictive, but in the wind it is crucial that no skin remains exposed, otherwise frostbite is inevitable.

Like a spaceman, I was ready to venture outdoors. I unzipped the inner part of the tent and then the outer door. The wind howled and screamed as I clambered out into the blizzard. I could make out the other red tents, but little more. The sky was obscured by a flat white mist of snow. It was noticeably colder and I felt my fingers quickly numb with the chill. This was the image of Antarctica I had been expecting.

Inevitably, everything takes longer in the wind. Our pulks were buried under a foot of snow and a large drift had developed up one side of the tent. Slowly we packed our pulks and took down the tent.

As I bent down to remove one of the poles, my world disappeared in a white fog as my goggles steamed up. This was my first experience of what would become the bane of our lives. We had been warned by other polar adventurers that misty goggles would drive us to distraction, but I hadn't realized how fast it could happen. We hadn't even started skiing.

The real problems start when you combine goggles or sunglasses with a balaclava and face mask. The hot air from one's breath heats up the material, sending a warm stream of air towards the eyes. The extreme difference in temperature on both sides of the lenses then mists and freezes it, rather like a car windscreen. We had been given plenty of advice on how to avoid 'goggle fog', and I had just broken the cardinal rule: 'never, ever bend down in a pair of goggles'. The heat from the body streams up through the top of your jacket, fogging the lenses before you've even got anywhere. The only way to defog a pair of misted lenses is to remove them and stick them down your thermals with the lenses to the skin. The body thaws the ice, and you then have to try to dry and clean the lenses before they freeze again. As with everything in Antarctica, it is a battle against the elements and a game of management.

JAMES Stian and Rune were already out and about, wearing what could only be described as a furry tunnel over their heads and looked annoyingly toasty; they'd clearly brought a combination of modern Gore-tex and old-school explorer gear. The latter seemed perfect for these conditions: apparently, the fur created a small microclimate that meant you couldn't feel the wind or cold, and they were complaining it was too hot. My heart bled for them, and selflessly I offered to swap my woolly hat for one. My offer was politely declined.

The award for best headgear, however, went to Mark Pollock,

who emerged from his tent with his head covered in a full bala-clava. Up until then he'd been wearing the same hat and goggles as everyone else, but overnight had decided to dispense with the goggles, saying 'I feel like an idiot [pronounced eejit] wearing them, it's not as if I can see anything.'

Taking down the tent ('pulling pole') and packing up the pulks took much longer than in the sun. With our ears covered up, the noise from the wind and the lack of peripheral vision made communication difficult. We learned some valuable lessons that morning because every other time we'd taken down the tent the weather had been good, and it hadn't mattered if we weren't all ready at the same time. This morning Ben was ready first and was left standing around getting cold, waiting for Ed and me. We also lost a valuable roll of toilet paper. Ed had been busy getting rid of the excess food his body didn't want, and put the loo roll on Ben's pulk. He said he told Ben it was there, Ben said he didn't hear – either way, it showed us that we couldn't assume someone had heard something. We needed confirmation from the other party that they'd heard.

Unfortunately, it wasn't the only thing Ed lost that day. We'd stopped for a drinks break after a couple of hours skiing. I was chatting to Ed and saw Inge skiing downwind like a maniac, chasing what looked like a glove. I nodded towards Inge: 'I think someone's lost a glove.' A minute later Ed went to put his back on and realized one was missing. Meanwhile Inge had come back and was apologizing for not catching up with the rogue handwear, but if he'd gone any further he would have lost us in the whiteout. I'm not sure Ed thought that was a good enough excuse to give up the search.

I felt for Ed. He'd had a bad couple of days, during which time he'd broken his tracer – the metal rods that attached the pulk to the harness. Now he'd lost a valuable glove. Luckily we'd brought a spare pair of outer gloves just in case, but hadn't figured on having to draw on them two days into the acclimatization trek. Personally, I was amazed I hadn't been the one to have lost the glove. At school

I was the last in my class to stop having my mittens connected together with elastic.

I enjoyed skiing in the whiteout, that first time. Don't get me wrong, I didn't want them all the time, but my Gore-tex 'gorilla' mask was keeping the wind off and my goggles weren't steaming up – I was happy in my own little world. Navigating was a different matter – with the sun blocked, there were no shadows to steer from.

BEN   Skiing through a blizzard isn't as miserable as I'd imagined. The only real difference is that you feel as if you're in a video game rather than Antarctica. Cocooned in layers of wool and Gore-tex is a little like walking around in a diving bell, looking through a window into another world.

While skiing in a blizzard is relatively straightforward, taking breaks is a different story. Up until now we'd had the luxury of a warm sun on our backs during our breaks. Now, in the absence of the sun and with temperatures of minus 40, the long breaks became an ordeal rather than a rest.

I would sit on my pulk with my back to the wind, swathed in my thick orange down coat. The body temperature begins to plummet as soon as it stops working, and, as with a car engine, it can be difficult to start again once it is cold. I would sip from my chilly water and munch on some ice cubes of cheese. The main problem of eating during the break is that the body redirects all the blood to the stomach. This then leaves all peripheral areas, like fingers and toes, dangerously depleted of blood.

My body gave me about five minutes until my fingers went numb and my body began to shake. I sat on my pulk, cartwheeling my arms in an effort to get the blood flowing through my icy fingers.

By the time we started off, I had invariably lost all feeling in my hands. I would find over the weeks that followed that it took me up to half an hour of vigorous hand-swinging to regain feeling. I hated stopping during blizzards. Breaks then always seemed to do more damage than good and the recovery time was almost as long as the break itself. I usually needed a break after my break.

Another hazard of skiing in a blizzard is ensuring that no skin is exposed. Even the smallest gap between the face mask and the balaclava can lead to frostbite, and since even covered skin becomes numb in the cold, it is almost impossible to tell when gaps appear. In fact the only way was by peering into a teammate's reflective goggles. I would stare into James's or Ed's glasses and analyse my face for any exposed skin, while they did the same.

This was a little like staring into a bank robber's face. Without eye contact it is impossible to read mood or emotion. They could have been crying with laughter or weeping with sorrow. For all I knew it mightn't have been the person I thought it was. With identical kit, I had to read the embroidered name on their jackets to identify who was who. Occasionally, I found myself checking my own jacket to make sure it was me. Blizzards are wonderfully impersonal, stripping you of your identity and encasing you in a world of fabric.

*

Taking a break is one thing, but setting up camp in a blizzard is a nightmare. Many expeditions have failed not because the team couldn't get out, but because they couldn't get in. We had learned the hard way in Norway the perils of setting up a tent in a howling gale. The main danger was that a team would strike the tent, set out in a medium-strength blizzard and then, as the storm worsened, find themselves unable to erect the tent. This kind of knowledge separated the experts from the novices and we knew it was our weakness. In a blizzard the fabric of the tent whips and snaps in the heavy gusts, creating a deafening noise that only adds to the chaos. One wrong move, and the precious tent could blow away: a disaster on the training leg, certain death in the race.

We had come a long way since Norway and even Switzerland, when we had struggled to erect the tent even in fine weather, but now, under pressure, we worked like clockwork. No words were needed. There was no shouting or hollering. We each had our task and we got on with it. It was immensely satisfying and, above all, reassuring.

*

As we had worked our way towards the mountain range in the distance, before the whiteout hit, Inge had called us to the front one by one to teach us how to navigate. Compasses are not particularly useful in Antarctica, especially as we were racing to the geographic South Pole. The magnetic Pole is somewhere in the Southern Ocean near Australia, meaning that down here, on the bottom of the world, magnetic 'south' is not necessarily where it should be. To use a compass, you need a chart of 'deviations' according to your longitude and latitude, and the few times we were forced to use our compass in bad weather the difference was sometimes up to 50 degrees – a huge discrepancy, with a correspondingly large margin of error.

Instead, we began to learn how to use the wind and the sun to find our way. The wind is one of the simplest means of navigating in Antarctica. A thin piece of silk on the ski poles acts as a wind direction indicator, and since the wind rarely changes direction, then once the GPS has given you a direction to point towards you simply keep the wind on the same side of you.

Even the dreaded sastrugi became useful. As the wind direction rarely shifts, the patterns and sculptures in the ice are always cut from the same angle, creating long tentacles of snow and ice. Combine this with the thin layer of spindrift driven across the plateau by the wind, and you have a huge visual wind compass.

All of these tricks gave us a pretty accurate direction, but without any landmarks it is nonetheless extremely difficult to ski in a straight line. You think you are going straight until you look back at your track and see that you have been weaving wildly. A 1-degree deviation from a straight line might not sound much, but stretched over 800 kilometres it's a huge amount. If we didn't keep our wits about us, we could end up miles off course.

Inge taught us a clever way of maintaining a steady course across the icy tundra.

'Look ahead,' he said to me. 'What do you see in the snow?'

I squinted through my sunglasses at the blinding white terrain. There really wasn't much.

'Keep looking, and tell me when you see something,' he continued.

'I can see a Tyrannosaurus Rex head,' I announced sheepishly.

'Exactly,' he smiled kindly, 'now make sure you remember it and look for another.'

Before long I pointed out a crocodile, and a long-haired hippy. 'Right,' he said, 'keep the dinosaur head to the left and the hippy to the right and create a highway.' It was brilliant: I could create a runway using these wacky images, and I would find my way to the South Pole, the South Pole of Scott and Shackleton and all my heroes, using images of Donald Duck and Barack Obama.

Wednesday 24 December

JAMES Navigating by staring into a white abyss got nauseous after a while, and I wouldn't want too many long days like that. But no weather system hangs around for ever, especially near the mountains. We started the day skiing in a whiteout, had beautiful sunshine for five hours in the middle of the day, and then the weather closed in again and the temperature plummeted. We pitched in almost zero visibility – some Christmas Eve. Santa was going to struggle to find us.

14

WHITE CHRISTMAS

Thursday 25 December

BEN   I had been dreading Christmas Day. I had missed family Christmases before – memorably on the rowing boat with James, when we attempted to bring cheer to our wretchedly dehydrated state by wearing Santa hats – but it didn't make it any easier this time. It's the one day of the year when you know exactly what everyone is doing, where they are and what they are eating. It pained me to think about Marina without me, and, as James pointed out rather annoyingly, I had spent more Christmases with him than I had with my wife!

We had got into a routine over the last few days. I had resigned myself to being away and I'd even stopped missing home – but Christmas Day would take me back to square one. I wouldn't be able to escape my emotions and once again I'd be forced to confront the reality of how far from home we were.

It was a balmy minus 1 in our mountain campsite as we awoke on Christmas Day. Minus 1! I'm not sure if it was global warming or a Christmas present from Antarctica, but with kit that was designed to resist extraordinarily low temperatures, this felt like the Caribbean. I got up and wandered around in my thermal top, luxuriating in the warmth of the sun.

JAMES   The orange glow in the tent was back, as were the burning retinas and the broiling sleeping bag. I got up and took my sleeping bag outside to let sublimation work its magic; within ten minutes all the moisture in my sleeping bag had vaporized. I wish I could fully explain or even understand the physics behind sublimation, but basically it is caused by the temperature being well below freezing, which turns certain solids – ice being one – into gas without a liquid stage. Soaking wet clothes could be hung up and then retrieved totally dry. Antarctica's freeze-drying laundry service had already put the continent in my good books before I'd looked around to see where we were. For the first time, I truly understood why the early pioneers came back here despite the risks. We had unknowingly chosen the most beautiful campsite imaginable.

BEN   Vast grey peaks protruded from the white plains below, the wolf's teeth of Fenriskjeften sharp as razors against the cold blue sky. It was a treat for the eyes after so many days of bleak white plains. A few clouds clung to mountaintops that were sprinkled with a frosting of snow. This was *Lord of the Rings* country.

JAMES   Scott would have been making his way to the Pole at this time of year, while Amundsen was already on his way back. The year they battled to the Pole the weather wasn't kind to them to say the least, but with all the hardship they both endured on their respective journeys they would also have had days like this. It was moving to look out on this magnificent view and imagine Scott and his men awaking to a scene like this, and feeling the same lift in their spirits that we were experiencing.

BEN   Tony and his team visited each tent with a tiny bottle of brandy and a slice of Christmas cake. I downed the shot and gobbled the cake in seconds. Wrapped around it was a small piece of paper. 'A special Christmas message,' said race organizer Sarah with a wink as she disappeared and made her way to the next tent.

'Happy Christmas, darling,' read the message, 'thinking of you and wishing you were with us, love Marina, Inca and Maggi xxx'. That short, simple message cut through the pressure of my worries in an instant, a beautiful, brutal reminder of what I had left behind. I burst into tears.

Ed took hold of his small message and unwrapped it. I watched him as his eyes scanned the paper and a tear formed. He walked off to be on his own. It must have been hard for Ed, away from his family at Christmas for the first time. One of four children, the Coatses were a close family and Ed was struggling.

'I can't believe you're both crying already,' sighed James, 'what are you going to be like during the race?' Here was a typically blunt response from James, who until now had reined in his thoughtlessness. Knowing James as I do, I suspect it was his own way of keeping his own emotions and thoughts of home at bay, but I was annoyed by the lack of sentimentality. It was a difficult day for the film crew, too, and even Alexis, a real rock for us, was in tears at being away from his four children over Christmas for the first time.

JAMES Not surprisingly, I didn't feel particularly 'Christmassy', probably because I was trying to put it out of my mind. It was my choice to be here, though I desperately wanted to be back home to see the excited look on Croyde's face when he came piling into our room, probably at 4 a.m. What was also making me feel low was a realization that no photo, video footage or description I gave of what I could see this morning (or indeed any day out here) was going to do it justice, and I desperately wanted to share it with the people who meant the most to me. Not that I didn't love Ed and Ben, but it wasn't quite the same; I consoled myself that Bev doesn't like the cold or camping, so no matter how beautiful the view, the lack of a toilet, running water, a bed and normal food may have spoilt the experience for her.

I hadn't got a message from Bev, but I had a little Christmas cake that I shoved into my day sack, trying to put Christmas on hold until the evening while thoughts turned to home. The stunning scenery and weather made it a special day. I thought about the fun things that Bev and Croyde would be up to. I thought about my sister and her husband, who had been expecting to be spending a first Christmas with their daughter. It hurt so much when I thought of the horrible seven months they had endured since Eva's untimely death less than a week after being born. It made me appreciate how lucky I am and then wonder what I was doing down here, missing two months of Croyde's life when they had had only six days with their daughter.

BEN Apart from the morning's short celebrations, there was little to distinguish this day from any other. We set off at ten, and broke every two hours. Once again we set camp at six and settled down to a Christmas dinner of rehydrated food. We had decanted all the evening meals into plastic bags, three meals in each bag. We had bought a large Tupperware container in Cape Town into which we would decant the evening meal, add boiling water and then serve up the rehydrated contents. The only problem with this was that we never knew what we were going to get, or indeed, what we got. Christmas day's dinner was green and tasted like . . . rehydrated food. It was impossible to even guess what was in our bowls, but it did the job and filled a ravenous gap.

Tony and the race organizers had one final gift to give us: a telephone call home. We would be accompanied and we only had five minutes, but it was a call home nonetheless. I both couldn't wait and dreaded the call in equal measure. I had resigned myself to a complete absence of communication, and now we were about to be teased by a tantalizingly short conversation, and reminded of what we were missing.

'Happy Christmas!' I bellowed down the phone. Marina was with her parents and sisters in Henley. 'Jeremy Paxman prayed for you in church today!' she sniggered, explaining that the priest had included us in her Christmas prayer, and as Paxman and his family had been in the small congregation, he had therefore technically prayed for me. Cool, I thought, he usually shouts at people.

It was a good chat, but it had reignited my homesickness. I put the phone down heavily, lost in my thoughts.

JAMES I was determined to make the most of the call home, not be sad and try to paint a proper picture for Croyde of where I was and what it was like out here. Ben and Ed came back from their respective calls downbeat. They were always going to be difficult conversations no matter how hard you try to ignore it – a countdown from five minutes will start as soon as they pick up, an awkward goodbye already hanging over the conversation. But talking to an adult and a five-year-old high on chocolate is a totally different experience.

'Miss you, Daddy,' said Croyde, possibly under instruction from his mum, followed by, 'have you seen a penguin?'

'No penguins, although I did see —'

'Have you done a poo in the snow?' Now we were on to his questions.

'Yes, it's very cold but . . .' I nearly made it to the end that time.

'Has Ben done a poo in the snow? Has Ed done a poo in the snow?' He was like a little John Humphrys.

'Yes, we all have. Did Father Christmas bring you any presents?' I asked.

'Oh, Granddad and Poppy are wrestling in their sumo suits, bye,' he trailed off as the phone hit the floor.

Bev picked it up.

'Sumo suits?' I said.

'Yeah, it's all fancy dress round here. It's not the same without you.' She sounded as though she was trying to be cheerful whilst not feeling it. I felt the conversation was about to get emotional when Croyde grabbed the phone from her.

'Daddy, can you bring me back a penguin?' he shouted down the phone.

'I'll try but . . .'

'A chocolate one. Bye!' That was it; I could hear his little feet disappearing down the hall.

'Baby, I've got to go, my time's up, do you want a chocolate penguin as well?' I asked, going for a happy goodbye.

'Why not, I've eaten every other type of chocolate today,' said Bev. I could picture her smiling. 'You're allowed, you're pregnant,' I said. 'Bye, baby, I really miss you and thank you. I'm very lucky.' I really wanted her to know how much I appreciated her sacrifices.

'You enjoy it, I'm off to watch the sumo wrestling, and I'm the only one that doesn't need a suit.' She blew a kiss down the phone and that was it, the last contact until the end of the race.

It was brilliant to talk to them and I tried to forget that the next call wouldn't be until after the race at the end of January. I decided to cheer myself up with the Christmas cake I was given earlier. I didn't even look at the piece of paper stuck to the side, assuming it was a Christmas message from the organizers. As interesting as that would be, it wasn't as exciting as a good bit of cake. 'I think that letter might be from Bev,' said Ed, 'mine was from Karina.' Cue a frantic search of the rubbish dump that was my sliver of the tent. This would be my only letter from Bev. I'd hoped she'd hidden some in my bag but she hadn't, and I desperately wanted to hear her voice in my head again.

'Got it!' I shouted, unfolding a piece of A4 paper. It was beautifully written, and made me far more emotional than the phone call, possibly because it wasn't interrupted by a five-year-old asking about poos and penguins; or maybe Royal Mail were right all along and it really does mean more by post.

I thought about the best way of showing the effect the letter had on me, and decided the best way was to ask you to imagine you're in a tent on Christmas Day in freezing temperatures, over 10,000 miles from home. You're reading the following letter from your wife/husband/girlfriend/boyfriend and can hear their voice as clear as a bell as you read:

Dear James,

Hope you had a longer lie-in than me this morning! Guess there are advantages to being away on Christmas Day! By now, Croyde will probably have woken up the whole of Turner Towers, opened all his presents – pausing only to try on various outfits or take all the bits out of complicated board games – eaten most of his selection box and asked to watch every new DVD. And it's only 7.45 a.m. . . . I can only imagine how weird your day must be. Hope you and the boys are trudging along enthusiastically. PLEASE don't go off too hard at the start. Bernie says you will be fine – as long as you don't do that! We don't care a jot about positions. Just get back in one piece and not several little ones in Tamara- [Ben's sister] designed fabric bags. Please don't worry about us. We will be absolutely fine. Obviously, we will be missing you very much and no doubt Croyde will be misbehaving at times without your booming voice to pull him into line, but there will be nothing that cannot be ironed out in the fullness of time. You're such a fantastic daddy. You have huge reserves of energy that Croyde needs (!!) and enjoys and thrives upon. It's vital that you get home safe. And I've been really touched by the way you have made time for me in the run-up to the race. I know it takes a conscious effort to do that with your ridiculous schedule and I do appreciate it. How astonishingly different to when you went away on that long rowing race! We will talk about you every day and I will explain to Croyde why daddy needs to go away and do his 'work' in the South Pole and how we will have a lovely time when you are back. You may drive me slightly mad with your ridiculous schemes but you are an inspiration to me and I feel very lucky to have a husband who feels such loyalty and commitment to his family (and has really good thighs plus an excellent store of sarcastic one-liners). Mum and I are probably rowing about parsnips by now; Adi has been banished to the shed for gassing us; Cal will have been watching a crap film whilst texting various boys; your dad will be polishing off another bottle of Jacobs Fizz and I'm trying to remember why ONE meal is not such a big deal. So I'd better go and have a calming hug with my dad! Wish it was you but hey ho, dad gives good hugs so don't worry too much. Massively

*impressed by your superhuman efforts and willing you on
every step of the way. Don't forget to look at the beautiful
sky. Love you so much.*

   Bev, bump and the bunny rabbit xxx

I had tears rolling down my cheeks the first time I read it, and it has
had a huge effect on me every time I read it after that. Sometimes it
made me laugh, at other times inspiring me to get stuck into the
race and stop thinking how hard it was and how exhausted I was;
but I never tired of reading it. Lucky, as it was my only one.

15

TENT BRÛLÉE

JAMES Up until now the pace had been that of the slowest person, and I was champing at the bit to start the real race. A steep twenty-minute climb straight out of camp encouraged some metaphorical 'willy waving', either because teams were beginning to test their 'rank' and see how fast they were, or perhaps because of excess energy due to last night's Christmas. I was faffing around with my harness and was slightly late in leaving – a trait that seemed to stay with me throughout the race. I could see people starting to push up the hill and gaps opening up. 'The race hasn't started yet,' I told myself, 'I don't need to get involved.' That mature attitude lasted for about a minute, until I decided I wanted to see if I could make it from the back to the front of the group by the time we reached the top.

Halfway up the hill I was sweating for the first time and enjoying the feeling of my lungs being opened up. The Norwegians were just behind me when I started off, and I told myself that whatever happened I wasn't going to look behind me; I'd only see them if they overtook me. I slowly overtook the rest of the racers. Admittedly not everybody was racing but I didn't let that minor fact take away any pleasure. I tucked in behind Inge, he stopped at the top and we turned round to look at the group strung out down the hill. I was pleased to see that Ben and Ed had followed me up and were in the next group to arrive. The problem of sweating was becoming evident – my thermal was wet through and starting to cool. As we had been told in Norway by Inge nearly a year ago: you sweat, you die. It wouldn't be long before the moisture froze and we still had a few minutes to wait for everyone to make it up.

*

The pace was up and down all day and as the hours went by some of those who'd gone too hard in the morning were starting to struggle. It taught us the importance of not going off too hard and hitting a steady pace that can be maintained all day. A nice theory, but I'd been telling myself at the start of every race for years not to go off too hard and I still hadn't managed to heed my own advice – maybe this time?

We climbed up through 2,000 metres for the first time, although the perceived altitude was more like 2,800 metres because of the lack of pressure at this part of the globe. Being at altitude caused a drop in temperature, and as the day wore on and the sun began to fall again towards the horizon, it fell further. The coldest time of the day seemed to be from 8 to 11 p.m. The light didn't really change, but slowly, stealthily, clothes we were happily skiing in a couple of hours earlier weren't keeping us warm enough.

Saturday 27 December

The cold mornings I'd dreaded were starting to become a reality. I wasn't in such a rush to get out of the sleeping bag and start the stoves this morning. It was a big day today. We'd be leaving the mountains behind us and making our way up on to the plateau the peaks would disappear and we'd get our first glimpse of the famous featureless horizon that had played with explorers' sanity for over a century. We were heading for the rendezvous point – imaginatively named RV1 – where the planes would pick us up and move us to the start line.

It took us all morning to get past the last of the peaks and there it was, our view for the next month: a white horizon cut off by a bright blue sky. If the weather stayed like this for the race, though, I wasn't going to be complaining about the view.

*

Over the summer leading up to the race, our standard of skiing had been a major worry for me. Every centimetre we could gain with good technique would make a massive difference. I bought us all roller skis and organized some lessons; although not a perfect solution, they should get us used to standing on skis, strengthen the ankles and simulate the movement. They definitely made a difference, since none of us felt totally like a fish out of water when we went to Switzerland, and that in turn helped us when we clicked the bindings in Antarctica. We didn't have the technique of the Norwegians, but with pulks attached the importance of technique diminished slightly. Dragging a pulk is like riding a bike with stabilizers and brakes always on – frustratingly slow, hard work, but nice and stable.

So far the conditions underfoot had been flat and not too icy, and there had been relatively few Eddie the Eagle-style elementary mistakes. But as we entered our first major sastrugi field my pulk was acting like a group of pit bulls on a lead, either yanking me off balance or barrelling into the back of my legs. I fell over more times in an hour than I had done in the first week. If I hadn't been sepa-rated from my pulk by my metal tracers I'd have taken my skis off and spent ten minutes kicking the hell out of it for constantly pulling me over and capsizing. The notion of a flat featureless plateau was being shown up for the fantasy it was.

The weather started to close in and as we'd been skiing for over ten hours Inge decided to make camp for the night – we'd ski the remaining kilometres to RV1 in the morning. Once we'd set up we got a visit from Tony.

'Stop cuddling and open up,' he said in his military tone as he approached the tent. 'You boys OK? Still up for doing this?'

'Yeah, why wouldn't we be?' I asked.

'If you go on from here, you're coming to the Pole one way or another, even if you're sitting in one of the support vehicles all the way. This is the last chance to get back to Novo if you don't fancy it,' he replied flatly. 'It's minus 40 at the start line and a whiteout.'

'No, we're good,' I said.

'Right, see you at the RV.' He was gone.

BEN If his plan was to psyche me out, it worked – and not for the first time. During treatment he had accompanied me to hospital. 'Of course everyone else is out training now,' he had warned me while the nurses injected me with my poisonous cocktail. I had hated him for those words.

'Do you think we're ready?' asked James, for reassurance. Tony gave an almost invisible nod of the head. 'Then we're happy to go on,' I replied.

Tony's words had worried me. We had experienced minus 30 out here, but that was with wind chill. What did minus 40 'still air' feel like in the wilds of Antarctica? How would our bodies cope in those temperatures, and, more importantly, what happened if you factored wind into the equation?

JAMES Ben didn't look great. 'You all right, mate? You look a bit shaken,' I said.

'Not really,' said Ben. 'He scared me: minus 40 is really cold. I'm not sure I'm ready for a month of that,' he replied.

'Mate, we'll be fine, the temperature is just a number. Don't get psyched out by it or by him. You know how tough he likes to make things sound,' I said, trying to make him feel better.

'Yeah,' he mumbled. It clearly hadn't worked.

'Were you cold today?' I asked, half rhetorically. 'It was minus 25. We'll eat up minus 40 no problem. Ed and I were at minus 35 to minus 40 in the chamber and the cold was way down on our list of concerns. There's plenty of things to worry about before that.'

'Yeah, I guess so.' He didn't sound totally convinced, but the only way he was going to believe it was when he'd experienced it and coped with it.

Our conversation was interrupted by someone shouting 'Get it out! Get it out!' I stuck my head out of the tent just as a flaming stoveboard came flying out of a tent; Team Danske Bank had clearly been doing a flambé in their tent.

BEN The timing of their accident couldn't have been worse. We were still struggling to make Ed feel one of the team, but James was being surprisingly generous with his compliments and we made sure we took turns with all the chores, including the one we dreaded most: lighting the stoves.

If I had one concern about the expedition from this point on, one thing that could instantly ruin our chances of reaching the Pole, it was the stoves. Crevasses, frostbite, hypothermia, starvation and getting lost all came lower down my list than those bloody stoves. From the very first time we used them at MIRA, I knew these dangerously temperamental pieces of equipment would be the bane of our adventure, as capable of killing us as keeping us alive. They scared James, too. No matter how much training and planning we had put into the race, we could fail simply because of the stoves, and he knew it. As a source of comforting heat and, even more importantly, drinking water, they are quite simply a polar traveller's most important piece of kit. Both James and I had had a number of opportunities to practise with them over the year, and indeed James had taken it upon himself to strip them and rebuild them in an effort to understand the minutiae of their workings. But the fact remained: we hated them.

Ed had been late entering the terrifying world of stove maintenance. His encounter had been brief, but colourful. It was in Switzerland, on the glacier. He had been preparing breakfast while James and I snatched an extra ten minutes in our sleeping bags. We were both deep in sleep when I became aware of a bright flare. I don't know how we did it, but in tandem, from the heaviest of dreams, James and I flew across the tent towards Ed. We grabbed pots and pans and were able to put out the flames that were licking the tent's highly flammable walls. It had been a near miss and only confirmed our fears.

JAMES The result of Danske Bank's impromptu campfire was only a small hole, but it could have been so much worse. A few more seconds and they'd have been digging a snow hole to sleep in rather than just repairing a hole in their tent. An accident like that was a far bigger concern to me than the temperature. Danske Bank was an experienced team and they'd nearly lost their tent. What chance did we have of making it through the race without making a similar mistake?

16

IN THE DOLDRUMS

Sunday 28 to Monday 29 December

BEN We lay in our sleeping bags while the wind ripped across the icy plains, howling as the storm worsened. The tent shook like a jelly, its sides flapping angrily and I lay there, eyes open, ready to jump up and evacuate the tent at any moment. It seemed impossible that the flimsy thin material could stand up to such ferocity, and I felt certain the tent would rip at any moment. I could practically hear the guy lines creak under the pressure. If they snapped, the tent could be blown into the ether.

I imagined what it must have been like for Captain Scott, without the luxury of back-up, race organizers and support planes. The blizzard sounded like a hurricane as snow hammered against the tent, and we didn't sleep much that night. By morning it had worsened.

'Morning!' I shouted above the din, 'do you think we'll go out in this?'

'Yeah, course,' nodded James. I wasn't so sure.

JAMES I didn't think the wind was strong enough to stop us skiing the last few hours to RV1, so we ate our porridge, suited up in Gore-tex and were about to pull pole when Inge came round to say we weren't moving today; the wind was going to keep picking up all day and well into the night.

'Check your tent, pull your pulks round the back and put them on their sides to give some extra protection from the wind,' he said.

'How can you be so sure it's going to get stronger?' I asked. I wanted to know how he could tell as it may help us make important decisions in the race, and I was excited at the prospect of learning some traditional Norwegian method of interpreting the wind.

'I spoke to Novo airfield on the satellite phone and they have today's weather predictions,' he replied, simply. So much for ancient techniques. We were stuck with our method of sticking our heads out of the tent and guessing. Mentally, I knew it would be tough to sit and wait out a storm during the race. I knew I'd want to get moving, and the thought that we were in the tent not knowing whether others were skiing or not would be incredibly difficult.

For us, though, the next twenty-four hours was going to be a valuable lesson in when we should or shouldn't pack up and move. The meteorologists at Novo were right: the wind was getting stronger and stronger, and though a tent always exaggerates the noise of both wind and rain, it was taking a real battering. By the evening it was so strong we all wondered whether the tent was going to stand up to it, leaving us lying on the snow with the tent sailing off into the wilderness. It was then that we remembered this was first time this design of tent had been used in Antarctica. Hmm. We'd already replaced the guy ropes at Novo since the ones it came with looked as if they'd have snapped with a small huff and a puff from the big bad wolf. We may not have been able to make it as strong as the last little piggy's house, but we wanted something that put up some decent resistance.

As evening approached it was really blowing. The wind would lull, and we'd be hit by a massive gust. The whole tent would shake and I'd be about to dive for my boots. I figured I could either suit up and be ready to go just in case, or climb into my sleeping bag, zip it up, pull it over my head and pretend that it wasn't happening.

I chose the latter.

I spoke to the Norwegians in the morning and they were

equally as concerned but had done the former. Clearly, I was still serving my polar survival apprenticeship.

The storm blew itself out in the early hours of the morning. We all felt relieved that we'd got through the night and had more confidence in the tent after we knew it had held up OK and with no damage. My theory that it could have been weakened by the storm didn't go down too well, and I made a mental note to keep comments like that to myself in the future.

BEN   We were able to make a little headway, and edged our way across a further 18 kilometres of ice and sastrugi to RV1, the rendezvous point with the plane, while the race organizers began the long overland journey to the start line, still 500 miles away. Visibility had been reduced to just a few metres and the temperature had plummeted to minus 40. Once again we battled against the wind to erect our tent and settle down to another night in our storm-tossed shelter.

JAMES   It may only have been 18 kilometres but it was my worst ski of the whole trip thus far. By the time we reached our rendezvous point I was totally frustrated. Thanks to the wind in the night I'd got it into my head that it would be cold outside and wore an extra layer, but after ten minutes, skiing I was too hot and my goggles had steamed up. Not only was I uncomfortably hot, I couldn't see, couldn't get any rhythm and couldn't stand up properly. I just about kept my sanity because I could see other people were struggling as well, but that didn't stop a bout of Tourette's. Annoyingly, the Norwegians seemed to be gliding effortlessly over the surface while I waded in treacle. To an outside observer it must have looked like the cast of *Night of the Living Dead* going out for a ski. The ex-sportsman in me tried to put the last three hours of frustration into perspective – better to get the bad ski out of the system before the race starts – but that hypothesis never seemed to hold up in my previous life, and I wasn't convinced it was going to apply down here either.

Tuesday 30 December

JAMES   The race was supposed to start today, but it was a white-out and we weren't at the start line. Given that I could only just make out the nearest tent 15 metres away, I figured the plane wouldn't be able to fly in, and the race would be delayed.

That was disappointing, but a far more pressing problem was that for every day the race was delayed, we would be living on race rations. Our resupply bags were at the start line, several hundred miles away, and we'd eaten all the food apart from a manky bag of porridge that had split in the bottom of my pulk.

BEN   This wasn't the first time I had been stormbound with James. The last time, we had been stuck inside a small, stuffy cabin on a storm-tossed ocean. It had been a miserable few days plagued with seasickness and boredom. At least we didn't have to worry about seasickness.

I suddenly wished we had chosen a pretty, petite girl to be our team member rather than a six-foot plus sportsman with shoulders like breeze blocks. The wind pushed against the tent sides, further reducing the space inside. There really wasn't much room as we huddled in like sardines, but it was good to pass the time getting to know Ed. It was the first time we had really had the opportunity to talk, and the more Ed opened up about his job and his tight-knit family, the more I liked him.

The tent buzzed, hummed and vibrated with the strengthening wind, while spindrift worked its way inside through the tiniest gaps.

It rarely snows in Antarctica. It is the driest place on earth, with an average precipitation of just a couple of millimetres. It wasn't fresh snow that was falling, but old snow being funnelled across the ice. We had learned to build a snow wall behind the tent, on the windward side, to prevent the snow building up around us, so James jumped up, and made his way outside to start work on the Great Ice Wall of China.

JAMES   Building a snow wall beat lying in the tent thinking about food. I must have looked the part, as Pete and Tess commissioned me to build one for them in return for a bag of chocolate – an absolute no-brainer of a deal.

BEN   New Year's Eve arrived and the blizzard showed no sign of letting up. We were already running behind schedule and word had reached us that the support team were struggling in their vehicles, reduced to just a few kilometres an hour, not much faster than we had been skiing.

JAMES   It wasn't the most exciting New Year's Eve of my life. It was still a whiteout and windier when I woke up, so it was another couple of days confined to the tent trying to make Pete and Tess's chocolate and the manky porridge see us through the day. We decided the best way to make the chocolate last and to pass the time was to play poker – at least then we each had the chance of winning some extra food. That was, if any of us could remember the rules for Texas Hold'em.

We resorted to '21', which takes about as much skill as Snap, and after a couple of hours you'd rather give all your food away than keep deciding whether to stick or twist.

It's unusual that the same object can at times be so appealing and fill you with dread, but that's what the tent was like for us. When we'd been skiing all day I used to fantasize about pitching it, firing up the stoves, having a hot meal and getting into my sleeping bag. But any more time in it than that, and it was like being sent to your room for hours, knowing that everyone else was downstairs having fun (a situation I found myself in quite a lot when I was growing up).

An old adage says that you can survive three minutes without air, three days without water and three weeks without food. We'd run out of food and gone at least eight hours without eating, so we still had two weeks six days and sixteen hours left; let's call it two weeks, because of the demands lower temperatures place on the body in Antarctica. We had plenty of fuel so we could melt snow and make hot drinks, but too many drinks meant having to go outside for a pee, which at minus 40 involved getting suited up and then bringing back enough snow into the tent to build a snowman. It was a tricky balance to strike.

When you're stuck in a tent with nothing to do, food becomes a major issue. I'm not by any means comparing our bored hunger to that of Shackleton's men when they were stuck on the ice in 1915 following the crushing of their ship *Endurance*, but food became the major talking point for them way before it was an issue of survival. Frank Worsley, the captain of *Endurance*, wrote in his diary, 'It is scandalous – all we seem to live for and think of now is food. I have never in my life taken half such a keen interest in food as I do now – and we are all alike.' We were waiting for a plane to arrive; their boat had been crushed, there was no way of getting home and they were about to face the fury of the Antarctic winter.

Worsley was a truly amazing man, responsible for the unbelievable navigation of the *James Caird* from Elephant Island to South Georgia, by my lights the most amazing journey ever by a small boat. I was glad to see that we shared a characteristic, even if it was just that we have the same apathy towards food in normal life. For me food has always been a fuel rather than a source of pleasure or infatuation, but holed up in my tent I felt exactly as Worsley had done. Infatuation with food is a theme that runs through most of the exploration books on Antarctica.

There was some good news: Tony had come back to the camp. Nothing against Tony, but it wasn't him I was glad to be reunited with, it was our resupply bag on the back of his vehicle. It turned out there was no such thing as a free lunch though, as we all had to go and stand outside for a briefing. Tony informed us that there would be a delay to the start of the race, as I had guessed. That was the bad news. The worse news was that it didn't look as if we were going to get going until 4 or 5 January now. More time in the bloody tent.

With the dates of the flights out of Antarctica fixed (subject to the now-tired caveat of 'climatic conditions') he was going to shorten the race by 50 kilometres so that it would now be 750 kilometres: just a sprint, then. I asked why we didn't just dispense with the twenty-four-hour stop at the halfway checkpoint and keep the distance the same; luckily, he ignored my question.

Despite having a date for the start of the race, there was no guarantee that was going to happen. We needed the weather to be clear at Novo for the plane to take off, but also to be clear here, and at the start line too. To make that more likely we were going to move 10 kilometres to an area where the planes could land a greater percentage of the time. Having trekked for 200 kilometres an extra 10 kilometres would have made no difference, and I wondered why we hadn't just gone there in the first place. After the way my first question was treated, I thought it best not to air that one.

BEN   I now understand the term 'cabin fever'. We had only been tent-bound for a couple of days and yet already we were beginning to show signs of strain. Apart from a short trip out, we had hardly skied for a week. I enjoyed the relaxation, but Ed and James were like caged animals, raring to get out.

'I think we should go skiing!' barked James. An ever-eager Ed agreed, but I wasn't so keen. We were about to embark on one of the most physically demanding races in the world, involving up to eighteen hours a day of skiing. Wasn't this the time to relax and sleep? I wondered. The majority vote won, and before I knew it we were heading out into the whiteness.

Within a minute we were out of sight of camp. White, white, white. There was little to distinguish between ground and sky. In fact apart from the skis we could have been upside down. It felt a little like being in one of those snow shakers.

In single file we snaked due south. We had left the pulks behind, and without the weight behind us we sped across the polar tundra. 'Four and a half kilometres an hour,' marvelled James as we beat into the wind.

Already three days behind schedule, we were rapidly running out of time. The Russian Ilyushin was due back on 30 January and we had to be on it if we didn't want to spend the winter in Antarctica.

The sun shone for the first time in days, but the temperature had plunged. We were at the edge of the plateau and already at 2,500 metres, or 7,500 feet, which by a quirk of physics feels more like 3,500 metres or 10,000 feet.

Thursday 1 January

BEN New Year's Day came with lots of wind and little fanfare. The tent continued to shake and vibrate under the strain of the wind and we continued to wait. The organizers had planned a small celebration at midnight. We had been instructed to meet at 11.45 and join in the festivities with a dram of whisky.

As midnight approached, the wind intensified. Once again we were forced to battle against the drifting snow, which threatened to engulf and submerge our tent. A little like the Humber bridge, by the time you had worked your way around the tent, you had to start all over again. Things hadn't been helped by the colossal 'boredom wall' constructed by Ed and James.

They had reasoned on a simple science, 'the bigger the wall the better', and had proceeded to create a defence that was visible from space. They had failed to take into account the physics of wind and drift. The wall created a massive vacuum on the leeward side of the tent. This vacuum filled with snow at an alarming rate, burying our tent twice as fast as normal.

It was nearly eleven o'clock and there was just an hour until 2009. I could hear Inge shouting above the din of the wind.

'New Year's is cancelled', he cried, 'it's too dangerous out here', 'have a happy . . .' His final words were stolen by a gust of wind. It's not every day New Year gets cancelled. Does that mean I remain thirty-five for another year? I hope so.

JAMES New Year's Eve may have been cancelled, but that's not to say we didn't get to go outside, because the huge snow wall I'd built was now threatening to make a mausoleum out of the tent rather than act as a protective barrier against the wind. I now understood why Inge had shaken his head when I built it in the first place. It was about to bury us, so on went the Gore-tex and Ed and I went out into the 35 mph winds to dig out the tent. It was a miserable forty minutes but for five minutes of hilarity watching Ed trying to have a dump when it was nearly minus 40 in a blizzard. I was glad that, subconsciously, my mind had instructed my bowels there was to be no movement until the sun made a reappearance.

Once Ed and I were fairly sure we weren't going to be buried for a few hours, we dived back inside.

BEN Ed, James and I lay side by side in our sleeping bags. It was two minutes to midnight. I imagined all the different festivities around the world, welcoming in the New Year: the Thai beach parties, the firework displays, the countdowns. Jools Holland and 'Auld Lang Syne'. Marina had gone to Kate Humble's in Wales, and I pictured them around the fireplace with glasses of bubbly.

I stared at my watch as the second hand struck midnight. I swear I heard the sound of champagne corks popping. 'Happy New Year,' I whispered unenthusiastically as the tent swayed wildly above me.

'Happy New Year,' replied Ed and James in unison. And all my friends think I lead a glamorous life.

JAMES The New Year started pretty much as the old one ended, in a blizzard digging the tent out. I felt as if I'd been cooped up for weeks rather than days: I was pissed off and I shouted at the wind: 'This place is shit, nothing lives out here, there's nothing to look at, why does anyone ever come back?' I may or may not return to Antarctica but one thing was for certain: giant snow walls weren't going to be part of our tent routine, no matter how long we were camping in one place.

I'd just clambered back inside the tent when Inge came round and told us the plan for the day. He made the mistake of starting the conversation off by saying, 'This weather makes you feel alive doesn't it?' I don't think he was expecting the expletive-ridden rant that came flying back at him, especially as he wasn't even the bearer of bad news: we were going to move to the imaginatively named RV2, where the plane was going to arrive, 'soon'. I admired the optimism but noted the lack of specifics.

We pulled pole for the 10-kilometre ski and stood there in goggles and balaclava, waiting for the order to ski off, getting steadily colder as the wind blasted through the campsite. I decided I was born for Antarctic exploration as long as it was sunny, not too windy, with nice smooth terrain and temperatures not below minus 30 degrees. As soon as it fell outside those parameters, it wasn't nearly as appealing.

RV2 seemed a much better place to land a plane than RV1. I could actually see the horizon here, and having spent three days struggling to see more than a couple of metres I felt more positive – that was, if we could tempt the pilots out of Novo.

Friday 2 January

I needn't have worried about the pilots choosing another day with a vodka bottle over the throttle: the planes weren't going to be here until the 3rd at the earliest, so we had another day in the tent to look forward to. Great. There wasn't anything else for us to do, since we'd divided the food for the first half of the race amongst our pulks and picked out our personalized snack bags. I spent an hour checking my feet; I'd taped them up before we started, paranoid not just about the tight boots but because I seem to pick up blisters as easily as Russell Brand does girls. Amazingly, I didn't have any blisters this time, so I re-taped my feet, took a look at my Dr Frankenstein-style boots, shook my head at the state of them and hoped my feet would remain in that condition.

Ed, Ben and I stretched our legs and went for a walk. I didn't want the race to be a shock to our bodies, and it was important to keep the muscle memory we'd built up in the first part of the trek and remind the legs what was in store for them. While we were out on our stroll, Inge got the call that the planes were coming in the next day. As if to emphasize the point the sky started to clear, and four hours later it had turned into the most beautiful evening. Six of us chucked a Frisbee around beneath a stunning blue sky and a burning sun, complete with its own solar halo and 'sundog' or perihelion (literal translation: 'beside the sun'), a bright circular spot on the sun's halo. Having been horrible to me for a week Antarctica was now trying to win back my affections with a special demonstration of the refraction of sunlight. It very nearly worked, until I went back inside the orange tent and remembered how boring the last few days had been. There was no way I was going to forgive and forget that quickly.

Saturday 3 January

My resistance to forgiveness was being sorely tempted as I woke up to another beautiful day. I went for a 5-kilometre ski on my own, partly to have a little bit of time to myself because, once the race started, I was going to be within touching distance of the other two virtually twenty-four hours a day for three weeks. I also wanted to test out the GPS holder Roly, our amazing Austrian sound man and I had built: a triangular frame in which the GPS could be locked in place, and covered up if the screen started to freeze. Attached to a waist and neckband it worked like a dream, and meant there wouldn't be any faffing around getting the GPS out of my pocket. It wasn't going to be good for our reserve of batteries but it did mean that we would walk straight – my mantra for the trip.

*

BEN   We were itching to start after days of treading water, and now we finally had the news we'd been waiting for. There was a perceptible change in the camp atmosphere that night. Like a collective sigh, competitors left their tents and we enjoyed our impromptu game of Frisbee out on the polar plains. The spontaneity, the joy of that game, belied a deep feeling of relief. We were finally on our way.

We were on the edge of the plateau. Cloud encircled the horizon, while the sun beat down through the dark blue sky above. The plane was due in the early afternoon. Once again we packed our pulks, and waited for the 'air taxi' to arrive.

We were in the middle of nowhere, a tiny group of people hidden in the vast wilderness of Antarctica. Hundreds of miles from the nearest base and thousands from the nearest country. Like needles in a haystack, it seemed impossible that anyone could ever find us.

Air travel in Antarctica is not simple. An aeroplane needs five clear patches of fine weather to make a successful journey: at the departure point, the refuelling point, the pick-up point, the drop-off point and the return point. Given that conditions change from minute to minute and from mile to mile, any aeroplane requires its own meteorologist to avoid being stuck airborne, short of fuel or with nowhere to land. It's not surprising, then, that air travel in Antarctica involves a lot of postponement and cancellation.

It was early afternoon when we heard a dull buzz in the distance. Our ears, starved of manmade noise, had become much keener and a dozen heads popped from tents to stare at the invisible sky.

Soon, two tiny specks appeared on the horizon, reflecting the bright sunlight-like starbursts.

It's one thing flying to the middle of nowhere, and quite another landing. We were surrounded by uneven snow and ice, not to mention hidden crevasses. The race organizers had 'made' a simple runway by dragging heavy sleds behind their vehicles. The 'runway' didn't look any different to the rest of the landscape.

The two red-and-blue planes circled above our tiny camp while the pilots assessed the snow and ice below. Lower and lower they circled, shattering the polar silence and asserting man's power over this inhospitable place.

The first plane touched down, creating a blizzard of snow with its skis as it roared along the ice. The engines screamed and the plane came to a shuddering halt next to our tents.

JAMES The pilot got the manic reception only normally given by people stranded on a desert island. As the plane taxied over towards our campsite – the type of air travel I could get used to, where the plane pulls up 15 metres from you – we got our first good look at the Basler. It didn't appear to be state-of-the-art. The pilot, a 55-year-old Canadian, exited though the large rear 'door', the space where passengers, crew and cargo got loaded.

'How old is she?' I asked. I wasn't sure if planes were referred to as female, like boats, although I took an educated guess having seen 'Lydia' painted just below the cockpit window.

'This bird's ten years older than me,' he cheerily replied. I was marginally less cheery.

'Whoa, does it stay here all winter?' I tried not to sound concerned about flying in a sixty-year-old plane that was left outside in the coldest weather on the planet for over eight months of the year.

'No, we fly it back up to Canada at the end of the summer,' he said as though it was a short hop to the Isle of Wight. I wasn't sure what was better: the plane escaping the winter, or adding thousands of miles to the clock.

At least it was very clean, and I found that Paul (the pilot) hadn't really sold the best points about the plane. The Basler is a renovated DC-3, the plane that revolutionized air transport in the 1930s and 1940s because of its speed and range, and is regarded as one of the most significant transport planes ever built. Mind you, the Model-T Ford revolutionized the car industry, but it doesn't mean I'd want to drive one. Paul seemed very confident in her though, and he seemed like an honest guy – plus he was on the plane as well.

BEN   The second plane touched down and the crew helped us load up our pulks and kit. The atmosphere in camp was of huge relief. Boredom and frustration turned to excitement and jubilation as we took our seats for the six-hour flight to the start line.

We loaded the film boxes and helped the BBC and Norwegian film crews pack up their camps. I stared at the planes. In the dry atmosphere, they looked shiny and new despite their age. The inside was 'unintentional retro' – designers in London would spend a fortune trying to replicate it in trendy East London lofts, but here it was all original.

I crossed my fingers as the plane roared and bounced along the ice and soared into the sky. A smile broke across my face as we buzzed across Antarctica. I suddenly felt as if I was part of something very special.

For four or five hours we soared above the ice plateau just a few hundred feet below, while a pot-bellied Canadian fed us hunks of cheese. It was like stepping back in time, and I was reminded forcibly of *Raiders of the Lost Ark*, where a battered old plane dots its way across an exotic map. It was also the first time we had felt real warmth in two weeks and I luxuriated in the heat as we headed towards the start line. I closed my eyes and thought about everything we had experienced so far, and about what still lay ahead. This was only the beginning and things were about to get a whole lot harder.

JAMES   I felt the surge of adrenalin. Having sat in the tent with nothing happening day after day it was suddenly all action and I had to start getting my head around what was coming.

The co-pilot/steward did the cabin service by throwing biscuits and chocolate from the front of the plane, and we must have looked like a plane full of seals waving our hands in the air.

BEN   The pilot appeared from the cockpit and held his ten fingers aloft, and gestured for us to fasten our seat belts. We had just ten minutes before we were spat out to the elements once again.

I braced myself as I watched the snow and ice race towards the plane. The plane bounced and jolted as the skis raced along the uneven surface and again came to a shuddering halt.

We were met by an icy chill as we descended the old ladder. This time we really were in the middle of nowhere, and turning back wasn't an option.

'The race begins at 10 a.m. tomorrow,' announced Kenny. We looked at one another and smiled. 'Finally,' we sighed, before setting up camp.

PART THREE

BRITAIN VERSUS NORWAY: THE REMATCH

17

THE STRATEGY

JAMES   I looked at my watch as the plane abandoned us on the ice: 9 p.m. We had thirteen hours until the race started. I smiled, thinking 'Unlucky for some' – specifically anyone skiing all day every day for the next month.

It wasn't going to be a relaxed evening, because we still had some important decisions to make. We were required to allow enough food for thirteen days (that number again) for each half of the race, and must therefore decide how much to take with us on that basis, and how much of our rations to pick up at the halfway point. We thought we'd cover the first 375 kilometres in less than ten days, so we considered travelling light now, and picking up extra meals for the second half of the race.

It was a risky strategy. We could end up running out of food before the halfway point, and if our pulks were searched before the start, we would be penalized for not taking enough food. My mind was racing: we could get round that problem by dividing ten bags' worth of food into thirteen bags and having slightly smaller meals, but that would mean a lot of work, quite apart from the psychological downside of having to survive on smaller rations . . . In the end apathy won out, and we decided to leave things as they were and accept that we could well be hungry in the second half of the race. We'd still be eating more calories each day than the body could absorb, so any extra food would only be a psychological boost at best anyway.

After sorting the food out, we needed to make sure the weight distribution between the pulks was right so that we could all ski comfortably at the same pace – a bit like the handicapping system in horse races. For the acclimatization trek Ed and I had taken more weight to allow Ben as much recovery time as possible from his chemotherapy, and he'd coped brilliantly. Unlike racehorses, though, we had egos and nobody wanted to feel as if they were pulling less than anyone else. We'd spent time with QinetiQ in their human performance labs pulling weights whilst walking on a treadmill, and the initial results were obvious: I should take more weight than Ed, who in turn should take more weight than Ben – hardly surprising, as that pecking order exactly mirrored our different bodyweights.

Laboratory conditions at sea level are very different from the effects of altitude on the Antarctic plateau, however. It was important to remember that nothing was fixed; we were all going to have our good days and bad days, and weight could easily be shifted between the pulks. If someone was struggling, they needed to put their hand up without fear of judgement from the other two, especially as they could well find themselves in the same situation the next day. But would we stick to that agreement once we were up and running?

With meticulous, scientific precision we checked the loaded pulks by dragging them around for a bit and saying if they felt OK. We couldn't pack anything else until the tent came down in the morning, so it was time to get inside, have the last supper and talk about the elephant in the room – or tent, rather: what was our strategy for the race?

It had been a conscious, group decision not to talk about the race during the acclimatization phase. Whilst skiing up through the mountains I'd tried to prepare myself for the lack of sleep, boredom and exhaustion that was coming my way, but we hadn't aired many concerns or thoughts.

BEN   I was nervous as hell about our race tactics. Back at QinetiQ's HQ in Farnborough, we had been forced to discuss what we wanted to get out of the race. Did we want to win it? Did we hope to compete – or simply complete?

JAMES Having worked with psychologists in the past I knew they definitely have their place. They're great at seeing the situation from the outside and giving neutral, common-sense advice on how to resolve issues within a team. Having said that, I often wonder whether teammates say what they think the psychologist wants to hear, rather than what they are feeling – in which case the whole process is rendered pointless.

Ed, Ben and I all agreed on the primary objective, which was to reach the Pole; and having put a year of preparation into this, all of us wanted to enjoy the experience.

When it came to setting goals for the race I went first, making it clear that I wanted to reach the South Pole exhausted, put into practice everything I had learned over the course of the year and know that there wasn't anything else I could have done physically. Whether my statement made Ed and Ben revise their own replies or not, they basically said the same thing.

BEN I agreed in principle with the sentiment, but tried not to think too hard about the different ways James's statement could be taken. Wasn't pushing ourselves to the limit tantamount to trying to win? Don't get me wrong: I wanted to do well, but I would be lying if I said that I wouldn't also happily concede defeat. To win or come first would be a wonderful bonus rather than a primary goal.

JAMES If I'd been third to speak in that session with the psychologist and the other two had said 'We want to win, we'll do anything to make sure we get to the Pole first' I'm sure I would have become the all-American boy and said 'Hell yeah, let's go for it!' But as there was as much chance of their saying that as a plane leaving the Russian airfield on New Year's Eve, it wasn't a decision I was going to have to make.

If I'm honest, what I said about simply giving my all was influenced by my Atlantic voyage with Ben. I knew that if I said that winning was my objective, then every suggestion I made in

Antarctica would, in his mind, be geared towards trying to win the race. Not only would he struggle with that; he would actively rally against it.

Like this trip, the Atlantic voyage was a long race, and our primary goal had obviously been to get to the other side. But we had needed a plan if we were to succeed in any of our other ambitions for the race – setting a quick time, or even winning.

Before setting off from the Canary Islands, the three areas Ben and I spoke about were trusting each other to prepare properly, our daily routine and doing the best that we could do. We agreed on a strategy of rowing two hours on, two hours off, twenty-four hours a day and stuck religiously to that for virtually the entire 3,000-mile, forty-nine-day duration. The beauty of that arrangement was that, with space at the oars for only one person, we could row at our own pace while the other rested.

We'd been warned that our relative speeds would become an issue between us. People assumed I'd become frustrated if Ben was rowing too slowly, but to me that wasn't important: rowing had been my job for over a decade, and if Ben could row at the same speed as me I'd be a bit disappointed. The crucial thing was that we both did the best that we could do.

What we neglected to talk about then were our overall aims for the Atlantic race, and that's where the conflict started. Ben had made it clear that he just wanted to get across the finish line and wasn't really bothered where we came; I wanted to be towards the front of the field, but wasn't expecting to win, and was quite looking forward to not having the tag of 'favourite'. If I'd wanted to give myself the best chance of winning, I probably wouldn't have gone with Ben.

During final preparations in the Canary Islands and as the race started, it became clear that I hadn't been honest with myself or with Ben. Winning was far more important to me than I had realized and I quickly became obsessed with checking our position. Not only were our goals not the same, then; they had actually changed since starting the race. Ultimately it all turned out well. We got there safely and were the first boat to reach land. We got on well, too, though neither of us had really enjoyed the experience, mostly because our objectives had been so different. Expecting Ben to adjust to a new dynamic whilst out at sea simply wasn't fair, and I had learned from that experience. As a result I was determined to enjoy this race, push hard – and not change our goals as soon as we started.

BEN Having experienced James's competitive edge in the Atlantic, it seemed unlikely that he had simply lost it. Ed, too, had shown prodigious amounts of competitiveness during the selection process, and I couldn't help thinking that their relaxed approach didn't add up; they wanted to win the race, and I knew it.

I have never enjoyed competition. Like most people, I enjoy winning, but have always loathed the pressure of rivalry. This fundamental difference in character had almost driven James and I apart in the boat, and even now it threatened to poison our South Pole Race if we weren't honest with each other.

JAMES On a practical level there was a lot less to do for this race than for the Atlantic row. We didn't have to rebuild a boat for starters, and most of the kit was supplied by the organizers. It was up to us to get our skills, fitness and minds up to the job. Ben did a lot of training for the row, putting in the hours on the rowing machine according to a programme I had set him. But it wasn't until the last couple of months of preparation that he had really focused. We couldn't allow that to happen this time because, unlike the row, we'd be skiing together and there would be no hiding if either of us hadn't done the training.

*

Ben and I had come back from our first mini-expedition in Norway full of grand promises about what we were going to do not only to progress our skills but also our fitness. To help with the latter I entered all three of us – Ben, Jonny and me – in the London

Marathon back in spring 2008. Admittedly it wasn't skiing, but running is a tough sport; it meant time on the feet, and was a good medium-term goal for us to focus on.

I'd only known Jonny for a short period of time but he'd done plenty of marathons and it was easy to see that when he's committed to something he has a serious amount of focus. I can't honestly say I had the same confidence in Ben to prepare properly. I had total faith that he would finish even if it meant he'd have to crawl over the line, but I doubted he'd train properly; the South Pole was too far away for it to motivate him yet, and I didn't want to be the one telling him to train all year. I figured the marathon would either motivate him in his training or show him that he needed to pull his finger out. As far as the South Pole went, it was a win-win situation for our team.

A month before the marathon, I had my answer thanks to my spy network. Marina was moaning to Bev that she'd go out running every morning and Ben would lie in bed and not go with her.

BEN   I have never really enjoyed running, and by my own admission I'm a rather lazy trainer. I ran a little at school, but only because I fancied a girl who liked cross-country. I have run a few races in my life, but this would be my first road marathon and I was nervous, really nervous.

Without a pacer, I struggled to estimate my timings. I ran too fast and then I ran too slow. Jonny and James had stormed ahead and I was left to pace myself. I was still uncertain of what sort of time I should go for and plumped for three hours thirty minutes. How wrong I was: four hours later and I hobbled over the finish line. My legs had seized up in the cold and I was suffering agonizing cramps. The organizers led me into one of the medical tents where a kind nurse massaged my legs.

James was unimpressed, and he made sure I knew it.

JAMES   Jonny and I both had great races and finished a couple of minutes apart, running personal bests; Ben was over an hour behind and beaten by Ronan Keating, and only ten minutes ahead of Amanda Holden. Great athletes they may be outside of their day jobs, but they weren't planning to race to the South Pole. What frustrated me was that Ben is a far better athlete than that record suggests. I run like Frankenstein's monster and managed to lumber round in less than three hours, so there was no reason he couldn't as well.

BEN 'You took an hour longer than us. Do you know how far that would be in Antarctica?' scowled James. 'You were a full quarter slower than us. Someone just suggested we take Amanda Holden instead of you.'

Now, James and I have never tried to hide the fact that we are very different characters, with wildly opposing ways of approaching things. Like James, I am a workaholic, but I have a propensity to take on way too many things (which is why I am writing this in the car, in a field in the Peak District in between filming). I have always struggled to spend more than the bare minimum amount of time on any one project, and though I'd like to think it was the nature of the job, that would be being too kind. The real reason is that I don't have a huge amount of patience and/or concentration. I have an unhealthy ability to jump from one task to another.

The training for the South Pole had only gone to highlight the issue. Where James had been able to focus his workaholism on the South Pole Race, I continued to spread myself too thin. It was a trait I was aware of and I had struggled to suppress it during the year. My commitment to the task was unwavering but it was true, I should have trained harder. I was still hurt by James's attitude, though. After all, I had tried, and we were a team.

Either way, it looked as if I would have a lot of work to do to recover from the marathon disaster.

I stepped up my training regime to two hours a day, seven days a week and we both returned to our day jobs.

JAMES I didn't enjoy bawling Ben out, but at least the race had the desired effect: Ben was embarrassed by both his performance and the fact he was so far behind Jonny and me. Marina was annoyed by a comment I made on the BBC where I ribbed Ben about his performance – she is fiercely loyal and protective of him – but sometimes you have to let people fall over in order to pick themselves up, and for Ben this was the fall he needed. Alternatively she could have dragged him out of bed. I didn't need to say anything more: his physical preparation from April onwards was never an area of concern.

*

BEN I had shown dedication and drive with my training – I had spent a year in the gym and we had all taken six months off work – but even now, with just hours to go to the start of the race proper, I knew that James still doubted my desire to push myself.

'So – what do you want to get out of it?' asked James, like a broken record. It was a question we had been asked dozens of times, and like politicians with a soundbite, we could each reel off our standard replies without thinking: to push ourselves. To do our best. To be proud of our achievements. To fulfil a lifelong ambition . . . We had achieved so much together that we were terrified of upsetting the fine and often fragile balance. None of us was prepared to admit to our real hopes and dreams without this camouflage.

'How hard do you want to push?' asked James in an effort to pry deeper into our minds.

Before either of us had time to reply, James began to answer the question himself. 'I want to arrive at the finish line physically and mentally drained,' he began, 'I want to arrive having pushed myself to my limits with no regrets, in the knowledge that we couldn't have done any more.'

It seemed a reasonable goal, but it still skirted around the winning issue.

'I really don't mind about winning,' said James, 'as long as we have done everything we can.' This was certainly a very different

James from the one I knew. He never would have said such a thing before, but he had clearly matured since the Atlantic race.

I appreciated James saying that, but in our heart of hearts I think we all wanted to win; we just weren't prepared to admit it. Besides, how on earth would we beat the Norwegians, even if we wanted to? Rune and Stian had the benefit of knowledge and practice where we had guesswork and hope. These two former soldiers still taught Arctic warfare, for heaven's sake. Where we could hardly ski, they could do so while dodging enemy fire. Our only hope would be to simply push ourselves hard; but maybe, just maybe, if we could ski for a little longer than them for every day of the race, then stamina would triumph over speed . . .

We set about planning a daily schedule for the race, though since no one has raced to the South Pole for a hundred years, we simply didn't know what our bodies would be able to take. In Switzerland we had tried (and failed) to ski for eighteen hours a day, while many polar trekkers we spoke to had simply shaken their heads at our suggestion. 'Fourteen hours a day is the maximum,' warned one. Once again we were falling into the knowledge trap.

'Let's start by working out the minimum amount of sleep we can manage,' I suggested.

JAMES I genuinely believed that with the help of twenty-four-hour sunlight we could get by on four hours' sleep a day. This, together with the time it took to pitch the tent, melt snow for drinking water, eat and pack the tent away, meant stopping for around eight hours, so that left us with sixteen hours' skiing. Could we do that?

Ben and Ed were keen on starting the race on a tough regime, perhaps partly because they felt that if we got into a good position on the first day of the race, I'd be more relaxed; but understandably, Ben thought the competitive monster was going to reveal itself once the race started.

I felt we had two options: start off with a slightly shorter day and build up to doing sixteen hours' skiing, or go straight into a tough strategy and do everything we could to try to maintain it. The latter would be hard but at least it meant we wouldn't wake up tired, faced with the added mental hurdle of increasing the hours we had skied the previous day.

We decided to ski for sixteen hours, and then set up camp with the caveat that if someone felt they had to stop earlier, we would. We didn't think anyone else would ski for that long and it meant that we would be in a good position. We'd all been inspired by an email from Victoria, who'd made it into the final four, alongside Ed, to 'win' a place with us. It said: 'If Scott had walked a hundred extra steps every day, he'd have beaten Amundsen to the Pole.' We weren't sure if it was true or not, but it motivated us to take that extra step, no matter how hard it was.

In the end, I chose not to lead our team off; I wanted to keep the competitive beast in his cage for a little longer, just in case. I noticed that Ben didn't disagree. Ed was going to lead us out, with the plan to ski to our own pace and settle into the tracks of the Norwegians if possible; already, we were working to the assumption that Missing Link would be the first to take the lead, given their experience on skis. We would aim to stop every two hours for about ten minutes regardless of what was going on around us, and the time that we set up camp wasn't going to alter if a team was ahead of us and still skiing when we were due to pitch. We all agreed, shook on it and disappeared into our sleeping bags.

The last thing I did was to dig Bev's letter out of my pocket. One line stood out: 'PLEASE don't go off from the start too hard. Bernie says you'll be fine as long as you don't do that!'

Was our bold strategy going to take too much out of us early on?

18

THE HARES AND THE TORTOISES

Sunday 4 to Monday 5 January

BEN   Race day. The sun was shining and the wind had disappeared: a perfect day to begin our journey south.

We began to assemble on the start line, which was formed by a rope linked between two of the support cars. It was strange to think that this was probably the last time we would see everyone for a month. There was a noticeable sense of nervousness in the air. Comrades were about to become competitors.

JAMES   The atmosphere between the competitors before the start of an event gives an insight into what they are thinking. At the Olympics we rowers rarely spoke to our opposition; there may have been the occasional nod, but no interaction. As unsporting as it sounds, there were no wishes of good luck. Everybody was after the same gold medal, we'd all trained our butts off for it and there were no prizes for coming second. If there was any good luck floating around, you wanted it for yourself.

The start of the South Pole Race was totally different. We weren't lining up for a three-minute race or even a three-hour race, but three full weeks in a dangerously inhospitable place. With such a small field we all stood a chance of winning, but the handshakes, hugs and shouts of 'Good luck and be safe' and 'Look after each other' told their own story.

If you had been in a plane flying over the plateau, you would have seen twenty or so people strung out against the white backdrop like coloured beads on a necklace. We stood there in silence, a snowy, empty continent bigger than Australia before us. I asked myself, not for the first or last time, what the hell I was doing there. I did feel surprisingly relaxed, though; the competitive beast within hadn't yet surfaced. Was I going to be able to control the urge to race when we started? I had to. Ben would be watching to see if I meant it when I said 'The race is about us against ourselves.' If I started looking around, urging us not to lose touch or chase down the teams ahead, it was going to cause problems.

The lone horn of the race support vehicle started the race and, as we had discussed the night before, Ed led us off.

BEN It was really a rather comical start, like a three-legged race in an old people's home. Weighed down by 70-kilo pulks, we not so much raced off as lumbered off like tortoises.

We soon fell into single file and followed in the tracks of the Norwegians who, as expected, had raced into an early lead. I had been worried about polar etiquette; was it fair to follow in another team's tracks, given the exertion it takes to forge a path through fresh snow?

JAMES I applauded Ben's sense of honour. It was good to see that the old-boy ideals of fair play to which Scott was bound still existed. Sadly, I'm a different sort of animal. 'Hell, yeah, we'll use them!' I said. 'You think they wouldn't use ours? We've got 800 kilometres to cover and need every bit of help we can get!' I hoped that made my position clear.

The pace of the Norwegians didn't seem too fast, though admittedly my body was full of adrenalin and we still had fifteen hours twenty minutes of skiing left before we pitched the tent. What was surprising was the way the field was almost immediately strung out behind us; I expected most of the teams to be in a big group for most of the first day. Maybe the other teams knew something we didn't. Had we been lulled into a Norwegian trap?

BEN With a powerful sun on our backs and not a breath of wind, for the first time in weeks I felt a bead of sweat on my brow. The other teams had spread out across the plateau and there were already several hundred metres between them. I opened the vents on my jacket and we continued to close the gap between us and the Norwegians.

JAMES As if on cue, the Norwegians stepped to the side to adjust their clothing. Being a sceptical bastard my instant assumption was that they either wanted to see how fast our skiing pace was, or whether we could navigate. To be frank, these were questions I was quite interested in knowing the answers to, but not just yet.

Of course they could have just wanted us to break trail for a bit. In icy conditions, breaking trail is relatively unimportant, but in deep powder it can make a huge difference: it takes a tremendous effort for the lead man to lift his skis up instead of gliding, and it's a huge boost for those following him to ski on the compacted snow he leaves behind. The energy saving is not as significant as, say, 'drafting' in a cycling peleton, where riders shelter behind the lead man and use almost 40 per cent less energy, but it is still significant. It's also worth saying that if you're following, you can mentally relax and let the lead man navigate – if you trust him.

Whatever the Norwegians' reasons for stopping, we were now faced with a decision: do we stop and have a pee or fiddle with some clothes until they set off again, or do we just glide on by, making sure to look studiously unfazed, and take over the lead? I reasoned that if we stopped and waited we'd be showing a real lack of confidence – not just to them, but to each other. I felt sure that we were ready – and if we weren't, we had a whole load of problems coming our way over the next month.

As we passed the Norwegians, I shouted to Ed, 'OK fella, it's over to you now.' He punched the air and just kept skiing.

BEN Ed picked up the pace and suddenly we were several hundred metres ahead of them. The sweat continued to stream down my face, but nothing was going to stop us. We suddenly had an unexpected lead and we weren't about to give it up for a little sweat.

I fixed my eyes to the back of Ed's pulk and marched on. We fell into a nice rhythm and I made a point of not looking back. I couldn't, it was too stressful. We were finally under way. Every step forward was a step closer to the South Pole. Even a storm was unlikely to delay us now. We were finally doing what we were here for.

*

Two hours later and we pulled up for our first break. I stripped off my jacket and sat in just my thermal top. I gulped down some water and for the first time, took a look behind us. It seemed incredible but we were well ahead of the other teams, including the Norwegians.

JAMES   Had we gone off too hard? I felt great and asked the other two how they felt. They both grunted positive-sounding responses whilst frantically wolfing down a snack. It was my turn to lead, and I was fired up; I wasn't expecting us to be in this situation and knowing that we had some natural skiing pace was brilliant news. The other teams seemed to be following our tracks, so either we were navigating pretty well or they were just being sheep; but the most exciting part was looking forwards and seeing nothing but the ice stretching out to a blue-skied horizon.

I was jolted from my happy place by Ben's voice.

'James, wait up, Ed's struggling.' I looked round and Ed had fallen 100 metres behind. I'd kept the GPS on to make sure I kept the pace the same when I took over the lead. We stopped and waited for Ed. 'You OK, buddy?' I asked when he caught up.

'No, I feel dizzy,' he replied. 'I think I got too hot and didn't drink enough.'

I bit my tongue. Throughout the first two hours I kept asking Ben and Ed how they felt, and reminded them to grab something from the snack bags attached to our harnesses and keep drinking. We'd stressed the importance of stopping straight away and adjusting kit if we were hot; sweating out here was the worst thing we could do. We needed our bodies to conserve water like Antarctic camels, not sweat it out. With Antarctica's complete lack of rainfall we were technically in a desert, after all.

There was no point in telling Ed he should have drunk and eaten, however. He's an intelligent guy and knew that anyway; it was just the excitement of racing getting the better of him. The question was what were we going to do about it? Ed needed to take it easy for a bit. There were two ways of doing that: we could either slow the pace down, or Ben and I could take some of his weight.

'How are you feeling, Ben? Fancy some more weight?' I asked.

'I feel good but I think I'd struggle if I took anything else.' An honest reply and a nice bit of self-preservation. I wish I'd thought the same way, but with the Norwegians steadily bridging the gap between us the competitive beast in me started rising to the surface.

'Chuck us a couple of things from your pulk, Ed,' I said. 'How about the rope and the medical kit?' There was no argument from Ed, who obviously didn't feel 100 per cent. I suspected it was partly down to dehydration, but also the realization of how long we'd be skiing for today. In normal life, a two-hour training session is a monster. People train for months in order to complete a marathon, and the average finishing time is about four hours. We were going to try to do sixteen hours a day and we weren't even 15 per cent of the way through the first day. I'm not a psychologist but the reason I felt confident in guessing what was going through Ed's mind was because I'd been through it myself a couple of times. The first time was on the Atlantic row: after three hours we were in the lead. I was excited and full of adrenalin, convinced we were going to win, and any other rowing race I'd done would have been finished two hours 54 minutes earlier; yet we still had 2,994 miles to go. It took me a week to come to terms with the reality of what I'd taken on. I hoped Ed wasn't about to experience a week like that.

We set off again but I wasn't skiing with the same relaxed mind-set. I was worried about Ed, and it would be disastrous to keep pushing on if he was struggling mentally. It was up to Ben and me to help him through it.

After twenty minutes it was clear that Ed was still struggling. We stopped again. Ben still wasn't keen to take any weight and I felt great, so I took the meals from Ed too. I felt the difference as we set off again, and in hindsight it would have been better for us all to have slowed down as a group rather than overload myself and keep the pace up. Wonderful thing, hindsight. Leaving a rational decision to me with the Norwegians chasing us wasn't that likely.

BEN Ed and James turned frequently to check on our progress and the size of our lead. I kept my eyes down. Judging by their reaction there was no sign of the Norwegians, but the important thing was that they were behind – something none of us had expected.

We skied on, stopping every two hours. At 7 p.m. we were due to make our first 'sched' call-in, to notify the organizers of our position. We had been racing for nine hours now and our feet were red hot. Ed stopped to dress a blister, and the pulks started to feel heavy. We still had seven hours' skiing ahead of us, and we all knew the importance of completing our sixteen-hour strategy on the first day. We had to keep going.

JAMES It became clear that we had good natural pace over the ice, and judging by the fact the other teams were still following us, our navigation wasn't too shabby either. But we never quite got into the 'two hours on, ten minutes off' routine because we had to keep stopping. After Ed had treated his hot spot we got moving again, only for the clip on my pulk harness to suddenly break. With a couple of karabiners from the climbing harness I rigged something up that should see me through until I could do a proper repair job in the tent.

We'd been skiing for over ten hours now and I was starting to struggle with my pulk. The extra weight not only made it heavy but made the centre of gravity higher, and it kept capsizing as I skied over the sastrugi. If I was skiing first or second, the guy behind could roll it upright but if I was at the back and it rolled over it meant unclipping myself from the harness, which wasn't quite as easy with my karabiner repair. Swearing continuously I would go back, level it up, ski ahead, clip myself in again and then catch up the ground I'd lost on Ed and Ben.

Finally, at about 11 p.m., the Norwegians pitched their tent. We were planning to ski until 2 a.m., of course, and seeing their orange tent go up gave us a new lease of life. Ed had got a second wind, and even took some of his weight back for the last few hours.

I was exhausted by 1 a.m. and could feel a few hotspots on my feet; I figured we were so close to stopping I'd sort them out when we stopped, and forged on for that extra hour. I would come to regret that decision in the days that followed, but right now all I could think about was getting inside that tent. In the space of two days it had turned from a prison cell into an oasis.

BEN We had overdone it. We were in the lead, but everyone had warned us not to hit the start too hard, and we had totally disregarded their advice.

Not that I was complaining. I was shattered, but I felt strong and we were in the lead.

We dived into the tent and set about the camp routine. Stoves were fired and food cooked. We sat back on our elbows and luxuriated in the completion of our first day. We were in a state of exalted exhaustion. I smiled, Ed smiled and even James grinned, quite something from one of the toughest of sportsmen.

Novices and underdogs we may have been, but we had got through the first day, in first place.

JAMES I could tell I'd pushed hard. The dehydrated food actually tasted pretty nice, and I could have polished off another couple of servings, even though I had no idea what I was eating. Our policy of 'keep everything but the essentials in the pulk' had fallen at the first hurdle, though; virtually everything had come into the tent, which now looked like a Chinese laundry. Ed had the contents of the medical kit out on his sleeping bag as he taped up his blisters, while Ben had the repair kit out and was sewing a nose cover on to his sunglasses. I had a lapful of karabiners, and was trying to replace the plastic clip on my harness with a system that wouldn't require a Harry Houdini escape routine every time I wanted a pee.

I nearly fell asleep mending my harness, and resolved to sort my feet out in the morning. I zipped myself into my sleeping bag at 3.30 a.m., and was due to be on stove duty at 7.45 a.m. That meant just over four hours of sleep, and I didn't waste a moment of it. Even with the sun burning through the tent and Ed's feet kicking me in the head, I was out cold in seconds.

BEN   What felt like only moments later, the alarm buzzed me awake from a deep sleep. Days and weeks of anxiety were finally at an end. The race had started and not only could I keep up with Ed and James, I had also proved that I could survive our insane strategy. I decided not to dwell on the fact that we had only completed our first day.

*

JAMES   I was surprised how refreshed I felt when I woke up, and it was nice knowing we didn't have to rush out of the tent. Even if we'd wanted to get going earlier, we couldn't; we needed water to last us through the day and for that the stoves had to work their magic. Unfortunately, they were more Paul Daniels than David Blaine, so it took a while. We used the time to get organized, chat, do running repairs and contemplate the day ahead. Ed was clearly doing the latter. He'd been sitting there for fifteen minutes in silence, with a look on his face as if he'd been sent to his room without any TV. He hadn't even touched his porridge.

'Knackered?' I asked.

'Not too bad,' he mumbled.

'What's wrong then?' I asked, slightly disheartened. I'd woken up feeling surprisingly good physically and very positive mentally, and Ben seemed the same. Ed's demeanour was sucking that positivity out of the tent.

'I can't believe how far we've got to ski today,' he said, head down, not making eye contact.

'Ed, it was always going to be hard, but don't look too far ahead,' I said. 'We did 47 kilometres yesterday and are in a position none of us thought we would be in. It's all good,' I added, trying to sound positive and upbeat.

'Yeah, I know,' was his muted response.

I knew where he was mentally, and he had to fight his own way through those battles. I had every faith in him doing so, but the last thing Ben and I needed was to be reminded of how far we had to ski today.

BEN This was the start of things to come. That Ed and James respected one another is unquestionable, but they both had the ability to wind one another up. James often accused Ed of transmitting his pessimism to us like some disease, but in all honesty it never bothered me. I just hated the conflict it illicited.

*

JAMES Even after the long acclimatization trek, we weren't as efficient at leaving camp yet as we were at setting it up. It might have had something to do with the realization of what lay ahead: sixteen hours' skiing wasn't as appealing a prospect as a hot meal and a sleep. We concentrated on repacking my pulk with a lower centre of gravity, so it didn't roll over and lie there like a dog wanting it's tummy tickled every time I went over a sastrugi.

I pulled on my boots to go, and realized that I'd forgotten to sort out my feet. They'd stopped hurting as soon as I took them out of the boots and I'd not thought about them until now – a massive mistake, as Ed had packed away the medical kit. Once again I thought, naively, 'I'll see how they go.' As I exited the tent my head automatically swung north towards the horizon behind us to see if there was anybody in sight and, sure enough, there were two black blobs heading towards us. They were further behind than when we were skiing yesterday but to have made up the extra three hours we skied for last night they must have set off at around 7 a.m.

I was at the back for the first two hours. Ben didn't look over his shoulder once to see where the Norwegians were, whereas Ed checked on them every fifteen minutes. I wanted to look as often as Ed but, like Lot escaping the city of Sodom, I was determined not to look behind me; after a while though, I figured the risk of getting turned into a pillar of salt was worth taking, so I had a peek. Yep, there were still two dark spots on the horizon. It was impossible to tell if they were gaining or not, but I consoled myself with the thought that we at least had to turn around to see them.

The first two hours of skiing hadn't done much to Ed's outlook. He was still struggling with what lay ahead. I didn't want to bring up the conversation we'd had at Novo when Ed had said 'It won't be as bad as the chamber' because it would serve no purpose, but he now understood what it was like staring down a long dark tunnel. Ben and I had both been there before, and it is down to the individual to find that chink of light at the other end, and head towards it.

Ed would get there, but he couldn't withdraw into himself. His mindset was affecting his skiing and in the first two hours he'd been struggling to keep up with Ben. He was supposed to lead the next two hours and I wasn't sure he was up to it, but there was no point in driving him further down physically or mentally.

'Feeling any better, Ed?' I said. I knew the answer before asking the question. He hadn't said anything in the break, sitting on his pulk with his head down, but I wasn't sure how else to initiate the conversation.

'Not really,' he said. Not the chattiest response.

'You want me to lead for the next two hours?' I said, trying to sound cheery.

'Don't mind,' he said.

'Why don't you just cruise at the back and chill out for a couple of hours? I'll do this stint,' I suggested. Ed just nodded. I'd had enough.

'Ed, we know you're struggling today, but you've got to realize the effect it has on us if you totally withdraw. We'll do anything we can to help, but this situation takes extra energy out of us all. We're in a brilliant position, it's sunny and we should be making the most of it. You'll be fine, mate, just put one foot in front of the other. Remember what you told me to tell you when you were down? This is your Olympics. You've taken six months out of work; don't waste them.'

He nodded, this time more positively.

'Eddie,' Ben said, 'I promise you, when you are back home you'll miss these days.' I wasn't sure I totally agreed with that sentiment, but was happy to go along with the romanticism if it helped Ed.

'Thanks, guys,' Ed said. A few manly backslaps later and we were off.

*

As Michael Barrymore used to shout on the 1980s quiz show *Strike It Lucky*, 'What is a hotspot not?' Cue audience reaction: 'A good spot!' When that catchphrase started to go round my head, I knew it was time to check out my feet. I asked Ed for the medical kit at the next break. A hot spot was definitely not a good spot, although to be accurate the hot spot was no longer a hot spot – it was a blood blister. What an idiot. I'd felt the warning signs twenty-four hours early and did nothing then, forgot to do it in the tent and had skied on it for over ten hours. Had I learned nothing from the training we'd done over the last twelve months? I knew I was susceptible to blisters, having got them on every trip we'd been on. I hadn't got any throughout the acclimatization trek but I had one now that wouldn't have looked out of place on the Elephant Man.

On a positive note, the sight of blood seemed to fully revive Dr Ed, who'd become much more like himself once we'd broken the back of the day. He set about draining the blood out of my blister with the relish of vampire. You might think that bare skin would freeze right away, but if there was no wind you had a few short minutes to perform running repairs. Drained, taped and back in the boot, it was just the last five and a half hours to go.

After two of those hours, Ed said, 'They've set up camp. Every step we take now is one they've got to catch up in the morning.'

'Check out the motivator!' I said. 'Eddie's back!'

We pushed on until 2 a.m. and as a team felt even more confident than twenty-four hours earlier. Ed had come through a tough day and would be stronger for it. We had shown that our position at the head of the field wasn't a fluke – we'd covered 48 kilometres and, er, there was dehydrated chilli con carne for dinner. Well, you can't have everything.

19

RASH DECISIONS

Tuesday 6 January

JAMES   It already seemed as if I was stuck in Groundhog Day, and it was only the third day of the race – but the sun was shining, and we were in the lead.

When I'm doing normal training at home I know when I'm knackered because the first thing I do is work out how long it is until I can get back into bed again. Today I made it about twenty hours to go, sixteen of which would be spent skiing. I couldn't help but look longingly at the horizon, imagining the midway checkpoint: a twenty-four-hour enforced stay with a quick check by the doctor, new food for our pulks and twenty-two hours of delicious, uninterrupted sleeping and eating. After the success of the toilet roll questionnaire it was time to draw up another spreadsheet, using our daily mileage to predict when I could put on my sleeping mask and become Rip van Cracknell for the day.

In the first two days we'd covered 95 kilometres, at which pace we'd reach the midway oasis on either 12 or 13 of January. 'Six days!' I shouted to Ed and Ben, after doing some worryingly slow calculations in my diary.

'What! Where?' Ed said, as I startled him awake from his daily 'porridge avoidance' catnap.

'Six days to the checkpoint!' I said excitely. 'All we have to do is keep doing the distance we've been doing and we'll be there in less than a week.'

A less than enthusiastic 'Oh' in reply.

'That's great, but we've only been going for two days,' Ben said over the hissing of the stoves.

'Good point, but we can keep this up for another week, easy,' I said, trying to sound convincing. The lack of a response indicated that I may have made myself feel better about the day ahead but hadn't managed to persuade the other two.

Our eyes scanned the horizon behind us as we packed up the tent. Ed was convinced he could see the Norwegians on the horizon, Ben and I weren't so sure. Mind you, without the glasses that Ben claims not to need, they could have been 50 metres away and he'd still have struggled to make them out.

The morning followed a similar pattern to the previous day, Ed struggling early on but pulling through later. He was clearly coming to terms with the fact that it was going to be hard and horrible and that we had no option but to grind it out. Meanwhile, Ben was starting to return to something like full fitness.

His mood hadn't changed much during the first few days of the race and it was hard to gauge exactly how he was feeling. The amount he spoke varied, as it did with all of us, but whatever the damage the Leishmaniasis and the aggressive treatment had done to his body, I couldn't help but think that it had helped him mentally.

BEN James was right. I may have been quiet, but while he and Ed drifted in and out of gloom, I found myself riding the crest of a wave. My recovery from the illness had given me a new surge of motivation. I was determined to enjoy every second of the race and nothing was going to stop me. I sometimes wondered whether Ed and James appreciated just how lucky we were to be there. I had lived through the nightmare of nearly having my dream snatched from me, but it was clear that they were having trouble keeping the storm clouds at bay.

JAMES When Ed and I were going through a dark patch, wallowing in self pity and asking ourselves what the hell we were doing down here, Ben looked at it from a different perspective. Throughout the horrendous treatment the one thing that motivated him was getting to Antarctica and going to the South Pole and now it was as if he was determined to appreciate every second.

Perhaps Ed and I were taking the trip for granted, having not nearly missed out on coming, and didn't fully appreciate how lucky we were to be in Antarctica – and that meant we slipped into a darker place more quickly than Ben.

Both Ben and Ed were having serious problems with another dark place, however. It would have been funny watching them leave the tent for a 'comfort break', if it didn't look so painful; no, scrub that, it was still funny.

BEN The excess sweating had caused havoc, creating a large painful welt around my bum and between my legs. It's more commonly known as nappy rash, though I won't use that term because it belittles the pain. It was agonizing. Every movement, every step aggravated the angry red skin and the continual chafing created a raw wound. While I skied, blood trickled down my legs.

JAMES When we set off after a break it was like watching two toddlers who'd had an accident in their pants. They'd tried a variety of methods to ease the pain, from creams to lubricants, but seemed to have settled on wedging a piece of loo roll between their cheeks whilst they skied.

I wasn't hugely sympathetic, not because I'm a heartless bastard – well, not just because I'm a heartless bastard. Ben and I had experienced problems with our backsides during the Atlantic row, and we'd been warned that crotch rot was very likely here too. Our groin area stayed nice and warm whilst skiing and with very little washing or changes of pants – we only had two pairs for the whole trip – it wouldn't be long before a touch of 'fermentation' set in. During the acclimatization trek I was anal, if you'll excuse the pun, about having snow baths in the evening, whereas the other two didn't seem as keen to leave their warm sleeping bags and roll about naked in the snow. Who was laughing now? That's right, me.

BEN   Snow baths had been the subject of much amusement. On the trek to the plateau, James had taken every opportunity to strip naked and run around camp. I'm not sure if it's a sports thing in general, but James seems to relish every opportunity to get naked. Call me a prude, but I have always been a little more conservative when it comes to removing my clothes in public. It still makes me laugh when people refer to me as the 'naked rower' on account of the large amount of time we spent in the buff while we rowed the Atlantic. I don't even like showering in front of other people.

A snow bath involves stripping off in the tent, running outside and either rubbing snow into your naked skin or rolling around on the ground. The effect is more invigorating than it is cleansing. It involves no soap and very little water, as the snow doesn't melt at those temperatures. The result is the comedy sequence of a grown man running around in his birthday suit, screaming. Funny the first few times, but then just a little disgusting as James would invariably rest his naked bum on my sleeping bag.

I 'bathed' twice during the acclimatization. I use the word 'bathe' very loosely, as all I did was run around hysterically clutching my willy in modesty. Believe me, minus 30 is not the kind of weather to revel in nakedness.

Snow bath or no snow bath, we all stank; and while James gleefully ribbed us for our nappy rash, it was soon his turn to show some rather worrying signs of wear and tear as we rolled out of camp.

JAMES   My feet were feeling very sore but at least I seemed to have learned my lesson, and stopped often to tape them up. With both Ed and I taking boots off to try to stop the onset of blisters, and Ben and Ed examining each other's bums at worryingly frequent intervals, our ten-minute breaks were taking far longer and we'd slipped out of the slick routine we'd stuck to during the first couple of days. By the time it came to make our daily call to the organizers to update them on our position we hadn't covered anything like the same distance. For the first time, I agreed with Ed about the dots on the horizon: there was definitely something back there, and in a wilderness the size of Antarctica, there could be no doubt: it was the Norwegians.

I felt great mentally, and I was enjoying the skiing, and the knowledge of having ticked off a few more kilometres to our goal. Physically however, I was struggling, and it wasn't just my feet; I felt incredibly tired, far more tired than at any time during the previous two days, and we still had hours of skiing left. I was struggling to concentrate and that was leading me to make stupid errors of judgement.

A couple of examples will suffice: I realized that the repair job on my harness could be improved, and I stopped to attach an extra karabiner. I needed the full use of both hands, so my natural reaction was (for me at least) to pick up the shiny metal buckle, and shove it in my mouth.

BEN We were just about to move off when I noticed James hopping around, struggling with his mouth. He was silent, except for some muted grunts and groans. He was at the front and it was difficult to tell what was up. James had a habit of always being the last one ready, and I assumed it was his usual faffing.

'You all right, mate?' I hollered. He grunted and I saw his hand pulling at his mouth. It suddenly dawned on me what he'd done: in a moment of absent-mindedness, he had stuck a metal climbing karabiner in his mouth that had been cooled to minus 30 degrees. It fused with his tongue instantly. I watched James fight with the karabiner a little longer and eventually manage to pull it from his mouth, along with half the skin from his tongue.

JAMES What a schoolboy error! Not touching metal with bare skin is a golden rule in cold climates, which is why you always wear thin contact gloves, just in case. I'd been so careful since we arrived on the continent and couldn't understand why I'd allowed my concentration to lapse so badly. To have made contact with my hand would have been bad, but to have lost skin from my lips and tongue was disastrous. It would affect me every time I ate or drank anything, and as I was forcing food down rather than feeling hungry, I certainly didn't need any incentive not to eat.

The Tourette's was back as I gave myself a stern talking to, out there in the middle of nowhere on the ice.

BEN   If we missed the first signs that something was wrong when James freeze-dried part of his tongue, we should have heard the alarm bells at what happened next.

We had stopped for our two-hour break. Originally, James had been quite adamant that we would break for no more than five minutes, but Ed and I weren't sure this was long enough, and had negotiated a six-minute stop. This quota had long since been abandoned, as breaks became ten-, fifteen- and often twenty-minute affairs. I could never manage more than ten minutes though, as my core temperature plunged without the exercise. I had therefore got into the habit of leaving a couple of minutes ahead of James and Ed.

JAMES   Ed wanted to check his feet, so while Ben skied off, I watched as he unlaced his boots and removed the layers of socks, felt liners and vapour barrier – the highly technical plastic bag that was worn over the sock and under the felt. It was 10 p.m. and the sun was at the lowest point of its arc, so the temperature had dropped. I stayed with Ed to share my considerable medical knowledge with him.

'Whoa, that's a beast of blister! You've done well to ski on that!' I said. Having observed that my insights weren't really necessary and that Ed was more than capable of taping his own feet up, I skied off to avoid getting cold.

I couldn't believe how good I felt after that break. As they say in the army, I'd 'been on my chinstrap' at the end of the last two-hour ski, but felt like a new man now. I was catching Ben up hand over fist, and along with my new-found energy came confidence that I'd easily keep pushing on until 2 a.m.

I caught Ben up, and even had the energy to break trail and ski alongside for a chat. I was interested to know if he was having the same second wind as me.

'Hey, buddy, you doing OK?' I asked.

'It's hard,' he panted, 'but I'm just about OK at the moment.'

'I feel great now; my legs have had a new lease of life,' I said proudly.

'How are Ed's feet?' Ben asked, head down, pulling into his straps. Perhaps his legs weren't feeling as good as mine and he wanted to change the subject rather than talk to Tigger.

'He's certainly looking after them,' I said, pausing slightly. 'Amazing discipline to stop when he feels a blister developing. If I had that my heel wouldn't look like it does.'

'Is he far behind?' Ben asked.

I turned round to see where he was.

'Oh shit!' I half whined, half shouted.

'What?' Ben stopped, spun his head round and looked back at Ed. 'What is it?'

I could see Ed in the distance, making steady progress towards us.

'What?' Ben asked more urgently.

'I forgot my fucking pulk!' I cried.

There was no response from Ben – only a smirk that crept across his face that turned into a smile, and then laughter.

BEN   Now think about this. We're not talking about a briefcase or a school satchel; this was a six-foot sledge that weighed as much as a fully grown man. This wasn't like leaving your phone in the pub; this was like forgetting your wife on the train.

Antarctica has a way of piercing even the strongest armour; it searches for a weakness and begins to chip away at the toughest of defences. Once that shell has been breached, its downhill all the way. It was funny, though.

JAMES   I didn't hang around to share Ben's joy; I turned round and started skiing back to my pulk. The Tourette's was back.

That was the most disheartening ski of the whole trip. Not only was I retracing my steps and heading north rather than south, I had to face up to the fact that my new Tiggerishness was soon about to be buried beneath the weight of a pulk again.

Ed came towards me, pulling both his pulk and my own, tied behind. What a top bloke, I thought – until I saw that Fogle's smirk had transported itself onto Ed's face.

20

DR COATS, I PRESUME?

JAMES We forged on, but I was finding the going tough, despite the fact that it was only day three, and we were enjoying relatively mild weather. Annoyingly, I knew that the major reason I was struggling was that I simply wasn't eating enough. We'd been on the skis for twelve hours and I hadn't eaten even a quarter of my snack bag, meaning that I was missing out on nearly 3,000 calories. The lack of fuel had clearly caught up on me.

It wasn't just because of having lost part of my tongue that I wasn't eating. I'm sorry to say that it was an issue of taste, as well. Disliking the taste of something was an unacceptable excuse for not eating in this extreme environment; I'd almost had to force feed Ed his porridge in the mornings, and thought about pretending the spoon was a train going into the tunnel – it worked with Croyde. Ed in turn called me a 'Fucking food Nazi', yet here was the Führer barely touching his snack bag, and running out of energy with a quarter of the day's skiing still left to do. I thought back to our time in South Africa: I'd wanted to split sweet and savoury, but we didn't have the time – and that decision was now coming back to bite us. Two days spent relaxing in the sunshine of Cape Town after the pulks were packed and shipped to the airport was great for us, but meanwhile the chocolate, cheese and salami melted in the African heat and then refroze together on arrival at Novo. Add in some wine gums and cashew nuts, and even Heston Blumenthal would have struggled to make the combination work.

The exhaustion of the first two days meant I was struggling not only to keep pace with the other two, but to keep my mind in full working order. I was leading and turned round, lifting my ski pole in the air to indicate I was stopping. 'Anyone else think we're going uphill?' I asked. 'I'm really struggling to maintain pace.'

'It doesn't feel any different to me,' Ben said, before adding, helpfully, 'I think you're imagining it.'

'Hmm, thought that's what you were going to say,' I said. 'I'm finding it tough at the moment. How are you guys feeling?' I asked, hoping I wasn't the only one.

Ben gave what was now becoming his normal response, 'I'm really tired, but can keep going.'

'I'm really good,' Ed said, sounding upbeat. For all his negativity and insularity in the first few hours of skiing, once we'd broken the back of the day he had quickly switched, becoming the positive and outgoing guy we'd first seen at our selection weekend.

*

When Jonny had had to drop out of the team the summer before, Ben and I had adopted the ostrich technique to finding a new teammate. In our defence, we'd been burying our heads in the sand for a good reason: a fundamental disagreement on how to choose the third person. Ben wasn't keen to go down the route of choosing a member of the public, after previous experiences of people signing up for the media attention rather than the challenge. I thought the chances of our finding anyone at this stage was remote among people we knew. They had to be very fit, get on with Ben and me, have the time to prepare properly and take two months out from their life. We had to widen the search. I called up Tony Martin, the race organizer. Anyone we selected would have to be passed fit to race by him, and he'd run a similar competition in the past for a place in a race to the North Pole. It soon became clear that we'd left it late, and it was going to be a race against time.

BEN The advantages were obvious: we got to select from a potential pool of sixty million people, we could find someone who combined sportiness and humour and above all we'd be giving the opportunity of a lifetime to a member of the public. The cons, however, were rather more stark: we could end up selecting anyone from a tiresome bore to a mass murderer. It was a gamble. We would be spending six months training with this person and we'd then be spending two months in a very small tent with them.

JAMES We made the announcement through the *Daily Telegraph* and BBC *Breakfast*, both of which had huge audiences, and had been brilliant partners when we rowed across the Atlantic. The obvious downside of this route was the sheer number of people who put their hands up for this amazing opportunity. (Not, I should make clear, the chance to team up with Ben and me, but a free place in an event that would normally cost £42,000 to enter.) We wanted only the really serious applicants, so we took a risky decision and gave just ten days between announcing that we were looking for a third person and the application forms having to be in. We insisted that the forms had to be posted and include a picture rather than being an easy email questionnaire. After all, the harder you make it for people to apply, the fewer will bother – and, ultimately, you want only the ones who can be bothered.

We didn't know until after Ed was selected that he drove to the South Pole Race office to drop in his form in person because he didn't trust the postal service to get it there. That could be taken as an insight into his character – either he likes a bit of a worry, or has a huge attention to detail. I'm happy to say it's a bit of both, and it makes for a great combination.

BEN The announcement seemed to fire the imagination, and despite our strict criteria we received sackfuls of applications – including one from my father, who rather embarrassingly thought it would be funny to send in a photograph of himself being awarded an MBE by the Queen.

JAMES Sitting down with Tony we talked about a potential selection method once we'd chosen a certain number of people from the application forms. As Tony had run a selection weekend for the previous competition he'd held, we decided to use the same venue in the Cotswolds. I gave a rough outline of what the weekend should look like, which was to tire people out and then test them physically and mentally so their real personalities came out.

Ben and I didn't want to be involved in sorting through the forms in case we got accused of picking someone we knew, so Tony and his team kindly looked through them and chose forty people, roughly half men, half women, for the weekend of fun. They would be observed all the time and those observations would be fed back to Ben and me. We'd have formed our own opinions having worked with everybody all weekend, and then we'd choose four people to come to QinetiQ's HQ to have some further psychological and physiological testing.

BEN   It was a rainy, cold July morning when I drove down from London. I was incredibly nervous. I knew we had to pick one of those forty people as a teammate, and apart from common courtesy we were now bound by the law, having advertised on the promise that one of them would be selected. What if I didn't like any of them? It was a tortuous drive. I knew nothing about any of them, or even what lay in store over the next thirty-six hours. At least all I had to do was to sit back and watch. After all, I already had a place.

JAMES   The joining instructions were to turn up with everything for a weekend outside; tents and food would be provided. Judging by the number of quality rucksacks by the door, the well worn-in boots and outdoor clothing, I was probably one of the least experienced outdoor people here. Luckily, Ben turned up in shorts and a T-shirt with the sort of bag that Paris Hilton carries her chihuahua around in, which made me feel better.

BEN   'Where's your kit?' asked James, sternly. It was pouring with rain and the applicants were sheltering under a marquee on the shores of the lake.

'What do you mean?' I answered.

'Sleeping bag, sports kit, towel!' he barked. My heart sank. We would be doing the selection process too. It seems obvious now, but it never crossed my mind that we would have to do it. I hate selection processes, especially when they involve physical activity. What's more, we had pushed the organizers to make it harder and tougher than originally planned to help us make a selection. I felt like an idiot in my shorts and Converse trainers, and Tony took great delight in saying that I'd have been the first applicant crossed off the list if I didn't actually have a place on the team already.

We spent the first hour meeting all the applicants. Bomb disposal officers, doctors, climbers, expedition leaders, prison governors and naval officers were just some of the professions that jumped out. There were winners of Ironman competitions, Everest climbers and ocean rowers. I suddenly felt rather fraudulent among such distinguished company. What's worse, the majority of the applicants were better suited for the South Pole Race than either James or me.

JAMES The first morning consisted of building rafts in teams and racing around a series of islands on which there were a variety of challenges requiring teamwork, good communication and lateral thinking. Ed was in the group I went with and he stood out straight away, striking a great balance of listening to what other people had to say, communicating his thoughts well but not speaking for the sake of it. I could tell that the rest of the team liked him as well. When I swapped teams with Ben so we could try to spend time with everybody, I told him, 'There's a great candidate in that team, see if we agree on who it is.'

Ed showed his hand again in the afternoon's 'beasting' by Tony's Special Forces mates. The session started off with a run to a lake, and as the first people stopped at the edge I heard one of the instructors roar, 'I didn't say stop!' Like lemmings we all jumped in one after the other, only to be told to swim around before being run ragged for three hours in a field.

It wasn't a nice experience – and the fact that Ben and I had forked out for the whole weekend meant we were paying for the pleasure to boot. In the sprints and strength exercises Ed showed everyone a clean pair of heels, not surprising when we found out he used to represent Britain in the decathlon at U21 level. I suddenly felt less bad about his skinning me on the shuttle runs.

The never-ending day carried on into the night for a navigation exercise. None of my team had heard the final instruction that there was a cut-off time of 3 a.m. whether you'd reached all the checkpoints or not, and that there would be a group run at 6.30 a.m. We reached all the checkpoints but didn't get back into camp until 6.15 a.m. – just enough time to change into some trainers and then hit the road (or rather, field). What inspired me was that nobody complained all night. Surely this was nobody's idea of fun? And if it was, then how worried should we be that they might be our team-mate?

Narrowing it down to four people for the next stage at QinetiQ was incredibly difficult. We decided to take two men and two women, since we knew the most important criteria was that the new team member wasn't too similar to either Ben or myself. As long as the person was physically up to the challenge, we didn't have a preferred gender.

Ed was one of the six names that kept cropping up, and as any football pundit worth his salt would say, 'He'd be the first name on the team sheet.' The worst part was telling the group who was going to the next stage and disappointing thirty-six people, especially when Ben and I hadn't had to prove anything to get our places. That said, it was our ball so we had to be in the team!

BEN   Tony and his team laid out eight Polaroids of those they felt deserved to go through to the next round. The four whom James and I had selected in our minds were all included: Sarah, a six-foot Amazonian triathlete who had competed in the notoriously tough Eco Challenge; Victoria, a former bomb disposal officer with nerves of steel; Matt, a trainee army doctor; and Ed.

JAMES Three days later we met the final four again at QinetiQ's headquarters in Farnborough where they were put through a series of tests: simulated pulk-pulling on a treadmill, cold weather tolerance in a climatic chamber, and a flat-out 'VO$_2$ max' fitness test on a treadmill. Last came the psychological evaluation, by both questionnaire and interview. The aim was to get baseline data on their fitness and find out how their personalities fitted in with Ben's and mine as we underwent the same profiling. Ben and I would also spend the day with the final four and get a better idea of who we got on with on an instinctive level – equally as important as any test.

After the testing was done and results analysed we sat down with the experts and they went through how all the candidates performed. Ed's physical strength shone out, as did Matt's, but they differed markedly on the psychological profiling. Matt was very similar to me: incredibly competitive, which we were trying to avoid. Ed's profile showed that the way the team worked was key to him, citing the importance of inclusion and communication. He was competitive but not overly so, unless he was a bloody good liar.

I asked everybody in the room to write down one name on a piece of paper and we'd all turn it over at once. Every piece of paper had Ed's name on it.

BEN Ed had made an impression on me from the start. I had been impressed by his ability to stand back during different challenges and allow others a chance. He had been keen, kind and determined.

James and I have always been very different, he the competitive sportsman, me the complacent presenter. Where our see-saw of friendship rocks wildly from side to side, we wanted someone who could hold the balance somewhere in the middle. Ed fitted the bill and offered the best of both of us.

As well as his background in athletics and his job, Ed had also found time to squeeze in a law degree, all at the grand old age of twenty-eight. Apart from this he was also clearly a nice bloke, or so we hoped. It was a bold move, and one we hoped we wouldn't regret.

Starting with a Hollywood actor we had ended up with a doctor specializing in women's health. Useful for James and I, we joked. Little did we know how indispensable Ed would become.

21
HUNTERS AND HUNTED

BEN Back on the ice on the afternoon of day three, James was showing worrying signs of deterioration. He had developed a nagging cough, he was beginning to hobble, he wasn't eating his food and now he had stopped stone dead in the snow. What had happened?

JAMES From nowhere I heard Ben say, 'You OK?' His voice jolted me awake. I didn't remember stopping or know how long I'd been standing there doing nothing. The evidence was starting to mount that I was dog-tired.

'I'm feeling pretty knackered,' I said, not wanting to tell them that I'd actually fallen asleep whilst skiing. 'I just stopped for a quick mental regroup. How are you guys going?'

'Yeah, really good!' shouted Ed from the back.

Ben's answer had a slight variation this time. 'I'm really tired and can keep going, but I'm starting to get a teeny bit cold.'

I wasn't sure where 'teeny' was on the scale of coldness, but it could have been a result of either fatigue or because we were stopping too much and not skiing enough.

'Let's keep going then,' I said. 'Sorry for the unscheduled stop.' I took a piece of caffeine chewing gum we'd bought for situations when we were either struggling to stay awake or concentrate. It worked brilliantly, but I required more than just mental stimulation. I barely had enough energy to put one ski in front of the other, but the thought of salami-infused chocolate made me feel sick.

BEN 'Give me some weight from your pulk,' I said to James. It was an order rather than an offer. He looked visibly shocked, but we had an agreement that if one of us was struggling with the pace, then we would simply redistribute the loads in our pulks. It was a tried and tested rule, sharing the load according to bodyweight, strength and ability. The fact that I was 20 kilos lighter than James meant that, ordinarily, I would take less weight.

In Switzerland we had managed our 'team output' – the amount we could pull between us – with an individual scoring system between one and five, one being the least strain, five, the most. If you felt good, you would score yourself a 'one' and ask for more weight, and vice versa. We aimed at maintaining an average 'score' of no more than three for each of us.

Here in Antarctica it was particularly important to stick together. Crevasses and the danger of losing one another in a white-out meant we must ski together in a tight unit of three – so close together that often I'd accidentally crash into the pulk in front if Ed or James stopped too suddenly.

The scoring system worked well but had been largely abandoned, on account of it becoming really rather annoying. It was now used as a euphemism for 'I'm struggling'. 'I'm a three and a half' simply meant 'I'm knackered, will someone stop and take my bag?'

James hadn't said a word. He couldn't, he was a hundred metres behind. It was obvious he was struggling. Not only was he suffering from his blistered feet, but his lips had also blistered in the sun. 'They used to call me "hot lips" in the boat back when I was rowing,' he added, helpfully, but this was no joke; they had become so painful that eating was becoming more difficult by the meal. Lips were the subject of much debate and intense discomfort during the race. The sun burns them, the wind dries them and the cold cracks them. Unless you keep on top of your 'lip management' you are left with a scabby, blistered pair of smackers that drive you wild with a sharp, incessant snap of pain and discomfort.

With the cough and the injured tongue, James was in a sorry state after only three days in the harness.

Shortly before we left England, James had been to a charity dinner in East London with his wife, Bev. At midnight he had slipped into the Gents, changed from black tie into his training kit and proceeded to run home to Chiswick in West London. 'I'm going to need the strength to pull Ben's pulk for him,' he'd explained to Bev as he'd packed her into a taxi to go home alone.

And now here I was, demanding to take weight from James. I could see the bewilderment in his eyes. This was the wrong way round. It was like a parallel universe.

'What do you mean?' he asked.

'You're falling behind and we're getting cold,' I explained. 'Let me take some weight.' He shrugged and sighed, and if there had been a pramful of toys, he'd have thrown them out. There was a long pause.

'It's a stupid idea, you'll knacker yourself out,' he replied.

'I'm feeling strong,' I said.

'Yeah, but you've got to keep going for sixteen hours,' he continued – as if I could ever have forgotten.

'What shall I take,' I repeated, ignoring him. We had an agreement and James wasn't about to break it for the sake of vanity. Antarctica is no place for egos, and all three of us knew it.

Reluctantly, he handed over a bag from his pulk. It was a small but significant moment. Until now I had always felt our friendship was based on physical inequality. We both respected each other, that I knew, but I had always felt there was a physical bias towards James, perhaps not surprisingly since he is a world-class sportsman and I am not. For all that we are the best of friends, I still felt nervous around James. My butterflies before the marathon and the Great North Run were largely due to the presence of James at my shoulder, rather than the events themselves.

By his own admission, James has never been particularly generous with his compliments. A hard taskmaster, he is difficult to impress. After all, how can you impress someone who can't impress himself? It was a character trait that James had become more and more aware of since retiring from professional rowing, however, and he had certainly improved. He had become warmer and seemed to appreciate things more, and I had come to know a kinder James than the one I'd rowed across the Atlantic with. He had been a tower of strength and support during my treatment, and had called every day after Marina miscarried.

'What was the worst week in your life?' James had asked out of the blue shortly before the start of the race. Ed and I had both replied that we needed time to think about it.

'Why, what's yours?' I'd replied.

'The week Louise lost Eva,' James replied.

JAMES   My little niece had suffered from oxygen deprivation in the last few minutes of labour, and was born with limited brain activity. She fought for her life and the hospital tried to save her, but after six days she died. She was my sister Louise's first daughter, and her death in 2008 destroyed all of us. Throughout that week, and since her death, our lives had been suspended in some kind of hell.

BEN   'When things get tough out here,' said James, 'all you have to do is think of the worst week in your life and know that things can't get any worse.'

For someone who finds it hard to be emotional, by his own admission James had been hit hard by the loss of his niece, and the race had taken on a different significance since her untimely death. More and more, I could see an appreciation in my friend of how precious life is, and a realization of how lucky he was.

But for all that James may have softened, admitting to weakness was still a massive mental hurdle for him, and not one he had prepared for. By handing over weight from his pulk, he was conceding something, and in his mind I had no doubt that such a moment amounted to some sort of self-defeat. I don't think I fully realized the significance of that simple action for some time.

*

JAMES The other two had missed big chunks of the pre-race training and so I'd done a lot of training on my own, or with either one of them while the other was ill or injured. Given that I'd driven the training so hard, it must have been surprising for Ben, to say the least, to see me grimly hanging on. Even so, I found myself unable to be honest about how bad I felt, not wanting to show weakness or make us stop early. We'd set ourselves a hard, ambitious goal of skiing sixteen hours a day and none of us wanted to give up on that after only three days, especially now that we also found ourselves in the lead.

BEN I was feeling good, and above all I was feeling strong. I was thriving in an environment I had feared, and the months of anguish and trepidation had been replaced by the excitement of reality. But even after the weight had been redistributed, James continued to drop further behind, and his humiliation became keener when Ed also took some weight from his pulk. It hadn't been a good day for James, and things were about to go from bad to worse.

Apart from a couple of indistinct dots on the horizon, we had heard neither sight nor sound of the other teams since the Norwegians pitched their tent on the first evening. The weather had been kind to us and, according to the GPS, we had been making a steady progress of 3.5 kph. We had stuck to our strategy with rigidity and had covered an impressive 49 kilometres per day, but we were beginning to feel the strain, and our bodies were starting to tell us to stop.

It was 11 p.m., and we'd been skiing for thirteen hours. 'Can I make a suggestion that we stop early?' announced James. I was staggered, not at the suggestion, but that it came from James. This was not a man to give up early and it was a bold, if not worrying, suggestion from Mr Motivator.

Ed and I agreed at once. To stop early seemed an obvious remedy to our aches and pains, both physical and mental. We set the tent and clambered inside. It was midnight and we had turned in two hours early.

JAMES   I fired up the stoves, frustrated that I'd been the one to make us stop. If I'd looked after myself during the day and kept myself fuelled up (as I insisted others did), we'd still be out there. To make it worse, I knew that if either Ben or Ed had been that tired and I had felt OK, I'd have really challenged them about exactly how tired they were rather than allowing them to say – as I did – 'I'm really struggling.' I wondered whether my sometimes overbearing personality made it hard to ask me those questions.

Ben and Ed were both really positive when they came into the tent, and didn't seem nearly as concerned as I was that we'd stopped. In fact Ben thought it was a real positive.

BEN   'We've made great progress, and we're leading the race. It would have been easy to have kept going—'

JAMES   He could speak for himself on that one!

BEN   '—but I think that it was a very mature decision to stop,' I finished.

I was proud that as a team we had recognized the need to rest. To continue would have been inefficient and potentially damaging in the long term. A race of this length and magnitude is all about pacing. We had agreed on a strategy, but it had always been on the understanding that we needed to be flexible according to conditions and ability. I was amazed – and secretly pleased – to see how relaxed Ed and James were. This certainly wasn't the James I had known, nor was it the Ed I had anticipated. We set about mending damaged kit, repairing sorry-looking feet and for my own part, tending to the painful welts that had formed between my legs. This 'nappy rash' was no fun at all.

JAMES   Feeling revived after a warm meal and a protein shake mixed with custard, I put our mileage for the day into the spreadsheet in my diary. My dad would have been so proud that some of the accountancy genes had been passed down after all; it was just a shame it took Antarctica to bring them out. We'd covered 36 kilometres, 25 per cent less than the 48 kilometres of the previous day; it was such a significant drop in distance. There was nothing we could do about it now though, other than rest up and kick on tomorrow – well, in a few hours' time, to be precise.

I fell asleep and dreamed for the first time in weeks.

*

We knew we were still leading the race – or at least we knew the Norwegians weren't ahead of us. What none of us said out loud was that with such a big drop in daily distance, we'd opened the door to them. Our goal hadn't changed; we were still aiming to arrive at the South Pole totally exhausted, unable to do a step more. But after leading the race since the beginning, I'd be lying if I said I'd not thought about getting to the Pole first and I was sure that Ed, if not Ben, thought the same. It wasn't something I was going to bring up, though . . . just yet.

Over the first couple of days I was desperate to know what was going through the Norwegians' minds. As the clear pre-race favourites they wouldn't have expected to be behind us, so how had it affected them? The night before the race started, Rune had shouted out to all the tents, 'See this Norwegian flag? The next time you see it will be at the Pole.' I was going to point out that that would be the case whether they were there first, or last.

I was glad I didn't know what they were thinking that night, or I'd have felt even worse about stopping early. I spoke to them when the race was over, and Stian said that after that third day they had a conversation about what they were going to do. They felt they couldn't match our pace and weren't sure what would happen to them if they kept pushing this hard. They spoke about whether it was time to back off and simply make sure they got to the Pole and enjoyed the trip. Their conclusion was to push hard for one more day and then make a decision. So, we learned with hindsight that if we'd pushed on until 2 a.m. there was a chance that we could have broken their spirit and taken them out of the race. Was that the night we blew our chance of victory?

22

IN-TENT CORDIALE

BEN   It was day six.

'Norwegians!' hollered James from outside the tent.

My heart sank. They'd caught us.

We couldn't be sure we were leading the race up to that point – the organizers had banned communication with the outside – but we all hoped we were in the lead. We had been pushing hard, we were navigating well and we hadn't seen any sign of the other teams, so it was an educated guess that we were up at the pointy end of the pack.

The arrival of the Norwegians would soon put an end to that.

'They're about a kilometre away,' James continued. It was 9 a.m. and we still had an hour's work to do before we could get away. They would be with us within fifteen minutes. We were like rabbits caught in headlights.

JAMES   I wasn't surprised they had made up ground on us, but I didn't think the previous day's skiing would have allowed them to make such massive inroads. Three days earlier, when we covered just 36 kilometres after I'd eaten my karabiner, I fully expected to wake up and see their tracks running past our tent. The next morning I'd come out and looked for marks in the snow, but I don't know why I bothered. It occurred to me that if I was going to overtake someone, I wouldn't leave tracks outside their front door; I'd try to make them think they were still leading. Because our bright orange tents were visible from space it would have been impossible not to spot us, change course slightly and, to quote a leading authority – Maverick, in *Top Gun* – 'Fly right by'.

The morning after our early stop, though, I had been less concerned about the Norwegians and more keen to see the lie of the land outside the tent. Having been convinced we'd been skiing uphill I was looking forward to showing the other two I'd been the only one reading the gradient properly the previous night.

I was greeted by a perfectly flat landscape.

Ed stuck his head out of the tent. 'Mate, have you got the crampons on? It looks pretty steep out there.'

'What's that? The wind's really blowing out here, I can't make out anything you're saying,' I said, getting ready for a morning of ribbing.

'Any Norwegians?' Ed asked.

'None on the horizon, and no tracks either,' I replied, keeping to myself my theory about their skirting round our tent.

When we set off that day there was still no sign of life on the horizon, but a couple of hours later two dots appeared directly behind us. Over the next couple of days they seemed to stay roughly the same distance behind, right on the limit of the horizon, disappearing for a few hours and then suddenly coming back.

Trying to resurrect my topological credibility, I posited a new theory: that the Norwegians didn't come in and out of view because of a change in the distance between us, but because of subtle changes in gradient caused by a variation in the length of the horizon length. Ed and James weren't buying it, so I was left with either admitting I was wrong or that they just weren't in touch with the environment around them. Obviously, I went for the latter.

Being pursued by those mercilessly persistent dots on the horizon reminded me of *Butch Cassidy and the Sundance Kid*. Pursued by a posse formed by the President of the Railroad after they kept robbing his train, they try every trick they know to evade them, wading through rivers, scrambling over rock and doubling up on one horse – but none of them work. Our situation was slightly different in that we knew who was chasing us and we only had one tactic – keep skiing – but some of the conversations were spookily similar to those in the famous film. You could substitute any of our names into the script below, although I'd appreciate it if I was allowed to be Sundance.

> *Butch: I think we lost 'em. Do you think we lost 'em?*
> *Sundance: No.*
> *Butch: Neither do I.*

Ben was relaxed about the arrival of the Norwegians, but Ed was very disappointed. Clearly, as I had done in the Atlantic row, he seemed to be using the race and his competitive instinct for motivation and focus. And me? I knew the race wasn't going to be won in the first few days but the longer we stayed ahead, the more we had come to feel that it was our position by right. My reaction to seeing the Norwegians so close on that sixth morning surprised me, then. I thought seeing our lead evaporate would have wound me up and put me in a foul mood, but it didn't.

BEN 'We always knew they'd be faster,' reasoned James. He was right, but I think we'd all got carried away with our thoughts and dreams of winning the race. I certainly had and Ed's reaction, head in hands, suggested he had too. The imminent arrival of our rivals shattered any grand illusions of changing history.

'I wonder whether they'll ski with us?' suggested James. We had been alone, starved of company except for our own for nearly a week, and he was right, it would be good to have some new conversation.

I stepped from the tent and watched as the two figures grew nearer and nearer. It was heartbreaking to watch our lead disappear, but it was good to see some new faces. I wondered how they would react to us. Would they say hello? Would they simply skirt past us and ski off? Or would they, as James suggested, ski with us?

My heart pounded as they approached. One of them waved a ski pole in the air. Was this a sign of greeting or a sign of aggression, like a farmer with his stick? James and Ed packed the tent while I filmed the approach of our Scandinavian friends.

'Hi,' I shouted as they approached, 'good to see you guys!' They remained silent. Friend or foe? I wondered.

As they approached I held my hand out to welcome them. Any concerns I had about their reaction disappeared as I was enveloped in a bear hug.

'It is so good to see you guys,' smiled Stian. He looked tired, his long curly beard was encrusted with ice and his face was already heavily weathered by the sun. We must have looked pretty similar to him.

'You guys are fast,' marvelled Stian. 'When did you become so good?' I beamed with pride. 'We've been trying to catch up with you for days,' he explained. 'We have had you on the horizon every day and got up five hours ago to finally catch up.'

My mind raced to do the maths. They had got up five hours ago to catch up with us. At an average speed of 3.5 kilometres, that meant we had been 17.5 kilometres ahead of them, and what's more, if they had got up five hours before us, they would also have to stop five hours before us. They may have caught up with us but we still had a potential lead. All we had to do was keep that distance between us. My smile grew into a grin.

JAMES The hugs we shared were genuine, not just because it was great to see them but there was a bond there borne of a shared experience that hadn't existed before, mutual respect for what we were pushing ourselves through. Don't get me wrong, I'd rather have been waiting at the South Pole to give them a hug, but I didn't have that option – yet.

'Leaving camp late today?' Stian said with a grin.

'Haven't you got anything better to do than spy on us?' I joked. 'If you're so clever, what time do we stop? Harder to see that when you're already tucked up reading each other bedtime stories.'

'Around 2 a.m., we think.' Stian's grin was still there.

I was impressed but tried not to show it. 'Smart arse! How did you know that?' I said trying not to sound too surprised.

'We know the speed you ski at and how far behind you we are.

In the morning we see how long it takes us to ski to your campsite and then we work out how many hours you skied for after we finished, and what time you finished.' He recounted this as if he was telling me how to cross a road. I couldn't work out what I was more impressed by, the tracking, the fact that they had the energy and concentration to work it out, or the fact he could explain it in his second language. It was all I could do to ski up imaginary hills.

BEN   'Shall we ski together?' asked James like a child in the playground.

'Sure!' smiled Rune, 'we had wondered the same thing as we approached. We weren't sure if you'd want to,' he added, 'we thought you might just ski off as soon as we arrived.'

A little like the famous wartime football match in no-man's-land, we were to suspend rivalry while the Brits and the Norwegians skied together. I wondered what Scott and Amundsen would have done had they had a similar encounter. Theirs was never a planned race, and they had fallen into competing with each other almost by accident. I felt sure they would have done the same thing.

Rune and Stian sat on their pulks while we packed up camp. They gave us some of their granola bars and quizzed us about the previous few days.

'James has bad feet,' said Stian – a statement rather than a question – 'and Ed is a little dehydrated' he continued. 'Ben, your skiing is strong,' he added. How did they know so much about us? I wondered as we lowered the tent.

JAMES   The analogy with *Butch Cassidy and the Sundance Kid* had become more realistic, except in place of a sheriff in a white hat and an Indian tracker we had two Norwegians analysing our every move. Their revelations were about to get worse.

'You can tell a lot from the tracks,' said Stian.

'You've been skiing in our tracks, eh? Surely you'd want to break trail rather than take the easy route and just follow!' I smiled, feigning indignation, but chuffed that our navigation had been consistent enough for them to stick in the grooves we'd cut into the snow.

'Why not? Your course has been really straight,' Stian said as though he'd followed us down a road. Worryingly, I felt like Luke Skywalker being paid a compliment by Obi-Wan Kenobi, not normally a bad thing but when it's your competitors paying you a compliment it shouldn't have that effect. 'Your routine has been steady. You ski for two hours and then have a break. We can tell your speed by the distances between your stops and how far apart your ski pole marks are in the snow. The further apart each of you pushes, the faster you're going. We can also tell from your piss whether you're dehydrated.'

Bloody hell, it was as if I was being hunted rather than followed, although I felt a small victory in the urine analysis since I'd had a Berrocca vitamin pill every morning, which gave me fluorescent yellow urine. God knows what they made of that.

'Have you seen anyone else?' I asked. If they were that good at tracking people in front, there was a good chance they'd have an idea what was going on behind them.

'Not since the second day. I think we are both many hours ahead,' he said, simply. It wasn't as impressive a dossier as they'd compiled on us, but he seemed certain nobody else was close. Good news.

BEN We packed up camp and headed off as a group of five.

As would become the norm over the course of the race, I led first to warm up, and set the pace and direction. It was always easy to navigate between ten and twelve because the sun was directly behind us, casting long shadows on to the skis.

Stian skied alongside me as I cut a trail through the virgin landscape.

'So how are you feeling?' asked Stian.

'I'm feeling good,' I replied, 'but I'm worried about the others.' I surprised myself with my honesty. This was a rival and I was already giving away information about my team members, but I needed to talk. For days I had kept my worries to myself and now I had an opportunity to share them with someone else.

'Rune is the same,' he replied candidly. I looked behind me and saw James and Rune skiing alongside one another. Both were hobbling awkwardly. Stian explained that the blistering had become so bad on Rune's feet that they had been forced to stop early and call in the doctor.

It had never crossed my mind to call in a doctor. After all, we had one in our team, but he had become part of the sick party. Besides, we hadn't chosen Ed on account of his medical abilities. He was a team member, not the team doctor. I was overcome by a wave of guilt.

For two hours Stian and I chatted. We talked about the race, home and food. We were skiing much slower as we gabbled away, but I didn't care. It was good to have new company, and it was therapeutic to chat through our problems together.

Until now, the Norwegians were people we were scared of, like a fox chased by the hunt. They had appeared untouchable in their knowledge and unapproachable in their superiority. These barriers came tumbling down as we talked about life and dreams and aspirations. I smiled as Stian told me about their efforts to find sponsorship and generate interest in the race.

'No one was interested,' he said. 'We'd go into boardrooms full of bored people with stern faces, and we'd jump about with excitement as we enthused about this great race.'

They were just like us. We were exactly the same young men, driven by adventure, divided only by language – though Scandinavians being Scandinavians, they spoke even better English than we did. It was a startling realization that two people from two different nations could share the same dreams and hopes. Not for the first time, I thought of Scott and Amundsen, forging across the same continent a hundred years before.

'What would you do if Rune had to pull out because of his feet?' I asked.

It was a difficult question. It was one I had been asking myself.

James, and to a lesser extent Ed, had both been plagued by health issues and I had begun to wonder about their ability to go on. We still had hundreds of kilometres ahead of us, and I couldn't help but wonder what would happen if one or both of them had to pull out.

I had never discussed it with the boys. It had always seemed inappropriate. I felt it was bad luck and bad form to discuss such a negative and gloomy subject, and had therefore consigned all doubt to the back of my mind. Until now.

'I have asked myself that many times,' said Stian in his perfect English. 'I would go on alone,' he said, simply. 'And you, what would you do?'

'I'd do the same.' We paused while we digested what we'd said. Before the race there had been so much discussion about what would happen if I couldn't go, and yet here I was in the middle of Antarctica, debating the same question about my sick teammates.

We had lost track of time. We'd been skiing for three hours without a break, so we pulled our pulks alongside one another and shared snacks. I still craved conversation, and dropped back to chat with Rune.

'I have a secret,' he confided. 'When I get home, I'm going to propose to my girlfriend!'

It was a uniquely intimate moment; not just that he had confided such monumentally life-changing information in me, but because I could relate to his feelings and sentiments. I had proposed to Marina after rowing the Atlantic. I had decided I wanted to marry her on day one of the adventure, and it had been a tremendously challenging crossing, made slightly easier by the drive to get to the finish and ask her to become my wife.

'I get quite emotional when I think about it,' he continued. 'I just realized how much I love her.' I told him about my own experience and how I'd proposed to Marina using a tiny piece of rope from the boat. An expedition is like a love story. It is a journey of love found, love lost and love suspended. We all pretend to be hardy adventurers, but the reality is that we are more like love-sick puppies, lost without our other halves. In many ways the culmination of any expedition is not geographical but physical, in the reunion of loved ones.

Since I married Marina, we have spent an unhealthy time apart as filming and writing assignments have taken me around the globe. It never gets any easier, but we have developed different ways and means of coping with long absences, and above all we have learned to love the reunions. Like first dates, we relish the buzz of excitement and flutter of hearts when we're finally together again.

It is always harder for those left behind, and no matter how many times I tell her, Marina will never truly know how often I think about her or long for her when I'm away.

23

SCIENTIFIC PROGRESS

JAMES   Had I undergone a complete personality transformation? Had I finally lost my competitive instinct? Having driven us so hard to get into this position in the first place, I didn't think so. If we started covering the same mileage we were managing earlier then we had every chance of regaining the lead. The Norwegians had got up early that morning to catch us; they had to stop some time.

We had to remain confident in our ability and remember that the race, at this stage, was against ourselves rather than anyone else. If we committed all our energy into staying ahead this early, we might not even make it to the Pole.

I must have been ill: first I saw hills where there weren't any, and now for the first time in my life I was starting to be sensible. Skiing along talking to Stian and Rune about what they'd made of the first part of the race it was the excitement in their voices about racing in Antarctica and how lucky they felt to be here that made me realize I had to give myself time to enjoy the environment (if such a thing is possible in minus 30 degree conditions). Surrounded by endless plains of ice and surviving in such basic conditions, no matter how hard it got I couldn't forget how lucky I was to be here.

Our progress had been slower over the last couple of days as we struggled to cope with some health issues. Ben and Ed were still having trouble with their nether regions and I'd developed big blisters under the heel, ball and big toe of each foot, the three areas that take the weight through the propulsion phase, so it was impossible to get any respite from the pain in my feet no matter how I shifted my foot in the boot.

I'd tried to prepare myself mentally for painful feet, but I wasn't ready for this level of discomfort. Ed reckoned my blisters were caused by the fact that I wear flip-flops at every available opportunity in ordinary life, and therefore my feet can't cope with boots. With flip-flops not being a viable solution in minus 30 degrees, I was going to have to suck it up and get on with it. But it wasn't just causing me pain; the constant taping and maintenance took time and had cost us valuable minutes on the move and delayed our departure in the mornings.

Somehow, in a virus-free continent, Ed and I had managed to pick up a chest infection over the first few days of the race, though it didn't seem to be having too much of an effect on our skiing – yet. The constant coughing was a pain, however, and our bodies were using energy fighting the infection so we had to be careful not to make things worse. Most doctors would suggest lots of rest; instead, we tried to get over it by skiing for sixteen hours.

BEN James has never been particularly good at looking after himself. His concern after he burnt and blistered his lips during our training camp in Switzerland was not about his appearance or the pain, but about his wife's reaction. 'Hot lips' had been a metaphor for his general welfare and hygiene and Bev knew it was the first indicator that he hadn't been looking after himself.

His approach to his feet was typically cavalier, and by his own admission he went for the ostrich approach (a worrying theme in most of our preparations, as you can see): if he didn't look at his feet then they would be fine. This meant leaving his feet heavily bandaged and enveloped in a damp sock until the morning. This would give them enough time to steep in their own moisture overnight, thereby softening the skin and creating even more blisters . . .

Somehow I had escaped that particular problem, and I resolved to keep it that way by covering any hot spots in Compeed (a sort of second skin), and ensuring there were no seams or folds in my socks or boots.

As the veteran of more than a dozen expeditions across the

globe I am only too aware of the power of blisters. I had been plagued by them during the Marathon Des Sables, a 250-kilometre race across the Sahara desert. Somehow I had finished the race, but not before losing most of the skin on my feet to the debilitating rampage of blisters the size of golf balls. The pain is still etched on my memory.

Over the years I have found various ways of preparing my feet before expeditions, from barefoot running along sand to simply wearing thick socks and boots twenty-four hours a day. Nappy rash aside, I was pleased that my preparation had paid off, for once.

JAMES I was just pleased to know I wasn't the only one with sore feet – Rune had been struggling too. My unsportsmanlike joy in his discomfort didn't last long, though, when I learned that he'd reduced the impact by putting silk over the blisters. Apparently, it's an old Norwegian trick. Despite the boot still feeling tight, the silk reduces the friction that causes blisters, and Rune was already starting to get back to top form. Unbelievably, I'd left my silk pyjamas at home – what was I thinking of?

Like us, the Norwegians were skiing for a couple of hours and then having a break, but their nutritional regime differed slightly from ours. They seemed to drink much less than we did during the day, for a start. I was rationing myself to around three litres over the sixteen hours' skiing because of the time spent to melt the snow each morning; they were drinking about one to one and a half litres, 'How can you cope with that little fluid, especially in the dry air up here?' I asked, referring to the thinner atmosphere at altitude.

'In the Norwegian army,' – ah, all the secrets were coming out – 'we have to ski all day on a litre as part of our training, so the body gets used to working without water,' Rune said.

'That's clearly cheating!' I responded. That meant they were boiling less water every morning and the hour they were saving could be spent either skiing or sleeping.

*

During a break I thought I'd use the opportunity to palm some of my snack bag off on them. I'd got better at forcing down my salami-infused selection box, but thought Rune might have some goodies in his pouch. I offered him some chocolate and in return he handed me some reindeer tongue. Unbelievably, I'd managed to find something less appealing than my manky chocolate. The Norwegian delicacy tasted like a fattier, saltier, chewier version of biltong; hardly surprising, as it was virtually all fat, giving vital calories in a form the body craves in Antarctica. Per gram there are twice as many calories in fat as carbohydrate or protein, meaning twice the energy can be carried for half the weight. It wasn't all good news for the Norwegians, though; the downside was that it tasted horrible. Suddenly, my chocolate-cheese mix seemed a lot more appetizing.

Rune and Stian's more traditional approach to their nutrition was mirrored in much of their clothing, with warm traditional Norwegian wool worn over modern thermals and the fur 'tunnel' hoods that I had so admired at the start of the race. They looked like a couple of granddads, but who was laughing now?

Our preparation had been much more scientific, but which approach was best? Our performance had clearly surprised them. We had improved so much since they witnessed our shambolic efforts in Norway eleven months earlier, and that was down to the way we prepared, with QinetiQ's help.

We were faced with a juggling act in the lead-up to the race, needing to learn so many new skills in such a short time while the Norwegians, pastmasters at skiing and cold-weather survival, could concentrate on the finer details of polar preparation. The ideal solution for us would have been to move to Norway for six months, but that wasn't feasible if Ben and I wanted to still be married and have jobs at the end of the year. We had to make the most out of a couple of shorter trips abroad and use everything we had at our disposal.

The race was expensive to enter primarily because of the logistical difficulty of holding a race on the ice and getting the competitors there. Ben and I had needed sponsorship. Luckily two idiots

rowing across the Atlantic naked seemed to capture people's attention, making it easier for us to approach companies and, well, beg.
When we announced our intentions to race to the South Pole one
company approached us to see if they could help. I was determined
not to make the same mistakes we had in preparation for the
Atlantic row, namely underestimating the challenge, not focusing on
developing the right skills and leaving everything too late. QinetiQ,
the company in question, clearly thought along the same lines, on
top of which they were the perfect partner to make sure that didn't
happen.

QinetiQ was formed when DERA (the Defence Evaluation
and Research Agency) was split up in 2001. How can I put this?
There was a little bit of James Bond about them. Not only was the
centrifuge that appears in *Moonraker* a part of their facility (they
promised us a ride, which sealed their partnership for me), but
with their gadgets and giant freezers, I wondered whether they
had even inspired the character of James Bond's quartermaster, Q?
Its mission statement emphasizes 'determination to develop and
provide innovative technology solutions' – and boy did we need
some solutions.

Unfortunately, there are no short cuts to fitness – that was
down to us – but the physiology tests we undertook in QinetiQ's
'human performance labs' monitored our progress, checking that
the training we were doing was having a worthwhile effect and
identifying areas we needed to focus on. We simulated pulk-pulling
on a treadmill, worked out what we thought would be workable
weight ratios for each of us and also measured our basal metabolic
rates so that we could work out exactly how many calories we
would each need per day.

Despite being rubbish at all polar-based skills, however, we
were also way behind the Norwegians in another crucial area. Rune
and Stian have been friends since they were six. They grew up
together, were in the same class at school and went into the army
together, so have well over twenty years of friendship and shared
experiences to draw upon. We met Ed for the first time five months

before leaving and had spent only about thirty days in his company. The work we did with psychologists at QinetiQ gave us the ability to resolve conflicts and stop problems escalating by spotting the warning signs and defusing the situation, but our team understanding could only ever be artificial. It was genuinely gratifying to find that things were working here out on the ice; clearly, those sessions with the psychologist had been among the most successful and worthwhile elements of our preparation.

What QinetiQ couldn't do for us was the training itself, pulling those tyres up and down the beach in Devon. Hard and boring it may have been but it did the job. A major part of the training for me was getting my body used not only to being awake when it didn't want to be but exercising then as well. I'd get up and run for a couple of hours at two in the morning, which also had the added advantage of being time efficient. I could do work, see family at normal times and train when they were asleep. The downside was I didn't sleep much, but depriving myself of sleep was all part of the training. As I was running in the dark I kept telling myself, 'I'll feel less tired in twenty-four-hour sunlight.' Bev was supportive in her own way. When I got up at 2 a.m. for a run she'd mutter 'Bloody psycho'; and when I climbed back into bed a few hours later she'd say it again.

I even went tyre-pulling by night, in Richmond Park. Annoyingly, the six-week deer cull coincided with the period I was putting in the most training, and so the park was closed at night. I didn't think they'd mind if one bloke pulled a tyre round, so I threw my tyre over and then climbed the fence. It added a certain excitement to the boring sessions knowing what else was going on in the park; I just relied on them being good shots. Talking to Stian, he and Rune used to do exactly the same (apart from avoiding snipers) and pull tyres at night. It was funny to think there would have been nights when we were doing the same thing at the same time, them in Norway and me in Britain.

Race instructor Inge gave the impression that all Norwegian babies are left outside in the snow for their first night and those that survive are true Norwegians. As Rune and Stian were still here, they obviously had what it took.

*

BEN I had enjoyed the Norwegians' company, but I began to worry how it would end. When did friends turn back into foes? And how? We still had the benefit of sleep. They had got up five hours earlier than us and would probably need to stop before us.

'Just so it won't be awkward,' I ventured, 'we've loved today, but we have a strategy to stick to. I hope there's no hard feelings if we don't stop when you do,' I said rather presumptuously.

The Norwegians shrugged and shook their heads.

'Of course not.' This was a race, after all. We had all enjoyed the escapism, but the armistice was nearly over, the honeymoon ended.

It was mid-afternoon and the Norwegians had regrouped. I was skiing behind Ed when I noticed a shadow stride past first me, and then Ed. It was James. He had removed his skis and he was marching across the ice in his boots with his skis bound to his pulk.

He stormed past us in silence, creating large, deep footprints as he went. Ed and I were forced to pick up our pace to keep up with him. It was an impressive pace, I had to give him that, and the fastest we'd been in days. On he strode as we struggled to keep up. Slowly he began to pull away from us and before long he was just a speck on the horizon.

Ed and I were baffled. Why had he removed his skis and marched off at such a ridiculous pace? And why had he not stopped? It was almost laughable – if it hadn't been quite so annoying.

'He's so bloody selfish,' muttered Ed.

'That's James,' I shrugged, as we watched him disappearing into the glare of the sun.

JAMES Hearing about Rune's lovely, comfy silk plasters for his blisters had done nothing for my own private battle with my mangled feet. Norwegians or no Norwegians, I couldn't carry on like this, it was killing me. I had to take my skis off, but could I walk over this terrain without sinking into the snow? It was pretty icy underfoot and it would be more tiring – I'd be lifting my leg rather than sliding it forwards and there would be absolutely no free distance from gliding, unless my walking style had changed considerably since I'd been here. But if I could manage it, a slightly different movement would at least change the pressure points on my feet.

I strapped my skis to the top of my pulk and set off walking. A change wasn't quite as good as a rest, but it was much better. It felt great to be able to work off some aggression after feeling like I was slowing the other two down.

BEN   We had spent the last few days stopping frequently to allow James to catch up. Ed had spent hours dressing his feet each day and we had even lengthened breaks for him. But now, suddenly and for no apparent reason except for the fact he had removed his skis, we had been abandoned by our teammate, who seemed oblivious to us as he forged ahead. We were breathless and angry when we finally caught up with him.

'What was all that about?' I asked in bewilderment.

'It's easier and less painful without my skis,' replied James.

'I can see that,' I snapped, 'but what's with the ridiculous pace? Ed and I can't keep up.'

'You mean it was too fast?' he said. 'I thought it was too slow and I was holding you guys up.'

How could you be holding us up if we were a kilometre behind? I thought. There's no way James could have thought it was too slow. He was in charge of the GPS and would have known it was far faster than our average. Ed and I both felt it was his way of venting his frustration. He must have been annoyed about removing his skis, and irritated by his new self-inflicted limits.

I had no problem with his walking – there were no rules about skiing, and indeed we had been advised to remove skis through the larger sastrugi fields – but we still had to work as a team. And meanwhile, hanging back to give us some room, the Norwegians had witnessed our first bust-up.

'We're all feeling a little tired,' said Stian when they caught up. 'Why don't we set up the tents and have a game of cards?' It seemed a logical idea and in any other circumstances I would have jumped at the chance – but we were in a race.

For the first time, I wondered about their sincerity. They had been skiing for longer than us and would naturally be more tired. It was in their interest to rest and put up the tent. I wondered whether 'cards' was an excuse to get us to stop early. These were rivals who had tracked us for days, after all. I smelt a rat, and we declined their offer.

*

At 7.40 p.m. we had a natural split when the Norwegians stopped to make their daily call. We watched as they pitched their tent, and then pushed on south.

We had enjoyed the distraction of the day, but it had thrown us all out of kilter. Our usual routine had been abandoned and the result was that we were tired, hungry and above all dehydrated.

James was still walking, and we were making good progress. We had the psychological advantage. We knew when the Norwegians had stopped, and that we had the ability to create our own distance between us. What's more, they wouldn't know when we stopped. Or so we thought.

JAMES   As we set off, I noticed the Norwegians were about to have a main meal. I spent the next hour trying to work out their eating strategy. If they ate their only main meal of the day then, what did they eat when they got into the tent? It was like my efforts with a Rubik's Cube: I'd complete one side only to muck up the one I'd finished earlier. No matter how I reorganized the meal system, I couldn't work out how they were eating in the tent and on the go; I always seemed to be a meal short.

It wasn't until we got to the South Pole that I worked it out – well, they told me. When they set up camp they'd have some biscuits and go straight to bed, then wake up and have porridge and make their water for the day. At lunchtime they'd have their dessert and about 7 p.m. their main meal, the latter two meals with hot water from a thermos. This way they saved between one and a half to two hours in the evening. For the first few days of the race they were operating on the system we used for the entire race – eating a main meal when we pitched up, porridge in the morning and snack bags throughout the day. When we disappeared over the horizon at the start after a couple of days, they realized they would have to change their strategy to catch us up. It was flattering that we forced them to endure a regime they hated, and indicative of the pressure and desire they had to make sure they got there first. We'd have really struggled operating on that regime for any length of time, especially without the Norwegian army camel training, where drinking water seems to be a sign of weakness. Or were we just being soft? As our SBS trainer Bernie had said in Switzerland, 'You've got to back yourselves.' What would have happened if we had? Unfortunately, we'll never know.

The Norwegians returned to their rightful position behind us on the horizon, setting up camp, and I was impressed with their self-confidence, watching the opposition ski on for another three hours. They'd underestimated us, but I expected them to regroup. I've been in the position of overwhelming favourite. It is not the easiest situation to cope with because there is always someone who does something unexpected, and it is your reaction to that which determines whether you can cope with the pressure. They'd been tracking us for a week and the last couple of days I'd got the feeling they were just keeping us in sight before planning their attack. Or perhaps they were simply no longer worried about our speed.

They might have been right with the latter assessment, as our pace dropped significantly around midnight. We spent more time chatting at breaks, were eating less and the danger of skiing with camels is that you forget to drink as well. The Norwegians also skied slightly faster than we were used to, and in no time at all we got tired, very tired. Ed seemed to be suffering from the same problem I had a few days earlier, and like me he was looking for someone to call it a day, but both Ben and I wanted to carry on. We decided to ram Ed full of fluid, chocolate and Kendal mint cake, wait fifteen minutes and see if he felt better rather than put the tent up and call it a night. I didn't believe Ed had hit his lower limit. It may have been the most tired and weak he'd ever been, but there was more in the tank and he was such a strong boy I had no doubt he'd crank out a few more kilometres. It was just his self-confidence I doubted at the moment.

Ben and I took some weight from Ed and we agreed to carry on for another 8 kilometres, which would mean we'd probably stop just under an hour early. Ed didn't look happy at the prospect, but there was no way he was going to call a halt. Did Ben and I take advantage of that? Probably, but it was really important to do some more distance today; those extra 8 kilometres would give us 42 kilometres for the day – a full marathon, which seemed like a fitting distance. It also left us with a nice round number until the midway checkpoint: 120 kilometres.

24

A DAY IN THE LIFE OF A POLAR RACER

BEN How do you describe a day that essentially has no beginning and no end? In a land of twenty-four-hour sunlight there was little to differentiate night from day. I will begin where most of our days ended, back to front.

2 a.m. was the witching hour, when men become pumpkins. It was the point at which our bodies failed us. From 1.30 a.m. I would begin clock watching, except that it was almost impossible to look at my watch through all the layers. To tell the time while skiing involved removing my poles from my wrists, and holding them in one hand. I would then remove my thick outer mitts that I had joined with a thin piece of rope looped around my neck, and tuck them into the pulk harness around my waist. Next I'd remove the windproof gloves and stick them down my front, and with my thin pair of woollen contact gloves pull my Gore-tex jacket sleeve over my fleece, and remove my thumb from the thumb hole in my thermal top. Finally I would get a fleeting glimpse of the time, which was invariably half an hour earlier than I hoped for. Then I'd repeat the above routine in reverse. I could do the whole process in about three minutes. I didn't look at my watch very often.

1, 2, 3, 4, 5, 6 . . . I would begin to count up to our finishing time, blocks of 1,000 which took around fifteen minutes. The numbers would swim in my head and the minutes felt like hours as we skied on towards the witching hour. Legs were heavy and backs ached as we stubbornly marched on through fatigue and pain. Strategy, strategy, strategy. How I used to curse our daily strategy during that long final hour.

2 a.m. would arrive not a second too soon.

'This looks like a flat patch of snow,' I'd announce, pointing to an area to pitch our tent. 'No, this looks flatter,' I'd be corrected by one of the others, pointing to an identical patch of snow. In reality it was much of a muchness, but in our energy-starved minds, the overall flat terrain would take on imaginary shapes and slopes, unidentifiable by anyone else. I'd usually give in without a fight; at the end of the day it was all flat.

We'd unclip the harnesses and skis and begin to unpack the pulks. James always carried the tent and I always carried the dozen or so bamboo poles. We'd pull the tent from the bag and invariably it would be the wrong way round, despite the fact we repeated this task dozens of times. One person would feed the pole into the canvas sleeve on the left side of the tent, while the other wrestled with the other end, trying to get it into a small plastic holder. We would repeat this process three times until all three poles were hooped through the tent.

Next the whole structure would be pulled taut, making sure the wind was directly onto the back of the tent. While two of us fixed the guy lines and shovelled snow on to the tent's skirt to help keep it down, the other collected up all the kitchen utensils and stoves.

Stove duty was usually given to whoever was the coldest, and involved collecting the stove board, the kitchen bag, dinner and breakfast, the drinks bag and all the thermos flasks.

We'd unzip the tent, which would invariably catch on the fabric. After a couple of minutes wrestling, we'd clamber into the 'porch' and unzip the main tent. First off were the shoes. This was one of my favourite parts of the day. The pleasure of removing the boots cannot be overemphasized, and was a surprisingly lengthy process. Steam streaming up from the boots, feet singing, I would allow them just a few seconds' respite before they'd be plunged into my soft, down tent booties. Time to set up the kitchen.

I took great pride in creating a tidy, efficient cooking space.

First I'd lay out the kitchen stove board, on to which were mounted the two MSR stoves. Next I'd attach the two fuel bottles, and empty the stove bag. I would take out the pans, the pan handles, matches, bowls, and funnel and then, once everything was in place, I would set about lighting the hated stoves.

The stoves required patience, and care. Each one required its own unique attention. First you would pump the bottles, before opening the small tap on the bottle. There was often a delay of up to ten seconds as the fuel worked its way down the fuel line and out of the stove. The lightee would need to stare closely at the small hole waiting for the tiny jet of fuel to squirt from the pinhole; as soon as the fuel appeared you would turn off the tap to ensure you didn't flood the stove, and indeed the tent. A couple of times we were caught off guard, creating a burst of flame in the large pool of fuel.

Ice cold from the pulks, the stoves would often take up to ten matches to light. As the metal of the stove warmed, the fuel would flame up like a school Bunsen burner, its orange flames licking the side of the tent, and we were forced to hold a pan lid above the flickering flame to keep it away from the nylon. Eventually the flame would die down to a hot blue with a loud hissing sound, rather like a jet engine, at which point the lightee had to be ready to turn the tap on full. If you missed this, the flame would die and you'd have to start all over again.

Once both stoves were flaming, I'd pour some leftover water from each thermos into a pan and place it on the stove, before filling the rest of the pan with snow. If you put an empty pan on the stove, it would immediately buckle from the extreme difference in temperature, but more strangely still it would also smell exactly like burnt toast. I sometimes did it on purpose, just for that smell.

While the snow began to melt, I would wriggle out of my race suit and set about laying the tent before the others finished outside, digging a snow wall and manoeuvring the pulks to the front of the tent. Neatly lined up next to skis and poles, we would be ready for a speedy exit a few hours later.

Sleeping bags, sleeping mats and tent bags would all be passed into the tent, where they would be neatly set into lines. James was always on the left-hand side of the tent. We had tried putting him in the middle, but he simply took up too much space. Ed and I took turns on the right and in the middle.

The tent was small with just one of us, tiny with two, and minuscule with three. I used to liken it to a reverse Tardis; it actually looked larger than it was.

Apart from containing 300 kilos of people, the tent would also be crammed full of three enormous sleeping bags, three sets of boots and race jackets, medical kit, ten bottles, and kit bags. At this point I should point out that I am not a naturally tidy person, but in Antarctica I developed OCD. I became obsessed about putting things away, while Ed and James created kit explosions as mountains of 'stuff' enveloped the tent. When James spoke to Inge back on the acclimatization trek it had become clear that one man's 'bare minimum' is another man's needless luxury. According to Inge, proper explorers bring in only a sleeping bag, a mat and food. As James said, it was lucky we weren't proper explorers, then, as we might fancy changing our clothes, cleaning our teeth, writing in our diaries or carrying out our daily skincare regimes. Inge just gave us a wry smile.

It usually took forty minutes before we were all inside, the tent shrouded in a fug of rotting flesh and evaporating sweat as the others removed shoes and socks and wedged themselves into their corners. The first pans of water would invariably be near to boiling, and it was chef's duty to empty the evening food into a large tupperware container, top it up with the boiling water and decant the gruel into three equal portions.

In any other scenario, what we ate would have seemed disgusting, but at 2.45 a.m., leaning on one shoulder and scooping the rehydrated meal into my mouth, it tasted like manna from heaven. How I would luxuriate over that hot bowl of steaming goo. Normally a fast eater, I would attempt to slow myself down and savour its glorious taste, but invariably finished first and salivated as I watched James and Ed finish theirs. There was NEVER enough food. Every couple of days we would treat ourselves to a double meal, and even then I was left wanting.

I still look back with fond memories on that hour we'd spend in the tent together. We'd chat, we'd laugh and, occasionally, we'd cry. It was the one time we could bask in the freedom of lying down with half-full bellies, and enjoy each other's company.

Pudding consisted of rehydrated custard and apple, or rice pudding, followed by a cup of hot chocolate and a litre of energy drink to rehydrate us. In the absence of a dishwasher, bowls and spoons were licked clean.

By 3.30 a.m we were fed and watered and it was time for two of the team to squirm into their sleeping bags while 'chef' spent a further thirty minutes melting snow for the morning.

I'd invariably slide into my sleeping bag in socks and thermals. I'd then stuff my fleece, GPS, spare satellite phone battery, tent booties and felt liners into the bag with me to keep them warm. The colder it was in the tent, the more 'stuff' would join you in your bag. There was often more kit than body in our bags, which led to an uncomfortable sleep.

The two most important sleeping 'accessories', however, were a pee bottle and a buff to cover the eyes from the intense light that penetrated the tent's bright orange fabric.

The pee bottle was essential. I'd always drink two litres of water before bed to rehydrate my body, which meant I woke like clockwork at 4 a.m., bursting for the loo. Given that it was an average minus 40 outside and that I was invariably wedged between James and Ed, a pee bottle allows you to relieve yourself from the comfort of your sleeping bag without disturbing the others and has the handy option of doubling up as a hot water bottle afterwards. It was, however, very important not to muddle your pee bottle with your water bottle. James made this mistake once and swigged on his own piss. How Ed and I laughed! How James retched.

We all developed our own technique for peeing into the bottle, and while Ed and James favoured the kneeling position, I became pretty agile at peeing on my side. Without going into too much detail, I would strip off my thermals and hold the bottle upright. I'd hold my breath to avoid any unnecessary movement, and relieve myself. I never ceased to marvel at the fact that I always peed to within a few millimetres of the top. Just once, when I foolishly waited until 6 a.m., did I have to 'abort wee' for fear of overfilling. Not an easy task I can assure you, and one I never repeated. 4 a.m. was the peeing hour.

We all learned the hard way not to leave full pee bottles out of the sleeping bag. They froze within minutes and it took the best part of a day with the bottle down your top to thaw out. Trust me, it is not a pleasant experience skiing with a litre of urine melting next to your skin.

According to the position of the tent, you were either hot, warm or cold. James always slept on the dark side and therefore avoided the heat of the sun's rays, but needed a woolly hat to keep the cold at bay. More often than not Ed was on the sunny side, which meant I'd wake to find him semi-naked on top of his sleeping bag. My place in the middle was just about right.

Beepabeep beep, beepabeep beep, beepabeep beep: three and a half hours later and the first alarm would go off at 7.45 a.m., followed by three more alarms. We never trusted just one.

First up was the designated morning cook. Puffy eyed and parched from the altitude, you would slide back into the same clothes you had worn for days, and then weeks. First job was to clear all the spindrift from the kitchen, the snow blown by the wind through any and all tiny gaps in the tent. This would vary from a thin smattering to several inches, depending on the speed and ferocity of the wind.

Once cleared of snow, it was time to light the stoves and set about boiling water. Morning duty involved making up to sixteen litres of water, which sometimes meant twelve pans of snow. It was a lengthy process and involved precious timing if you were to do it in the allocated two hours. The weakest stove was used for melting, and the fastest for boiling. James was keen on a three-stove approach that involved managing three open flames and three pans, which was often difficult and always hazardous, but saved us a precious twenty minutes.

Breakfast consisted of a bowl of porridge mixed with powdered milk and sugar. Half a kilo of porridge isn't the most appetizing start to the day, but it filled a ravenous hole and was swiftly followed by a cup of Earl Grey tea and a cup of hot chocolate and coffee mixed together to make a sort of Antarctic mocha. These would then be washed down by two litres of water to hydrate us for the day ahead. There is something very comforting about sipping a hot cup of tea. Scott, Amundsen and Shackleton all drank it, and my morning cuppa was as close to home comforts as I ever got.

While one of us got on with kitchen duty, the others set about fixing feet, a surprisingly lengthy process. Invariably, James's feet required the most attention, and mine the least. Dressings and socks would be removed and the tent would once again reek of rotting flesh. It often made me gag.

We were largely immune to the smell in the tent, but just occasionally the nostrils would give in to the stench of stale urine, decaying flesh and body odour. Ed estimated that with each pee we would inadvertently 'leak' a single drop of urine on to our thermals. Given that we were peeing up to eight times a day, he estimated it was the equivalent of more than a cup of spilled urine each. No wonder we stank.

Blisters were cut and drained and Ed would then patiently dress each of James's dozens of blisters before working on his own. This usually lasted an hour as the tent turned into something out of *M*A*S*H*, with reams of bandage and plasters. By now, we would all be bursting for another pee and so one of us would volunteer to go on a pee-bottle emptying journey. If it was really windy, we'd empty them in a corner of the kitchen, onto the snow. Hygiene was not part of our Antarctic vocabulary.

Once all the water bottles and thermos flasks had been filled, the stoves would be turned off and the kitchen packed away.

As with everything in Antarctica the weather determines almost everything. If when we woke up in the morning it was a lovely day we could just chuck our sleeping bags outside to air, and even do the final stages of dressing outside. But if it was bad weather outside then leaving the tent required careful planning. There were a number of tasks to be done both in and out of the tent, and we had to leave one at a time to avoid a bottleneck of shoe-tying, but you had to make sure that the first person out wasn't stuck outside in the cold for too long.

First out was usually 9.15 a.m., second, 9.25 a.m. and last usually 9.40 a.m. James was in charge of refuelling the stove bottles and packing the kitchen, while Ed and I packed up food and drinks and removed the snow from the tent's skirt. Tent bags, sleeping bags and mats were all packed into pulks and at 9.50 a.m. we 'pulled pole' ready for the off.

Once everything was packed, someone would invariably need a poo. There is a policy in Antarctica that all bodily matter is taken with you, but special dispensation is given to long expeditions because of the sheer quantity of the stuff. We were therefore permitted to bury 'biggies' in the ice, which was just as well; I don't know what rehydrated food contains, but we left a trail that a Tyrannosaurus Rex would have been proud of. We estimated that each poo weighed a couple of kilos, and given that we were going up to twice a day, I estimated we would have ended up hauling nearly half a ton of shit to the South Pole. A lovely image, I think you'll agree.

We always planned to leave the site at 10 a.m. James was always last, and we invariably left late.

One of us would lead up at the front, cutting a trail through the snow and ice, and navigating south. Ed and I favoured navigating using the sun, shadows and the wind, while James always used his beloved GPS.

In Switzerland, Bernie had recommended that I should set the pace at the beginning of each day as I needed time to warm up. I would set off using my shadow, aiming my skis to the left side of my head's shadow and chasing my ear. It was a simple, efficient and incredibly satisfying way to navigate.

I soon learned what shadow the sun cast for each phase of my stint at the front: at 10.30 a.m. I would ski directly into my shadow, at 11 a.m. I would chase my right ear and so on. James would monitor the direction using his GPS and occasionally you would hear him shout or mumble that you needed to go fractionally to the left or right. It used to annoy me when he corrected me.

For two hours we would ski across the vast white expanse. Hood up, hood down, outer gloves on, outer gloves off, woolly hat on, woolly hat off: you would constantly adjust clothing and equipment as your body heat waxed and waned with the conditions.

I always needed a pee after thirty minutes and ninety minutes, but we never had a set peeing routine. Sometimes we'd all stop, and at other times the others would ski on ahead and you'd have to catch up.

Being in the front was always the worst. Not only did you have to work harder cutting a trail, but you had to focus on direction, speed and ensuring everyone was close behind. It was always a relief to reach the end of that two-hour period, happy in the knowledge that it would be another four hours until you had to navigate again. I would always give warnings ahead of a break. I would call out at thirty minutes and ten minutes ahead of time. It always bugged me when Ed or James forgot to give a warning. It was painful not knowing how long to wait for a break, especially if you needed the loo.

At 12 noon, we would all pull alongside one another and remove our harnesses. We'd take our skis off, walk over to the pulk and put on our big orange duvet jackets, straddling the pulk in silence as we caught our breath, sipped from our thermos flasks and munched on some chocolate or salami from our snack bags.

After ten minutes I could feel my body temperature begin to drop and for five minutes I would sit on my sledge propelling my arms like windmill sails to keep the blood flowing. I was always the coldest and therefore the first ready to leave, and more often than

not I led for the first few minutes while Ed and James faffed and fiddled with kit. Once they had caught up with me, it was someone
else's turn to lead. It always took me twenty minutes to warm up
after a break, and I would lose all feeling in my fingers for ten minutes, skiing with my poles under my arms while I shook the blood
back into them. I hated the breaks for that.

Once I'd regained some of my body heat, I'd relax back into the
skiing. Focusing on the pulk in front, fixing my eyes on the red
fabric, I'd fall into a trance-like state as I forced my body into a
rhythm. On good days you could ski just a foot away from the pulk
in front with ease, but on a bad day you'd feel yourself slipping
back and struggle to keep up. I hated those 'off' days. We all did.

Each of us had our stronger and weaker hours of the day. Ed
and James hated the mornings, while this was my preferred time.
We also had our own way of entertaining ourselves during those
endless two-hour sessions. I would have endless daydreams about
holidays I had been on, and sometimes I would even 'go for a walk'
around the park, imagining every step and visualizing every tree
and blade of grass. So transported was I by my imagination that I'd
often crash into the pulk in front if it stopped unexpectedly.

These two-hour sessions would continue until 7 p.m. when we
had to stop for our daily 'sched' call to the race organizers.

We would break at 18.55 and Ed would assemble the satellite
phone, fitting the battery that he had warmed against his body into
the unit. We took turns calling the organizers and were required to
give them our coordinates, our status, our distance covered and our
planned position the following day. It was usually Ed and I who
called in, as James was the 'captain' of navigation and in charge of
the GPS. James would call out our longitude and latitude and we
would repeat it down the phone. Sarah, one of the race organizers,
would then repeat the coordinates down the phone and we'd con-
firm them even though we didn't have a clue what she'd said. She
could have read out the coordinates for the North Pole and we'd
have said 'correct'.

19.10 was 'audio diary' time. We had to call a number in the

UK and leave a message, 'not more than sixty seconds'. Tony had given us strict instructions to keep them general and not make them personal. Sentimentality has never been an army trait, and Tony clearly didn't want his website audio blogs peppered with messages from lovelorn couples.

We had no such qualms and before long, we were dedicating messages to friends and family, which were then uploaded on to the Internet for people to follow our progress. It was difficult to gauge who or how many people were listening to those blogs which became more and more farcical with time. To begin with, we left unstructured, rambling, often incoherent messages, and it was only after I had listened to James leave a waffled message with a mouth full of chocolate that I suggested we put some thought into the messages. We didn't realize it at the time, but millions of people heard James's message to his son about me pooing in the snow next to him.

19.30 and we were off again. With the sun never setting the only noticeable change was a drop in temperature from 19.30 until about midnight, and by now the sun was in our faces. The evening created shadows of the front of the skis. The curves created 'dog's' ears of varying sizes, starting with sticky-up collie's ears and ending with big, droopy bloodhound ears. This was made all the more surreal by the portrait of Nansen that so disturbed James. In my mind, Nansen's husky ears at 8 p.m. became a bull terrier's at 9 p.m. and so on. I'm not sure if anyone has ever skied to the South Pole using this technique, but I can highly recommend it.

As the temperature dropped, I would pull my hood, with the fur ruff up, over my head. It was only once we arrived in Antarctica and I asked Inge what kind of fur was sewn into my jacket that I discovered it was dog. I never did get used to wearing man's best friend. Of course it hadn't been killed for this reason – the fur was the by-product of a working husky that had died – but as a dog lover I never felt entirely comfortable, particularly when the dog fur froze to my beard.

It was, however, exceptionally good at creating a micro-climate around my face. The sun warmed up the air and the fur kept it close to the face, and even when the atmospheric temperature plunged to minus 45, my face remained relatively warm.

Snack bags usually began to run out around midnight, and with them went the last of our strength and energy. Efficiency began to nosedive, and the final couple of hours always dragged on.

'It must be nearly 2 a.m.,' I'd think, removing the poles, the outer mitts, the windproof gloves, pulling up the jacket, taking the thermal off my thumb and flicking up the wrist.

1 a.m.

'Damn.' I'd shake my head and begin counting down again.

And thus the process would begin again as we rolled into camp at 2 a.m. There was very little change from day to day, except for those times we skied until 4 a.m.; in which case, you just cut out two of the sleeping hours. It was Groundhog Day.

25

OUT ON OUR FEET

BEN At 3 a.m. the morning after we left the Norwegians behind, we finally set camp. There was just 120 kilometres between us and the midway point. If we could cover 50 kilometres the following day then we estimated that we could attempt the final 70 kilometres in one go. It was ambitious to say the least; but at least we had a plan. We knew the Norwegians were somewhere behind us, but we had failed to take into account how early they might pack up and leave. It was painful waiting for them to appear on the horizon, and though Ed and James frequently checked behind us, they never materialized.

JAMES It's amazing the difference a few millimetres of nylon makes. Our tent was a bubble shielding us from what was outside, not just physically, but mentally too. Once inside I felt instantly protected from, and able to forget, the agony of sixteen hours' skiing.

Despite not covering the distance we wanted to in the few hours that followed our meeting with the Norwegians, there was a positive vibe in the tent. Ed had fought his way through a difficult couple of hours and gained a lot of confidence, and it was great watching him tough it out. Ben, obviously bored with our company already, had clearly enjoyed the variety of skiing with the Norwegians.

In fact, I was the only one feeling down. That's a lazy description: I wasn't down about our position, the disappointing distance covered or missing home, it was more a sort of 'anticipated depression'. My feet had caused me so much pain as we skied with the Norwegians I'd tried hard not to show it or complain too much. It didn't help anyone else to know they were sore, and my competitive streak didn't want the Norwegians to realize just how bad they were.

Right now, I couldn't think of anything worse than putting my feet back in those boots and then locking the bloody things into one position in the skis. I was starting to hate the skis, with Nansen's face staring up at me, almost as much as I hated the boots. I daydreamed about throwing them down a crevasse, much like Scott would have done with Nansen if he'd made it back from Antarctica.

Up until this point, our race regime had been pretty simple: stick to skiing for sixteen hours and just keep fighting and grinding it out day after day, with an extra burst before the halfway point and the finish.

Looking back, I've no idea what made us think 120 kilometres was 'within shouting distance' of the checkpoint. Our two longest days thus far had been 48 kilometres and 47 kilometres, which would still leave us with 25 kilometres to achieve the checkpoint, a total of around forty to forty-five hours' skiing and not exactly what you'd call a sprint finish. We were definitely honouring our commitment to each other that we'd get to that finish line with nothing left. I felt pretty empty already, but the thought of giving my feet a rest for twenty-four hours and not skiing sounded better than a two-week holiday on a Caribbean Island with Cameron Diaz and Scarlett Johansson instead of Ben and Ed.

Our plan for the last 120 kilometres showed that the powers of our nylon bubble not only helped us forget what lay outside the tent, it suspended reality as well. We came up with the cunning plan of ignoring the time and covering 50 kilometres the next day, no matter how long it took us. We'd then have our normal overnight routine, get up and ski the 70 kilometres to the checkpoint. The only problem with this masterplan was that we hadn't skied 50 kilometres in one session yet and our biggest daily distance was on the second day of the race when we were all fresh. At least we were optimistic – or deluded. We'd know which in two days' time.

*

When we woke up a few hours later the special powers of the tent must have disappeared, because the atmosphere was muted. We were all worried about how we were going to get ourselves through the day. Unless we kept a perfectly direct line to our target we'd be covering more than 50 kilometres, so it was vital to stick to our new mantra – Go Straight!

I hadn't exactly leapt out of my sleeping bag at the start of the race, but now I entered it like an overfed caterpillar and wanted to sleep for ever. Unfortunately I didn't exit like a butterfly; instead I dragged myself out in the manner of someone who had been cryogenically frozen for a century. Two hours of zinc oxide tape, painkillers, porridge, antibiotics, tea, coffee and various creams lay ahead.

For the first few days, the medical regime had been fairly quick. Ben and Ed would pull their pants down and show each other their butt cracks like a couple of baboons, before Ed and I went to work on our feet. Ed had just about stayed on top of his blisters, unlike me; but rather than blame myself, I cited the lack of seven years' funding by the taxpayer that had helped Ed be so proficient at looking after himself. There was little chance of my feet getting better – it was a case of firefighting rather than curing – but even that was a tough task. I needed Red Adair to help me get them under control, but as the legendary firefighter passed away in 2004, it was down to Dr Ed Coats to step up.

BEN   James has an uncanny – and rather worrying – ability to march on through pain. Pain is the body's way of telling you to stop, but James shows a remarkable deafness to those warning bells and battles on regardless. His feet were in tatters, and his cough had worsened. As early as day three he had awoken with a worryingly swollen face, eyes and cheeks so puffy that he was almost unrecognizable, but now he was coughing and wheezing his way through every hour in the tent, while Ed spent more and more time slicing and dressing his blisters.

I knew how important it was to manage and take care of my feet since without them we wouldn't be going anywhere. To use the analogy of a car's tyre, it is vital to fix any puncture, whether it's a blow out or a slow puncture. There is no point driving on for days with a slow leak as the tyre will eventually become worn and useless and need to be replaced. You can't replace your feet.

One of the main problems encountered by polar travellers is 'trench foot', more commonly associated with the muddy living conditions of the First World War and jungle travel than the driest, coldest place on earth. But even in these freezing conditions the feet sweat, and all the moisture trapped in the sock by our highly technical plastic bags created the same effect as spending sixteen hours in a bath. The feet 'shrimp' and the flesh eventually begins to rot. Without care, the soles begin to crack, creating painful welts and sores. The decision is a fairly stark one for the Antarctica traveller: forfeit the plastic bag and risk frostbite, or retain the moisture and risk trench foot.

JAMES The fact that Ed was a doctor was a massive bonus, over and above the fact that he was our favourite candidate to join us in the race. It was too much to ask Ed to watch over us, but I can't deny that when we divided up responsibilities he took control of the medical kit in the same way I did navigation. Poor guy, he wasn't duty-bound to look after my feet or apply cream to Ben's butt, but desperate times call for desperate measures.

Ed cut his way through the mummification job I'd done on my feet and when he eventually peeled back the final layer, it wasn't exactly like winning 'pass the parcel'. The stench was awful and worryingly the toe smelt of rotten flesh rather than the stale cheese aroma they normally gave off. The blisters were a combination of fresh ones filled with blood and old ones that had burst and had the skin ripped off.

'Bloody hell,' Ed said, 'how can you walk on these?'

'They're sore when I start off, but it doesn't get any worse. I could do with a few more painkillers if you've got any, Doc?' I smiled.

Ben turned round to see what Ed had exclaimed about and was hit with the double whammy of Ed lancing a huge blood blister, and the stench that followed. Ben retched and I felt a certain sense of pride in evoking such a reaction.

Ed did a grand job. Apart from reducing the chance of infection and having much better taped feet, I was glad that my tax hadn't been totally wasted on his education. My feet though weren't the only problem: both Ed and I were suffering with our spluttery coughs. Ed was coughing whilst skiing, whereas I didn't feel too bad on the move; it was in the tent I felt awful. It might have been the change in temperature but I was having massive coughing fits, causing me to throw up and leaving me really short of breath. During the night I woke up a number of times struggling to breathe, and having never experienced anything like that before it was really worrying to do so out there in the middle of nowhere. But it was reassuring to know Ed was there: though I have a lot of time for Ben's first aid skills I knew whom I'd be waking up if I required resuscitation.

Ed put us both on a course of antibiotics to go along with the anti-inflammatories and painkillers that we were all on. The only disadvantage of having a doctor on the team was that he wasn't quite as free with the painkillers as my feet would have liked.

BEN Ed had been struggling over his breakfast. Even in the acclimatization stage he had been complaining about the porridge, and today he finally refused to eat it.

'It makes me nauseous,' he said simply. Turning down a bowl of porridge is not normally grounds for debate, but in the Antarctic when you're burning up untold numbers of calories, every meal counts. Our sweetened porridge counted for 1,000 valuable calories.

'Stop being so negative,' snapped James, 'I've had enough of your negativity.' Ed had been struggling with his own worries for a number of days now and it had been bothering James, who was clearly fighting his own demons.

James had already berated Ed for projecting his pessimism on to the rest of the team, of course – which I thought was rather harsh of him. There had been a number of disagreements between the two ever since, and I had made it my business to reassure Ed each time. The porridge episode was the final straw for James and he vented his frustration at an incredulous Ed.

He had a point – Antarctica was no place for pickiness – but James had failed to mention his own issues with his snack bag, which he wasn't finishing each night. Frankly, it was like travelling with two anorexics.

*

Tempers calmed, we got ready to set out to cover our first 'half ton'. The temperature had been slowly dropping, as shown by my high-tec thermometer: my beard. The more ice there was in it, the colder it was . . .

At first I had loved the icicles in my beard, but my childish wonder soon turned to frustration as the icicles grew. It wasn't long before I loathed them, particularly when they fused my mouth together. I used to spend my breaks cracking icicles with the pliers on my Leatherman.

JAMES   It was time to get going, and even without my silly spat with Ed we weren't exactly bouncing around in anticipation. The situation clearly required some of my legendary amateur psychology:

'We're skiing a set distance today rather than a time, so if we crack on we might finish before two and get an extra bit of kip.'

Ben's non-committal exhale of breath told me he hadn't really bought it. My attempt at a positive outlook was tested when I squeezed my feet into the boots. 'How am I going to get through this?' I asked myself. The same question went through my head again – but with more expletives – when I snapped the boots into the ski bindings. Luckily though, the human body has a tremendous ability to get used to discomfort. The first five minutes were terrible but the pain subsided and after an hour I could actually think about something else other than my feet.

*

I switched between skiing and walking throughout the day and although we weren't skiing as fast as we had on some days, we were making decent progress. Ben and Ed were worried about my feet, but the only way I could alleviate their concerns was by making sure I walked at the same speed they were skiing. That wasn't a problem over uneven icy ground – I was actually faster – but when the snow was deeper or the ground smoother I had to work much, much harder.

After about ten hours and 30 kilometres had been ticked off we comforted ourselves with the thought that we hadn't yet seen the Norwegians on the horizon. Ben and Ed seemed confident they were still behind us, but I wasn't so certain. They'd seemed very organized yesterday and lovely blokes as they undoubtedly were, there was definitely some competitive espionage going on to see how we were holding up, and whether our routine indicated any problems.

Right now though, my battle was with the terrain, not them: my imaginary hills were back. I was desperately trying to show the other two that they weren't a figment of my imagination and that if they looked at the horizon in front it seemed much closer. Surely that was proof of a hill?

I conveniently ignored the fact that the pulks didn't slide down the 'hill' when we stopped for a break.

Hills or not, I was struggling to keep pace with the others. Ed was storming along and Ben was exhibiting the same Energizer Bunny type momentum he'd had from the start. There's no doubt he was benefiting from having looked after himself in the first few days of the race by not taking weight when he felt he couldn't, and speaking up when the pace was too high. He had been by far the most consistent force in the team, and butt crack aside he hadn't suffered any other problems. The bastard didn't even have one blister.

That's not to say he wasn't exhausted or fighting his own battles, though. Ben generally keeps his feelings pretty close to himself until he can no longer contain them, whereas I let the emotion out and move on quickly. Ed was easy to read, emotional and happy to cry in front of us which, from a team perspective, is a great thing. It shows that you're truly comfortable and trust the people around you. In fact, Ed spent so much time crying we were thinking of renaming him Tiny Tears, a homage not only to the little girls' doll but an extension of the first nickname we gave him. When we met up for tyre-pulling on the beach in Devon he turned up with what must have been the tyre from a Smartcar, and was instantly nicknamed 'Tiny Tyres'.

If Ben had a weakness it was missing home, hardly surprising after what he and Marina had been through literally on the eve of his departure. Out of the three of us he's the one who spends the most time away from home, and when he did *Castaway* he'd spent a year on an island away from his loved ones. For this trip, Marina had given him an envelope to open every day with a picture, a lovely thought and if it helped to motivate him, then brilliant. Everyone is different but I think it's often better not to be reminded about home; park it at the back of your mind, yes, draw on it for motivation but don't think about what you're missing all the time.

I wasn't sure having a different picture and note every day was very helpful, but then I was of course saying that from the totally jealous position of having no letters whatsoever. When he opened his envelope, I programmed the GPS.

Ben's emotions weren't slowing him down though: the Energizer Bunny was in full effect, storming up what to me felt like the North Face of the Eiger. We'd been walking for over sixteen hours now and my feet were not easing up on me, despite squeezing an extra painkiller out of Ed and a significant drop in pace. I needed to take my skis off and walk the last few kilometres.

I saw Ben's head drop when I shouted. I could understand why; we'd had a number of unscheduled stops to either switch weight between pulks or for me to ditch skis and switch to walking. After a few changes, I had to change what I shouted.

'It's too close for missiles, I'm switching to guns,' I hollered in true *Top Gun* style to warn them I was stopping. It was an attempt to at least make them smile while they waited for me to faff around again, and I like to think it may have worked the first time. I didn't bother trying now; it was nearly 3 a.m. I'd done everything to try to make sure that I walked as quickly as they skied but it had been a tough day and I'd walked nearly 30 kilometres on rotten feet.

BEN   The witching hour had come and gone, and we had covered 45 kilometres. We had a least another hour and a half to go before we reached our target. It was cold and I had pulled on my hood to protect my face with its fur ruff. The final 5 kilometres seemed to take for ever. We had slowed our pace and by 4 a.m. we still had 1,000 metres to go. I put my head down and started my count-down.

JAMES   The GPS in the holder round my neck was showing our distance at just over 49.5 kilometres. '500 metres to go!' I shouted over my shoulder and got a couple of thumbs up in return.

I set off again and the first step I took set off an underground clap of thunder and the whole 5 square metres of snow around me sank a few inches. Three thoughts flashed through my head almost simultaneously: 1) What was that? 2) Shit I'm on a snow bridge over a crevasse 3) Fuck, I haven't even got skis on to spread the weight.

26

ON THIN ICE

BEN Whhhhhhhhhhhhhoooooooooooooosh!

I thought I had heard a sound like a distant storm, but the Gore-tex hood that covered my ears made it difficult to be sure. I span around, but there was nothing. James and Ed were well ahead of me, apparently oblivious to any noise. It must be in my head, I reasoned. I was tired, and hallucinations weren't beyond the realm of possibility.

Whhhhhhhhhhhhhhooooooooooooooooosh boomed the noise again.

'What was that?' shouted Ed. The hairs on the back of my neck stood on end and we all stood motionless, rooted in place, not daring to move an inch. My heart was racing.

'We're on a crevasse field,' said Ed. The noise we had heard was the sound of tons of snow and ice as thin ice bridges collapsed under our weight and fell into deep chasms below our feet.

JAMES The impact of the noise was weirdly exaggerated by the fact that, apart from each other's voices and the sound of the skis on the snow, it was the only sound we'd heard all day. Antarctica is totally silent. The only noise comes from the wind. In fact it was the silence rather than the miles of empty plateau that made me feel isolated; I've never been in a place so quiet. But right here, right now, I would have taken silence any day over that deep, thunderous noise.

BEN 'Look at the horizon,' warned Ed. 'Look how close it is; that means we're on a pressure ridge,' he explained. He was right, our crevasse training had warned us about pressure ridges and the high likelihood of crevasses nearby. We weren't supposed to find one here, though, out on the plateau. Despite the best efforts of the organizers, Antarctica still had plenty of tricks up her sleeve. We needed to get off the crevasse field and out of there fast.

To make matters worse, James was still in his boots. Skis spread the overall weight of the body over a larger surface area, whereas in his boots James was in grave danger of falling through the thin crust. He gingerly strapped his skis back on, and we edged our way slowly, carefully across the invisible minefield.

'Whhhhhhhhhhhhhhhhhhhooooooooooooooooooosh'. My heart missed a beat as I imagined great blocks of snow tumbling into the chasm. I tried not to think how thick the snow bridges were as I braced myself for each step, ready to fall at any moment.

JAMES   Ed was right: on closer inspection, the area looked different – but it looked nothing like the crevasse fields we had skied through during the acclimatization trek, where pressure ridges were easily visible as long snakes of shadow, ready to swallow you up.

*

It wasn't as though we didn't know what to do in this situation. We had practised in Norway almost exactly a year ago, and again in Austria in July. But knowing what to do and being able to do that under pressure are two very different things. I've done numerous first aid courses involving resuscitation and managed to successfully breathe life back into the rubber dummy, but would I be able to do it in a life-or-death situation? Under pressure would I administer the Heimlich manoeuvre, or just start slapping the patient on the back, asking them if they were OK?

I'm embarrassed to say that six months earlier, in Austria, the crevasse training itself was a secondary consideration. Ed had been selected to race with Ben and me less than a week before, and it was the first time I'd had to spend any proper time with him. We certainly got to know each other fairly quickly as we shared a four-hour drive in a hire car from the airport, checked into the hotel that night and were greeted with a double bed. Neither of us could be bothered to change rooms, so in we hopped. The next night we would be sharing a tent in the snow 2,800 metres up in the Austrian Alps, so this was no time for messing about.

What confronted us in the Alps wasn't so much a crevasse as an incredibly steep, snow-covered hill. We were roped together to simulate skiing through a crevasse field and then the lead skier, without warning, was supposed to throw themselves down the slope/cliff, forcing their teammate to instantly go down on one knee and anchor themselves in the snow. The challenge for the rescuer (or 'saviour', as I liked to call the role) in holding his teammate there in this 'arrest position' was to avoid tumbling down the slope after the lead skier, then get down to the serious business of hauling the lemming-like friend back up again.

To really secure yourself, a rucksack buried in the snow with a loop around its centre provides a great 'sarene' (anchor). Skis can also be buried and used in the same way. On our climbing harnesses were two prussic ropes, one attached to the rope from which your lemming friend is swinging, the other attached to the anchor.

The saviour can now get into a strong position and start hauling up the victim using the first prussic rope. A prussic knot is a friction knot where one rope is wrapped around another and if tied properly will slide freely in one direction, but lock tight if pulled the other way. So to pull someone out of a crevasse the rescuer will push the prussic knot down the rope the victim is on until the prussic rope is stretched against the anchor and then heave like hell and the victim will shift up a couple of feet. When slack comes into the prussic rope the rescuer quickly slides the knot down the rope so the guy down the crevasse is locked into position a couple of feet higher up. The technique is heave, slide the knot down, heave, slide, heave, slide, heave, slide . . . all in one smooth movement and eventually their ugly face will reappear.

One slight problem we were told we'd have to watch in Antarctica is that prussic knots don't work on frozen ropes because they require friction to function properly, so we'd have to look after them. There was a huge amount to remember: 1) Don't panic that Ben or Ed had disappeared, 2) Arrest (stop the fall), 3) Make an anchor, 4) Attach the rescuer and victim to the anchor with prussic ropes, knots, figure of eights and karabiners and 5) With freezing cold hands and brown underpants, haul like hell. The only way to ensure I could remember the knots and the order of doing things was by making it second nature – and that involved practice. Two days in Austria wasn't going to do that.

The alternative was to learn the secret of self-rescue; unfortunately the name is slightly misleading because in order to do it, someone at the top has to arrest your fall. Once that has been done, you can use the prussic ropes on your harness or make like James Bond and use your shoelaces. The rope/shoelaces are tied to the rope leading out of the crevasses using a prussic knot. Once they're in place you can ascend the rope as in the movies by sliding the knot up, putting your foot in the loop and use it as a step, repeating the process with the other foot . . . The only problem is that in the movies they don't have a pulk attached to them, which makes self-ascending a little harder. The bottom line was this: it's better to learn the full crevasse rescue technique.

We did practise the James Bond-style self-ascending rescue but without a real crevasse to hand, ascending a rope attached to a cable-car pylon. (Ironically, it was the very cable car used in *Moonraker* where Jaws and James Bond have one of their tête-à-têtes.)

Austria had been great practice, and I'd come away – as I had from Norway – confident in crevasse rescue. The problem was that I didn't have much need for crevasse rescue in Chiswick. Perhaps I should have taken a leaf out of Monty Python's book and tried to scale nearby Sheen High Street. Either way, I got to Antarctica knowing what I had to do, but it wasn't second nature. If I knew what it felt like to be standing on a snow bridge over a crevasse thousands of miles from anywhere I'd have made sure I could do them with my eyes shut before I stepped on the plane.

*

BEN I'm glad James remembered all that, because my memory of Austria was a blur of ropes and knots. I had been terrified at the prospect of crevasses and had had many sleepless nights worrying about them.

The bridges creaked and groaned, and we froze to the spot. What do we do now? For the first time on our long journey to the Pole, we were at a total loss for an answer. Until now we had relied on assumption, supposition and a little bit of training to get us through, but now, here in the cold and brutal reality of a crevasse field, we were at a loss. For the first time, I wished we had an experienced person on our team; now wasn't the time for trial and error.

'Shall we rope up?' I suggested. We had been carrying ropes and harnesses for just such an unlikely scenario but now, at 4 a.m. in the morning, just a few hundred metres from our daily goal and shattered from 49 terribly hard kilometres, digging around in the pulks and fiddling around with harnesses and ropes was a less than appetizing prospect.

JAMES 'If I'm really honest, I'm knackered,' Ben said, in answer to his own question. Like me, he clearly didn't feel mentally sharp enough for a roped-up crevasse rescue.

'I feel OK; if we go much further we should rope up,' Ed said, tilting the discussion back the other way. After yesterday's late-night blip he seemed strong this evening, and of the three of us he'd have been the one who'd have made sure the rescue technique was second nature – the same way he could resuscitate someone, do the Heimlich manoeuvre and perform a caesarean section.

I knew I didn't want to (or couldn't) ski much further, so I tapped on a solid bit of ground I had somehow found amidst the snow bridges. 'There's plenty of this type of terrain heading our way,' I said. 'Why don't we stick to that and see whether it's all as solid as this? If we find a big area of it we can set up camp and rope up in the morning. Sound like a plan?' I suggested.

BEN   I'm not sure how or why we came to the decision – and looking back, I have no idea what we were thinking – but we decided to ski on without harnesses and ropes until we made camp. It's not something I am proud of, and I can feel my cheeks reddening with embarrassment at the thought.

I was terrified, but absurd as it must sound, the thought of losing any more precious sleep seemed worse. For twenty minutes we edged our way across the invisible obstacle course, until we found a flat, firmish patch of ground. We were all delirious with exhaustion, and too tired to care. Fear had been usurped by fatigue, and so it was that we pitched our tent in the middle of a crevasse field.

Now, it doesn't take an expert to tell you that this was more than a little stupid and of all the things I've done, I'd probably rate it alongside getting a tattoo when drunk, and rowing the Atlantic.

It was only after we had pitched the tent that we thought about probing the area with our poles. It turns out that we were camped half on a snow bridge. I'm blushing again, but it is a stark testament to our mental condition that even after we realized where we had camped, we failed to do anything about it.

'I think we should call the race organizer to warn the others,' I suggested. We were tired enough to pitch our tent in the middle of a crevasse field, but we weren't about to risk other competitors falling to their deaths.

James rang the emergency number. It was 4.30 a.m.

'We're in a crevasse field,' blurted James. I couldn't hear the response. 'No, we've camped in it,' he continued. We left our coordinates, cooked dinner and fell into the deepest of sleeps. I dreamed I was falling.

*

JAMES   In just seven days we had covered over 300 kilometres, but I felt further away from the finish than ever. It's interesting how the human mind prioritizes problems. Until I felt that first snow bridge partially collapse, the pain in my feet was all I could think about; but trapped out in the middle of that crevasse field, I hadn't thought about them once.

I wish the crevasse field had taken the edge off my chest as well as my feet; I was having coughing fits during which I was struggling to breathe and kept regurgitating my dinner – sweet and sour chicken, since you're asking – which (every cloud . . .) turned out to be not the worst meal to swallow for the second time. Although desperate to go to sleep that night, I hadn't wanted to close my eyes – not because of the crevasse field, but because I was worried about forgetting to breathe. I asked Ed why it was happening. He thought it was a combination of my chest infection, the altitude and extreme fatigue. Hmm, not a lot I could do about any of them.

I had an awful night's sleep that night, out on the snow bridge. I woke up several times struggling for air, which forced me to sit up and try to relax and breathe slowly.

BEN Over porridge the next morning, James dropped a bombshell. 'I want you both to know that if I can't go on, I want you to continue without me,' he said. I was shocked by his honesty. I had been concerned about his failing health from day one and had made my own worst-case scenario plans, but I never expected to hear that from James. He was clearly in a great deal of pain and discomfort, and it broke my heart to hear him talk like that.

'Don't say that,' I said, as if it would make a difference. We had planned this together. This had been a shared dream and despite my unguarded admission to Rune, I realized that it was a dream that had to be finished together, as a team. I was supposed to be the one who would fall apart in Antarctica, not James.

I shook my head. A tear rolled down my cheek at the thought of such an unhappy ending. James patted me sympathetically on my shoulder. His eyes were brimming with tears too. This had become so much more than a race. There were so many people relying on us, so many people trusting in us, and above all, so many people waiting for us.

JAMES Time to pull myself together. Only 70 kilometres to go to the halfway checkpoint, after all. Only 50 per cent further again than our longest one-day ski so far. Only a whiteout outside, I realized suddenly, from the fact that there was no burning orange glow through the tent.

And then I remembered that we were still in the middle of a crevasse field.

Ice magic. The mountains of Antarctica were as beautiful as they were isolated.

Stormbound, waiting for the starter's pistol. We had to dig the tent out every two hours.

Skiing across the plateau.
From the position of the sun,
it looks like late morning.
Only twelve hours to go . . .

'Snoticles'.
I used to snap them off
with a pair of pliers
during my breaks.

James's face became painfully swollen from the combined effects of altitude and pneumonia. Either that, or he was hiding extra rations in his cheeks.

March of the penguins. The blue sky always lifted our spirits.

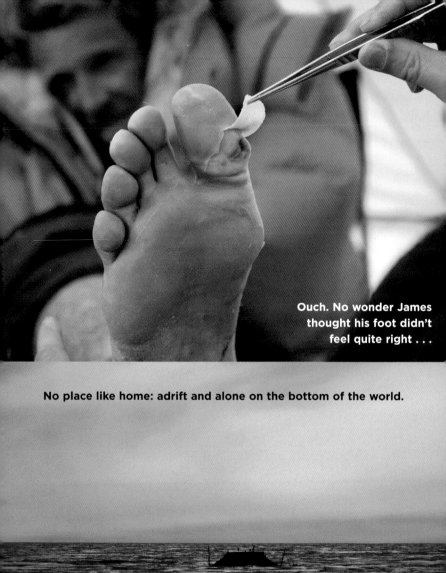

Ouch. No wonder James thought his foot didn't feel quite right . . .

No place like home: adrift and alone on the bottom of the world.

Rune and Stian approaching the South Pole – but in which position?

We came, we saw, we collapsed.

Team QinetiQ at the Pole: tired, hungry and weatherbeaten.

The South Pole Diet. Between us we lost 7½ stone in under a month.

27

FALLING APART AT THE SEAMS

JAMES We decided it was asking too much to go for 70 kilometres in one go, so we'd ski for 40 kilometres, quickly pitch the tent for an hour, have a hot meal, whip the tent down, head off for the last 30 kilometres and then sleep for Britain at the checkpoint.

It was a whiteout outside, but once I'd put lighter lenses into my goggles and got better contrast on the snow the visibility wasn't actually too bad. More annoying was the crosswind, constantly blowing the snow onto our left cheeks.

Having camped safely I voted to forget roping up, and instead prod and pick a safe route over the ice as we had last night. Whether through tiredness or because we were all getting cold, Ben and Ed agreed; there was less heat from the sun today and more wind chill, so we packed up and headed off.

In hindsight it wasn't the most sensible decision. The fact that I was nervous as I led us off indicated that we should have roped up, although a rope on its own isn't going to save anyone from a crevasse – only the people on the other end. I had a knackered Fogle behind me who hadn't practised a rescue since July; perhaps it was better to be solo than attached to him!

*

There were some small collapses as we skied over snow bridges, but without the horrendous noises underneath that we had experienced the day before. The terrain gradually changed, with more hard ground and less of the flatter smoother snow – we were nearly out.

'James!' Ben shouted. I turned round, surprised that he or Ed would want to rope up when we had virtually left the crevasses behind, but he was holding up his hand for me to stop. Ed had dropped back, skiing with his head down and shoulders slumped, looking as if he'd skied 70 kilometres rather than just started out.

'What's wrong, Ed?' I asked.

'I'm really hot; I'm going to take my fleece off,' he replied. So far we'd skied in a thermal top for warmth and our Gore-tex jackets to protect us from the wind. I'd made the mistake on the acclimatization trek of skiing in my fleece and it was uncomfortably hot, so I understood why he'd be frustrated. I had been surprised when he'd put the fleece on in the tent, since the old adage is 'start cold, get warm', but a desire to put on more clothes than you need is a sure-fire sign of fatigue in the Antarctic. I was getting to understand Ed better every day, and though he seemed worried about the distance ahead, I also knew that in a few hours' time he'd have fought through it; we just had to help him get to that point.

Changing a top is not a simple process, as you might have gathered from Ben's account of checking your watch. Harness, jacket and salopettes all have to come off, and the spare top packed away. None of that could be done in the open – it was too cold if we weren't moving – so we dived under the emergency shelter, which is basically a massive poncho that all three of us could get inside. It worked really well – too well. Every minute spent inside weakened our motivation to pack it away and go skiing. Nice as it was in the shelter though, it was no match for a day of rest so we stuffed it in Ben's pulk and set off.

Twenty minutes later Ben shouts and I stop to see Ed has dropped off the pace, skiing with the poise of someone heading to the gallows.

'What now?' I asked trying not to let my frustration show, especially after the duty of care he had shown my feet when he could have been resting. But stopping all the time made it hard for any of us to get into a rhythm.

'I'm struggling, boys,' Ed said, simply.

'Physically or mentally?' I asked.

'I'm coughing a lot, and struggling to keep up with you guys,' he said, looking down.

'OK, give me a couple of things from your pulk and we'll take the edge of the pace,' I said.

He nodded.

'I'm going to have to get moving,' Ben said. Now it was his turn to seem exasperated. The looming target of 70 kilometres was really starting to grate on our nerves and chip away at our resolve.

The sun started to burn its way through the cloud and over the next hour revealed a horizon that was back to a more natural position of miles in the distance. Snow bridges had given way to solid ice and snow and for the first time that day I could swap the full face mask for a woolly hat, and goggles for sunglasses. I turned round to see how the other two were doing and got a couple of thumbs up. On this crazy merry-go-round of changing moods, life was good, despite my feet and my chest.

We had been warned that the never-changing vista of the plateau would drive us mad, but I hadn't found that to be the case. For a start I could invent hills where there weren't any, while different light and weather conditions meant the same area could look totally different in a matter of minutes. When blended with a change of terrain – large sastrugi, small frozen wind ripples or perfectly flat snow – I never felt trapped in the same location. Trapped on the same bloody skis, with the same bloody pulk and the same bloody people, maybe, but never the same place.

That day we were treated to the full range of terrain and weather, from bright sunshine to a complete whiteout, via a dark grey sky that sat heavily on top of us. It may have been fatigue but I felt as if I was skiing through the bed of a dried-up river as we picked our way round big sastrugi. Then, suddenly, I was in an endless white desert, only to leave that and wander into a valley with rolling hills either side. As the plateau is a white desert any other perceived landscape is due to the effect of light and the tricks it plays on the mind, knackered minds being more susceptible than most, but it certainly gave the journey an epic feel as we pressed on.

*

BEN   The hours slowly ticked by, and 2 a.m. came and went. We were making good headway and it was deeply satisfying to watch the kilometres fall away on the GPS.

At 4 a.m. we stopped to melt snow and make some warm food. We pitched the tent in the bitter cold. It was minus 40 and we were deliriously tired and hungry. We'd covered 45 kilometres and had just 25 to go.

We piled into the tent in our thick orange jackets and made ourselves a double meal of curry for extra energy. For an hour we fired the stoves and took turns melting snow while we each power-napped for fifteen minutes.

JAMES   Unfortunately, setting up the tent was similar to sleeping with an ex-girlfriend; familiar, comfortable and good fun, but ultimately not the right thing to do. The hot meal was definitely rejuvenating, but my body was behaving like Pavlov's dog: I was inside the tent, so it must be time for a sleep. Both Ben and I fell asleep for twenty minutes, and it would have been for a lot longer if Ed hadn't shaken us awake. I felt as if I'd woken from a coma, while Ben just looked as if he wanted to slip back into one. There's always someone worse off, I reasoned.

The tent and stoves were quickly packed up and we were off. I just couldn't get warm, and felt terrible. We had worked with a sleep expert at QinetiQ when we were trying to establish the minimum amount of sleep we could manage during the race. We filled out sleep diaries for a week, the results of which were encouraging because we all got by on roughly the same amount in an 'average' week. I thought it was hard for the expert to make solid conclusions because that week Ed was working nights, my sleep was broken by Croyde's habit of coming into our room dressed as Spiderman or a pirate before 6 a.m., and I think Ben made his up.

We did learn about the 'circadian rhythm' though, the fancy name for the body's internal clock. Yet calling it a clock doesn't do it justice, as it also helps to control temperature, the release of enzymes and works with a neurotransmitter called adenosine that acts like a handbrake on the processes of the body that are associated with wakefulness – like the ability to ski. Adenosine is created during the day so that the body feels sleepy at night, making us want to go to bed. At the same time, the circadian rhythm is also busy making us tired by causing the body to release melatonin which, apart from inducing sleep, gradually decreases our core body temperature.

Right now my body was telling me it should be asleep, yet I was telling it to go skiing – and it wasn't very happy. Ed meanwhile was clearly operating on a different circadian clock because he was storming along. He took back the weight he'd given me at the start of the day and we set about knocking off the last kilometres.

BEN Our break had taken us nearly two hours, and in some ways had been a mistake. Instead of feeling full and rested, we were cold and exhausted. We had lost 7 valuable kilometres to feel worse than we did before!

JAMES I was fighting to keep up, telling myself to keep putting one foot in front of the other. It wasn't until 11 a.m., the time we'd normally be an hour into our ski, that I started to wake up. Suddenly I didn't have to fight to keep my eyes open; the downside was my feet were starting to really hurt. But only 15 kilometres left.

BEN 2 p.m. came and went, and still there was no sign of camp. We were stopping frequently because our bodies froze with exhaustion. We had become irritable and frustrated: where was the bloody checkpoint?

JAMES We sat on the pulks and for the first time speculated whether the Norwegians would be there waiting for us. Ed thought they wouldn't be, which was a logical assumption having been ahead of them for five days and having covered such a massive distance over the last forty-eight hours. Ben thought the same, whereas I wasn't sure. We'd lost a few kilometres when we stopped early, having skied with them all day, and although we'd covered masses of ground we'd done so in a start-stop fashion that had lost us, by my reckoning, about five hours. With a big push, the Norwegians were definitely capable of overtaking us.

Well, it wouldn't be long before we found out.

We must have looked like three drunks as we staggered, coughed and spluttered our way towards the checkpoint. We'd been skiing for twenty-five hours and were on our chinstraps, when I thought I saw something on the horizon. There was no point in asking Ben, he wouldn't be able to see it unless he was about to trip over it, so I checked the GPS: it said we had 7 kilometres left until the coordinates of the halfway line.

BEN 'Look,' said James, pointing to nothing on the horizon. My eyesight is bad at the best of times, but when I'm tired I can barely recognize my own wife. I stared and strained at the horizon. I wanted to see something, but . . .

'It's the checkpoint,' confirmed Ed.

'We've reached the top of the hill,' sighed James. I rolled my eyes and surveyed the flat white expanse of nothingness all around. Perhaps I could just make out the reflection of the vehicles in the sun. So near, and yet so far.

For half an hour we crawled along the flat expanse. It was tantalizingly close. We had split apart and agreed to reform as a close-knit team for the final push to the halfway point.

It was a significant marker. To date the trek had been peppered with 'targets', but this marked the final frontier. The last boundary between the South Pole and us.

As we neared the checkpoint we could make out a flurry of activity as the film crews and organizers sprang into action. We could make out the four vehicles and their little nomadic village of green tents, but just to the left of their camp was an anomaly.

Alone, about a hundred metres from the organizers' camp, was a lone red tent. Only the competitors had red tents. What was it doing there? I wondered.

I stared at the red tent as we edged closer to the checkpoint. As we got closer, I could make out a flag flapping in the wind. My heart began to race. There were only two teams who flew flags, and with the Norwegians safely behind us after our mammoth push, I reasoned that it must be Team Southern Lights' tent. We knew they would have struggled with the distance and pace and wondered whether they would need some help from the organizers. Maybe they had been picked up and dropped off at the midway point? I thought.

The flag began to gather shape and form. I crossed my fingers and hoped for Southern Lights' multi-coloured peace banner.

I could just make out the red colouring when Ed confirmed the seemingly impossible.

'It's the Norwegian flag.'

We'd been beaten to the midway point by the Norwegians. I was stunned.

PART FOUR

RACE TO THE POLE

28

IRON LUNG

JAMES 'How have they managed to get here first?' Ed's words could have come from any one of us, and yet there was the proof, ahead of us. Unless Tony had decided to support Rune and Stian by flying the Norwegian flag, they were already at the checkpoint.

Our team atmosphere altered as if Tony Blair had walked in, unannounced, to a party Gordon Brown was hosting for world leaders. I was less surprised than Ben and Ed to see the Norwegian tent there, but two things amazed me: first, how relaxed I was about it, and secondly that Ben and Ed seemed to be finding it harder to accept than I was. Had I truly tamed the competitive beast within, or was I just feeling too tired and ill to care?

BEN Three days ago we had seen them erect their tent five hours before us. That gave us a 17.5 kilometres lead. The following day we had busted a gut covering 50 kilometres in eighteen hours, and we had done the final 70 kilometres in one push. We had pushed ourselves beyond our physical capabilities. How could they have matched that? And more to the point, how had they bettered it?

I couldn't understand. We hadn't seen any tracks or trails. When had they passed us, and how? Why hadn't we seen them? I couldn't understand how they had crept through under our noses. That they had the benefit of experience and skill is undisputed, but these were two Norwegian soldiers, not superheroes. I even wondered whether they had pulled out of the race and been ferried here by the organizers.

JAMES   My relaxed attitude to coming in second might change when I found out how far ahead of us the Norwegians were. If they had only just got there, then those lost five hours while we faffed around with crevasses (oh all right, and with blisters and lung problems and . . .) would really change the way I felt. Being beaten is one thing; handing the race to your opposition on a plate is something else entirely.

That was something we'd find out in due course, though. Now it was important just to enjoy crossing the line. We'd worked so hard to get here and there hadn't been many moments of celebration in the last 400 kilometres, but this had to be one. We owed it to ourselves not to walk across the line looking as if we'd swallowed a wasp.

I don't know whether Ben and Ed were waiting to see how pissed off I was that the Norwegians were there before saying something, but I saved them the trouble.

'Fellas,' I said, 'we can't be disappointed. Our aim was to push ourselves as hard as we could, and we've done that.' I meant what I said. We'd made a few mistakes and were battered and worn-out, but overall we'd done a grand job.

It was as if Tony Blair had thought about staying at Gordon's party for a second drink, but decided to go. Their faces relaxed and as we crossed the line Ben shouted, in a way that only he can, 'Yes! That's it, the halfway line.'

Tony was less effusive. '15.23! Set up camp over there.' He pointed to the area next to the Norwegians' tent. 15.23 was the time we'd be heading off tomorrow, so it was twenty-four hours of relaxed recuperation – or so I thought.

BEN   As we skied past their tent, Rune's head poked through one of the airvents. I half expected him to say 'April fool!', but it was January and, to be fair, he looked like a man who had pushed himself to the limit.

'How did you do it?' I marvelled.

'We pushed really hard,' he explained. 'Didn't you see us? We skied beside you the whole day yesterday, just after the crevasse field,' he continued. I felt a little stupid. We hadn't seen anyone and what's more, at one point they had even dived behind some sastrugi to avoid being seen by Ed, who was busy with a comfort break in the snow!

'The day we said goodbye,' said Rune, 'we pitched our tent for an hour and then continued, we passed your tent and did 60 kilometres, and then another 60 kilometres yesterday. We pushed real hard.'

'When did you get here?' I probed. Rune tapped his nose, winked and disappeared back into the tent.

We set camp in silence. We hadn't really believed we could beat the Norwegians, but clearly we had all hoped we could. We had pushed hard, but it wasn't enough. I wasn't disappointed; I was stunned.

JAMES   We quickly stuck the tent up and all we had to do before I got to spend some quality time with my sleeping bag was to get checked over by the doctor.

We were about to head over when Tony's dulcet tones shouted: 'Quick kit check!'

The race rules stated that certain bits of equipment always had to be with us, like stoves, cooking equipment, tent, emergency shelter, safety rope and harnesses – items you'd be pretty stupid, if not suicidal, to throw away. There hadn't been any random checks at the start and if teams were going to try to save weight it would be by cutting the amount of food and fuel they packed – something we had decided not to do.

I began to dig harnesses, karabiners and other essentials out of my pulk.

'Who's got the rope?' I heard Ben shout.

'I haven't got it,' Ed chipped in.

I was pretty sure I didn't have it either, but went through my pulk again. 'Nor me, let's just check one more time,' I shouted back.

BEN   We went into the big green tent. The floor was covered with a white insulation foam, a fuel heater burned in the middle of the space, and three chairs had been set out for us.

Alexis, Roly, Keith, Georg, Petr, Martin, Sarah, Ian, Deidre, Tony and Kenny had all crowded into the cramped tent, waiting for us. It was like a circus freak show, and we were the exhibits.

We sipped on hot chocolate and luxuriated in the warmth of the tent.

'Right,' barked Tony, shattering us from Shangri-La, 'first things first, where's your rope?'

We had no answer to that one.

'How did you get through the crevasse field?' asked Kenny.

We looked at one another sheepishly and then James explained that we hadn't felt ropes and harnesses were necessary. We had simply probed our way out of danger using our poles.

There was a sharp intake of breath. We sat there like naughty schoolboys in front of the headmaster. 'This is a very serious issue,' said Tony. 'The rope is a compulsory piece of race equipment, as important in Antarctica as a gun [as a defence against polar bears] is in the Arctic. It also creates a problem for us,' he continued. 'You see, the race rules insist that you need to finish the race with all your safety gear. Without it, you can't be officially placed in the race.'

I could see where this was leading. We were about to be disqualified. My heart sank.

JAMES   It suddenly dawned on me why Tony had ordered a spot check now. Turning towards him, I said, 'How did you know we'd lost it?'

'Team Danske Bank told us they'd picked up a rope during one of their safety calls,' he said. 'They found it in the ski tracks.'

BEN   Tony went on to explain that some people had insinuated that we had 'lost' the rope on purpose, to save weight.

'Come on, Tony,' I said, 'if we were going to dump a rope, we'd at least bury it rather than leave it in the middle of a trail that we know everyone is following.' It was infuriating. We were supposed to be celebrating our achievements, not undergoing a polar Spanish Inquisition.

We hadn't lost the rope on purpose. We didn't even know we'd lost it in the first place.

The rope had been passed between us as a 'handicap' balance. Weighing a couple of kilos and easy to strap to the top of a pulk, it was a simple way of redistributing weight. It often changed hands half a dozen times a day and must have fallen unnoticed from the back of a pulk after not being secured properly.

JAMES It was a mistake we could have avoided and as such it was annoying, but inconsequential compared to the potential implications of having no safety rope. When we were debating whether to rope up in the crevasse field, the fact was we actually had no rope. What would we have done if we'd come across a more dangerous crevasse field?

'How did you know it was ours?' As soon as it came out of my mouth, I realized it was a stupid question. He'd have asked the Norwegians as well.

'The Norwegians had also seen it and marked its location on their GPS,' Tony replied.

'So they just left our rope in the snow?' I asked.

'Yeah,' Tony replied with a grin.

I asked myself what we would have done if there'd been a rope in the snow. I'm pretty sure I'd have left it, whereas Ben and Ed would have voted to take it – so on a 2–1 vote we'd have picked it up. By virtue of having two thoughtful and considerate teammates, I had the moral high ground to go and wind up the Norwegians.

'What happens now?' I asked. I knew we'd just contravened a race rule, but as I hadn't been planning on dumping vital equipment, I hadn't bothered to read what the punishment was.

'As another team has your rope, and because of your reaction when we asked you to look for it, I don't believe you deliberately dumped it. And even you lot could find a better place to hide it than your tracks. So no punishment – but you might want to buy Danske Bank a beer. Right, go and see the doc.'

BEN   I was too exhausted to feel relief and too angry to feel happy. To be honest I couldn't feel much. I was on my third cup of hot chocolate and we all longed for sleep.

JAMES   I was hobbling past the Norwegians' tent when Rune stuck his head out of one of the side vents.

'Hey,' he said.

'Ah I see, first you leave us in a crevasse field with no rope and now you can't even be bothered to unzip your tent to say hello. It's like that, is it?' I said, grinning.

'We marked it on our GPS in case you wanted to go back and get it,' he smiled back. 'We were going to bring it, but it looked very heavy.'

'You're big strong boys, you could have coped; Ben and Ed are really pissed at you,' I said seriously, putting on my best poker face – which clearly wasn't very good.

'Oh no! How can I make it up to them?' he laughed back. It was very annoying to be outsmarted by someone in their second language.

'Been here long?' I asked.

'About four hours,' Rune replied.

I'm sure my face changed then. Four hours! We gave it to them!

'Good job, man, I'll see you later. We've got to get checked over by the doc. Rest easy now,' I said, waving goodbye as I headed to the organizers' green dome tent.

Now I really was pissed off, not with the second place but the fact that we gave them that time. I could have made myself feel better by saying they lost time in the crevasses, and may have had problems we don't know about, but that didn't change the fact we could still have been here ahead of them.

BEN I had been dreading seeing the doctor. I was relieved that James would get the medical treatment he needed, but I also worried about the implications. What if he wasn't allowed to continue? James talked about his very real concerns about carrying on. He had been debilitated by pain for days now and in some ways I wonder if he was hoping the doctor would pull him out of the race, so that he didn't have to make the decision.

JAMES The change in temperature as I entered the doctor's tent sent me into a coughing fit, which, no matter how hard I tried to suppress it, didn't stop. Doctor Ian didn't look impressed.

'Right, let's check you over. Sats first.' 'Sats', or 'oxygen saturation of the blood' for those of a scientific persuasion, should be close to 100 per cent at sea level, but at altitude the figure drops slightly. Doc Ian clipped the device on to Ed's finger and repeated it with Ben: they were 97 per cent and 96 per cent respectively. He then clipped it on to mine and showed the digital readout to Ed, who raised his eyebrows – bloody doctors sticking together. My score was 80 per cent.

A value below 90 per cent can cause hypoxaemia, which is a reduced concentration of dissolved oxygen in arterial blood (blood going away from the heart) – which in turn means that a reduced amount of oxygen is being delivered to the lungs. I wasn't exactly sure what I could do with that information, apart from understand why I'd been waking up in the night struggling to breathe. Doc Ian listened to my chest and I almost let out a squeal as the cold metal touched my back. Fortunately I realized just in time that that's not the sort of thing hardcore explorers like me did, but the news was about to get worse: I had fluid on my left lung, and pneumonia. That explained why I was coughing and coughing until I was either sick or a load of phlegm flew out.

I'd come into the tent thinking I had a simple chest infection and that my feet were going to cause Doc Ian the greatest concern; we hadn't even got to my feet yet and he already looked very unhappy.

'Your chest isn't good,' the doc started, in a tone that sounded ominous. 'At the moment I'm not sure you can carry on.'

I felt physically winded. I couldn't believe what he was saying. I'd felt awful in the tent and definitely wasn't as strong as normal on the skis, but I didn't feel that bad – and then it hit me: not only was my eighteen months of training about to be wasted; so was theirs, because to complete the race you had to arrive at the Pole with the same number of people you started with. I felt terrible.

'I'm sorry, fellas, it didn't feel that bad, not compared to my feet at least,' I mumbled, head down, looking at the ground.

'We started as a team of three and we'll finish as one,' Ben said defiantly. I really appreciated the support but, ultimately, that wasn't going to be our decision.

With luck the state of my feet wasn't going to push Doc Ian even further towards not letting me carry on. Wisely, Ben and Ed took this as a cue to head to their sleeping bags. They'd experienced the ravishing scent of hot, slightly rotten flesh, and weren't keen to stick around.

'Which foot is less painful?' asked the doc.

'The left,' I replied.

He smiled, and started on the right, gently peeling off the tape and padding that Ed and I had put on over the previous few days.

The stench of steaming, bloody flesh made him cough, but I was slightly disappointed that I didn't make him retch. Mind you, making the race doctor sick with the smell of rotting feet wouldn't have done my chances of being allowed to carry on much good.

'I don't get paid enough to do this,' he said, in a voice that sounded as if he was trying to hold his breath and speak at the same time.

'I don't think anyone gets paid enough,' I answered. 'I'm six feet away, they're my feet and that's still far too close. I don't know how you're coping down there.'

Things were about to get a bit more painful. The flaps of skin from the burst blisters had stuck to the tape and it was going to hurt like hell when the last bit of tape came off. Or, as Doc Ian put it, 'You might feel this.'

I'd be rubbish at resisting interrogation. All you would need is a roll of zinc oxide tape and you'd have all the information in a couple of days. When the tape came off I let out a scream normally saved for people on either stage two or three of a back, sack and crackwaxing session.

My feet were now tape free and I was about to find out if my biggest fear had been realized and they were infected. If they were, my race was over; a blood infection out here could be life threatening. If they weren't then I needed to go back to the tent and give Ed a massive kiss for saving them with his care and attention.

'Well, they're not in a very good state. Did you not feel the blisters coming?' asked Ian.

'Yes and no. They came on very quickly,' I said sheepishly, and, thinking that a change of direction was required, drove to the big question. 'Are they infected?'

'Amazingly no!' he exclaimed, 'but you owe Ed a beer.' My bar bill was getting big: Danske Bank and now Ed.

Not all the news was good. 'You've got a deep sore on your big toe and some very raw blisters. Unlike your chest they won't stop you doing the race, but they'll hurt all the way to the finish and probably get worse,' he stated matter-of-factly.

The doc dipped out of the tent and I sat there wondering how I'd got into this position. I'd left the UK the most fit and healthy I'd been since the Athens Olympics in 2004, and here I was with pneumonia, horrendous blisters and no green light to carry on. Ben, who had been in and out of hospital for the last month before we left the UK, was cruising along. How did that work? Had I done it to myself? I felt so stupid and imagined the other two saying pretty much the same thing in the tent.

Doc Ian came back and handed me some antibiotics and oral steroids. 'Take these, and I'll give you the rest tomorrow. The best way to recover is to rest, so go and get some sleep. We'll leave the feet uncovered and sort them out tomorrow.'

I turned as I was heading for the door. 'What chance have I got of being allowed to carry on,' I asked.

'It's hard to guess. I definitely wouldn't let you go now, but if you show signs of healing then perhaps. It's a matter of how quickly your body heals,' he answered. I appreciated his honesty, hoping that my body mended itself as quickly as it had broken down.

The first thing my eyes focused on as I thanked the doc and headed outside was the Norwegians' tent. An hour ago I had walked away from it spitting nails about handing them a four-hour lead; now that felt totally irrelevant.

29

THE MUMMY'S RETURN

JAMES   On the way back to the tent I was intercepted by Petr and Martin, who were making a documentary about Rune and Stian for Norwegian TV. 'Can we ask you a couple of quick questions?' Martin asked.

'Sure,' I replied.

'You made yourself ill by pushing too hard. Has it cost you the race?'

Bloody hell, I wasn't expecting Jeremy Paxman. What could I say to that? I wanted to say no, but the answer was probably yes.

Martin's follow-up question was equally as sympathetic: 'How will you feel if the other two are forced to carry on without you and the team is disqualified from the race?' I started to see the wisdom of Sir Alex Ferguson's policy of talking only to journalists who don't ask him any tough questions. I ended the interrogation as quickly as possible, and went into our tent. The other two were crashed out. I had a quick look around and was relieved that I couldn't see any Cracknell-shaped voodoo dolls with pins in anywhere.

BEN   I can't even recall getting into my sleeping bag, but when I opened my eyes it was 7 a.m. I had slept for thirteen hours. My mouth was parched and my stomach ached with hunger, but my body had finally got the rest it craved. While Ed and James continued to sleep, I fired up the stoves, melted some snow, made some porridge and then went back to sleep for a couple of hours.

It was 11.30 a.m. when I next opened my eyes. We had just four hours until we left. Where had the time gone? Twenty-four hours had sounded like an eternity, but it had simply flown by in a blur of dribbles and snores.

James was still asleep. He hadn't moved for more than eighteen hours. We still had an hour of media calls before we could begin packing; but before any of that we still needed to hear the doctor's verdict.

JAMES   Exhaustion had clearly won out over stress. I had a great night's sleep – although I'm not sure you can call spending eighteen hours comatose just a 'night's sleep'; surely that's more of a hibernation. Yet even after that length of time I again felt like a caterpillar that's been dragged out of his pupal stage too early.

I was greeted by a laughing Ben. 'Your face is totally swollen,' he said, passing me the team mirror – the shiny back of his iPod.

'Shit!' I said, stunned. My eyes were the two proverbial 'pissholes in the snow'.

I couldn't put it off any longer: it was time to go and see Doc Ian. I definitely felt better, but figured my 'sats' percentage, rather than my opinion, was going to be the crucial reference point. Even better news was that my feet hadn't become part of the sleeping bag overnight. They didn't smell too good but I'd challenge any guy to have a sweet-smelling sleeping bag after eighteen hours.

BEN   'I just want you to know that I respect any decision you make,' I said to James. 'The selfish part of me wants you to continue, but I also want you to do what's best for you.'

He looked shattered. Deep down, was he hoping that he'd be pulled from the race? In his current condition, it would become difficult to maintain our strategy and even harder to beat the Norwegians. He was certainly quiet and withdrawn as he got himself ready to see the doctor. After all his problems over the first half of the race, had he mentally prepared for this to be the end of the line, when it was just the beginning? We still had nearly 400 kilometres to go.

We all agreed it was vital that the decision should be made for him, rather than by him. It was unfair to expect James to make the final choice. The coughing had abated, but he truly looked terrible.

Ed and I set about packing our supplies. Time was ticking away. I imagined the Norwegians cutting through virgin snow, making headway while we packed our porridge and counted our snack bags.

We had been at the checkpoint for nearly twenty-four hours and other than the Norwegians we had seen no sign of any other teams. As I had speculated, Tess and Pete of Team Southern Lights had struggled with the first half of the race and had indeed been picked up and relocated by the organizers, but there was still no sign of Inge and his team, nor Team Danske Bank. The Norwegians may have stolen a march on us, but at least we still had more than a full day's advantage over the next team.

JAMES 'Fingers crossed I'm good to go,' I said, trying to sound positive as I unzipped the tent.

'Hey, boys,' I said, walking slowly past Rune and Stian, who were preparing for the off.

'Hey,' Stian replied, 'you OK? They going to let you carry on?' Man, gossip gets round fast on a campsite; nylon doesn't make for a good sound insulator, but I should have remembered that from camping with a girlfriend when I was seventeen.

'I hope so,' I said solemnly. 'If they do, I'm only allowed to ski 30–35 kilometres a day, so you guys can just cruise along – the race is in the bag.' I was trying my poker face again; surely it would work this time?

'We were going to do the same as well; it's not all about winning,' Stian replied. Back to poker school for me.

'I'll see you at the Pole, you take care,' I waved, and wandered off to find the doc.

*

'Hey, Doc,' I said.

'Steroids are working then!' he said, seeing my puffy features and narrow eyes. 'How are you feeling?'

'Brilliant! Is that it? Can I go now?' I asked, hopefully.

'Sit down,' he said, pointing at a chair. 'Let's have a look at your sats.'

He produced his magic device and clipped it on while I willed every bit of oxygen in my body to head to the tip of that finger.

Doc Ian nodded his head in a vaguely positive way. '92 per cent, not great, but a massive improvement. Let's listen to that chest,' he said, getting out his stethoscope.

'There's still fluid on that lung, but you don't seem to be coughing as much. There's no point in asking your opinion as you'll say "I'm fine",' he said, adding, 'I'm surprised how quickly you've healed. I was expecting to say you couldn't carry on today, but the signs look good.' He fixed me with a keen stare. 'But you need to look after yourself to make sure you get healthy again.'

'Does that mean I can go?' I asked, in the same voice Croyde uses when he really wants something.

He simply said, 'Yep.'

'Brilliant, Doc!' I said. 'You'd better sort my feet out then.' There was a bounce in my voice that hadn't been there since I came into the same tent the day before. There was shouting outside the tent and a couple of people clapping; the Norwegians must have set off.

'We've got two options here,' said Doc Ian. 'We can either put a base minimum of tape on and you can replace it every day, or we can make sure it's clean and tape the bugger up and hope it gets you through. Your call,' he said, looking up at me.

'Go for the tape option,' I said. 'Less to do in the tent.' I wanted my health to have as little impact on the team as possible, especially Ed; he was here to race, not to be a personal physician to Ben and me. By the time Doc Ian had finished with my feet it was a toss-up between me and Tutankhamen as to who had the most bandaging.

At that moment Ed came into the tent. I gave him a thumbs-up sign and he grinned and handed me a bowl full of something hot: my guess was a curry.

'Great news, buddy. The food and fuel are all sorted and the tent cleaned out, we're nearly ready to get going,' Ed said. Having felt positive about being allowed to go, the amount of work Ben and Ed had done reminded me that I wasn't doing my share.

'I'm glad you're here, Ed. You did a great job in getting James to the checkpoint in a condition he could recover from, both his feet and chest. But don't take everything on: you're here to race and I'm the doctor. Don't be afraid to use me – I've got a bigger medical kit. It may take us a while to find you but we will get to you if you need us,' Doc Ian said looking him in the eye. Doc Ed had just been reduced to Ed.

Doc Ian then proceeded to hand Ed my antibiotics, oral steroids and inhalers, saying, 'You know the doses he'll need, make sure he takes them.'

'Bloody hell, he wasn't considered a doctor for about thirty seconds!' I exclaimed.

'Will you remember to take these all on your own?' Doc Ian asked.

I was back in the headmaster's study again and mumbled, 'Probably not.'

*

BEN   Ed and I were elated that James could continue. I felt sorry for him – he would be in a lot of pain over the next few hundred kilometres – but I was happy we would be able to continue together as a team.

3.23 p.m. came and went and we were still packing. With James 'out of action' Ed and I were swamped with admin, and I took special care to pack our 'replacement' rope safely inside my sledge.

JAMES   Time to get going, so we pulled pole and skied to the line. Doc Ian and Kenny were standing there, resplendent in reindeer skins. The Norwegians had clearly been shedding weight – we obviously had them worried. On the start line ten days ago I was full of anticipation and looking forward to the race ahead.

Knowing what was coming our way now, the sense of anticipation and excitement wasn't quite as strong.

BEN Ed and James seemed remarkably relaxed about our delayed departure while, conversely, I was anxious and on edge. It was like some hideous transformation. I was becoming competitive. I was becoming James Cracknell.

At 4 p.m. we dragged our pulks over the line and once again set off into the wilderness. Somewhere out in that white desert were the two Norwegians. They may have taken the lead, but we were in hot pursuit. The hunted had become the hunters.

30

THE DANGER ZONE

BEN Shortly before we left the checkpoint, Tony had briefed us on the next leg of the race.

'There's some bad news,' he barked, holding out a map. 'You see this?' he said, pointing to a large pie-shaped area. 'This is a restricted zone. We did have permission to pass through it, but the Americans have changed their mind.'

Tony pointed to the South Pole at the corner of the restricted area.

'You're going to have to skirt around the no-go zone, and then approach the South Pole from the north.'

He handed us some waypoints that would ensure we didn't stray into the restricted zone.

'Just how far is this detour?' I asked.

'About 75 kilometres,' shrugged Tony.

It wasn't a great deal in the grand scheme of things, but it would add an extra day or two at least to the race. Worse still, it meant we had to detour from our southerly heading. It would be a wicked psychological blow to have to ski away from the South Pole.

*

It was good to get away from the checkpoint. It had disrupted the careful balance of our daily routine and while it had been good to rest and recover, it had also been unsettling.

We set off just after 4 p.m., and our first major decision was how much ground to cover in the first day. If we stuck to our strategy and skied for sixteen hours, we wouldn't stop until 8 a.m. in the morning – our whole daily pattern would be out of kilter.

We all agreed that we would ease ourselves back into the race by skiing until 2 a.m., and then return to our original timetable. It may seem strange to stick to timetables, particularly when there is twenty-four-hour sunlight, but we all recognized the importance of routine. I craved it, and made sure the others knew it. I was happy to push myself to the limit as long as there was a structured routine.

On the Atlantic James and I had rowed two hours on, two hours off, twenty-four hours a day, every day of the week for over a month. It sounds impossible now, but it was something we got used to and within a couple of weeks it had become normality. I had been thrown out of sync, then, when James had suddenly suggested changing the routine to one hour on, one hour off. The effect was debilitating and I had become depressed and withdrawn as a result.

I firmly believe that routine is the key to success on any expedition. There has to be an element of flexibility around it, but it is vital for morale and motivation to stick to a broad plan. We had always allowed an element of flexibility within our strategy, and we all agreed that there would be days when we would ski for longer and others when we'd stop earlier. The key was to use 'the strategy', our sacred sixteen hours on/eight hours off, as a template.

James's condition had improved slightly. The coughing fits had abated as the antibiotics kicked in, and his mummified feet were beginning to feel more comfortable. He was on a high dose of morphine-based painkillers and he'd resigned himself to continuing. Our Norwegian friends, Team Missing Link, would be hard to catch, so we set about holding the distance between us and the third team.

JAMES   I appreciated I was incredibly lucky to have recovered sufficiently to be given the all-clear, and I made some internal resolutions. I wanted to show Ben and Ed that I was on the mend, and that they didn't have to keep looking over their shoulders to see if I was OK. I wasn't going to make an issue out of my blisters – unless something drastic happened, they were taped up until the end of the race – and I was going to look after myself. I didn't want to let them down any more than I had done already.

BEN It was cold out there on the plateau, bitterly cold. The wind was from behind, biting through our thin layers and chilling to the bone. For the first time since arriving in Antarctica I began to feel cold even while skiing.

Weight loss was undeniably a factor. Our bodies, starved of nutrition, had begun to eat into our fat reserves, but that was scientific assumption rather than a visual fact. We hadn't seen our bodies for a long time, as they had been either wrapped in layers of clothing or enveloped in a sleeping bag.

I certainly felt thinner, though. My bones had started to rub against the ground at night and I was always hungry. In fact, food had taken over most of our waking thoughts and conversation invariably revolved around it.

JAMES The temperature in Antarctica drops almost a degree a day from the middle of January as winter approaches, and we were heading towards the coldest part of the continent (and, therefore, the coldest part of the planet). I was skiing in my Gore-tex gorilla mask and goggles again, and while they were great for keeping the cold wind out, it's no fun spending hours dressed like that. If the temperature did keep falling then I would be spending much of the next 400 kilometres like an astronaut, unable to interact with the environment around me.

Though I'd obviously never been there, it struck me there must be certain similarities between the moon and the plateau; the sense of isolation, no life, the inability to interact with the environment you're in. Not to mention rubbish food and the arduous process of having a poo.

The ground underfoot, in sympathy with the weather, was very icy, which was good because it meant less friction and a higher speed, but bad because it meant less cushioning and put more pressure up through the ski and onto my blisters. If nothing else it was nice to see the Chinese philosophy of yin and yang was in good working order – the pleasure of easy speed balanced out by the pain of sore feet.

In just over nine hours we covered 32 kilometres, partly down to the fast icy surface, but also because of the lower temperature we didn't want to sit around too long during the breaks. I'd made sure that my pace was consistent, aiming to restore Ben and Ed's confidence in me, and I hadn't mentioned my feet; nobody wants to hear someone complaining when nothing can be done to solve the problem.

It was nice to be on our own again. We'd got used to seeing no one, and being part of a bigger camp for twenty-four hours had been strange. There's something unbelievably special about unzipping a tent and seeing nothing in any direction. The atmosphere was great in the tent that night. Both Ed and I slept better as we steadily recovered from our respective colds, and though my face was still puffy I had had one of my best skis of the trip when we left the checkpoint. Every cloud and all that.

*

Scratch that. Every silver lining . . .

At the end of the first two-hour session the next morning, it was clear that I was going to have to undermine what I'd tried to demonstrate with my skiing the night before by sowing some seeds of doubt in Ben and Ed's minds about my recovery. Although I'd kept pace it had been hard work and there was no way I could maintain that pace for fourteen hours, or even another two hours. I'd have to ask them to rein it in.

What frustrated me was that the pace would drop during the day anyway. I'd commented earlier in the race that it would be more efficient to be steady at the start of the day and keep that pace all the way. Better that than going fast for the first two or three sessions of the day and then slowing right down or even having to stop early. Repeating those same comments now sounded as if I was saying them only because I was struggling to keep up, I knew, but surely none of us would be able to ski this fast for the rest of the day?

I suggested the change of pace to Ben.

'I feel great,' he said. 'I could ski at that pace all day, but if you want me to slow down it's no problem.'

He wasn't being patronizing, but it felt like it. Throughout our preparation over the last eighteen months he had been asking me to slow down – and now, in the real race, it was the other way round. There was no offer to take extra weight to balance out the speed, but that had been Ben's way throughout the race. He'd rarely offered to take weight, though would always take it when he was asked and felt able. His attitude was understandable after the illness he'd fought through. It was up to me to ask, but even with pneumonia and feeling rubbish I was still too proud to do so.

BEN Over the course of two dozen expeditions I have developed, through trial and error, a system of self-management, varying my pace to my physical ability at the time. I watched as James and Ed yo-yoed wildly between the weights they pulled and though I was always prepared to take weight from either of the boys, self-preservation had prevented me from taking 'vanity' weight. I have struggled for years to accept that James is a naturally stronger and more able athlete than I am, and was often right on the edge of what I was capable of; I knew that adding extra weight might throw me over that edge at any time. I had often taken weight from Ed, but still felt uncomfortable taking it proactively from James, not least because I knew he would accuse me of bravado if I then fell to bits!

But perhaps that was unfair. I thought back to the charity event back in England, where James had told Bev that he was running home 'because when Ben struggles, I'll need to be strong enough to pull his pulk for him.'

Bev had told me the story, and I am still moved by its significance. James wasn't training for himself, he was training for me. This went beyond standard team dynamics. He could have told me to drop out of the team altogether. Instead, he was training double time to take the burden.

I thought about that story often and it seemed even more profound now, when James was at his weakest. I wished I had been able to put the extra training in to take his pulk for him but because of the Leishmaniasis, that wasn't possible. Our only option now was to slow down.

JAMES   We took the edge off the pace and I was still feeling pretty good at the end of the day, the last six hours of which were spent skiing into an horrendous whiteout, forcing us to steer exclusively off the GPS. It was an unusual day because we ended in the same high spirits that we started with. Normally someone was in a bad mood either at the start or finish, but we were a bunch of happy campers today. Unfortunately, it didn't last.

31

A NASTY CASE OF 'STUPIDITY'

BEN Next morning we woke at 7.45 a.m., ready for a 10 a.m. departure. James was on a cocktail of pills for his various ailments, and Ed made a little pile of tablets next to him, ready to go.

'There's something wrong with my finger,' mumbled James as he popped his medicine.

'What?' asked Ed. I had become used to this no-way conversation. James has a tendency to mumble, while Ed struggles with his hearing. The result is that James says something indecipherable, which Ed can't hear anyway.

It used to annoy James, who had suggested Ed get his ears syringed before the trip. Ed had refused and said that his natural response to any question was 'what?' whether he had heard it or not. But I digress. James held out his middle finger. The end was swollen and blistered, and the nail was dark red.

'Does it hurt?' I asked, examining it.

'No, I can't even feel it,' he replied.

JAMES We had all lost the sensation in the tips of our fingers at least a week earlier, and because Tutankhamen's feet weren't to be disturbed, I had used the extra time that morning to check out my fingers. The middle finger on my right hand didn't look that great. I'd never been that good at spotting frostnip – the initial, reversible stage of frostbite where the tissue becomes pale and numb, but crucially still has a blood supply. There was a blister covering the top of my finger which, in my experience of blisters, should have hurt like hell but didn't. I wasn't sure if that was a good sign, especially as I couldn't remember burning it or doing anything that would cause a blister.

BEN   Frostbite. The idiot had frostbite. I couldn't believe it. I had never even seen frostbite, but it was perfectly clear that that was what it was.

Ed examined it too, and concurred. James stared at the finger, as if he could will it away. It wasn't going anywhere. In fact, it was likely to get worse.

'How on earth did you do it?' I asked.

He shrugged his shoulders. 'Dunno.'

For me it was symptomatic of James's laissez-faire attitude to his health. Until now I had given him the benefit of the doubt for his physical deterioration – he had blamed his blistered feet on soft skin and his pneumonia on bad luck – but frostbite is eminently preventable. We had been taught how to avoid it, and warned not to get it at all costs.

That James had now added frostbite to his already lengthy medical CV was cause for more than just concern.

JAMES   I couldn't believe it; I didn't even remember getting cold hands yesterday and generally my hands stayed warmer than the other guys', probably a hangover from years spent rowing in the winter. I didn't want to believe it and was in denial. Ben said I should call up the race doctor and get either Doc Ian or Doc Deidre to come out and have a look. I didn't want a doctor to come out in a vehicle just to look at my little pinky but they put pressure on me, and after my recent track record I wasn't surprised. I agreed to mention it during our safety call that evening and see what they suggested.

The Tourette's was back as we skied off. Frostbite, on top of everything else – what an idiot! The words of Ben Saunders, an Arctic explorer we had spoken to before the race, came flooding back: 'There's no excuse for frostbite, I'd be embarrassed if I got it.' He was right with the second sentiment; if it was frostbite, I'd desperately be searching for an excuse.

BEN The weather had been getting colder still, and a thick bank of cloud had appeared on the horizon. We had been making reasonable headway but our efficiency and time management had been slipping. We had left late on both mornings since the checkpoint, and breaks were becoming longer than ever.

It was 10.45 a.m. by the time we pulled pole and headed off. The wind was strong and we were all preoccupied with James's frostbite. What did it mean? I worried. Would he lose the finger? Would he be allowed to continue? James seemed rather more preoccupied by Bev's reaction. 'Don't get frostbite' had been her departing words at Heathrow airport.

JAMES During our scheduled call I reluctantly told the organizers about the suspected frostbite; even though it was my finger, I had been outvoted 2–1.

In one of the only serendipitous experiences on the trip, Doc Deidre was with Alexis and the camera crew, who were on the way to find us and get some footage of our skiing in a whiteout. My call was clearly serendipitous for Alexis as well, because he got to film me being diagnosed with frostbite or 'stupidity' as we had renamed it. I wasn't budging from my diagnosis of bad frostnip, with the added caveat up my sleeve that it is a grey area between bad frostnip and mild frostbite.

My argument was severely weakened when Doc Deidre took one look at it and said, 'That's frostbite.'

Her advice was to keep it warm, hilariously adding, 'You might as well keep the other fingers warm while you're at it!'

I'd kind of lost the right for a witty comeback.

She also said there were some tasks I shouldn't do, such as lighting stoves and handling cold fuel bottles. One of my jobs was refuelling, so handling the bottles was in my remit. I felt like enough of a handbrake on the team already, so not all her advice was going to be heeded, especially as Ben and Ed hadn't heard the final part of our conversation. What they didn't know wasn't going to hurt them.

*

BEN   I had volunteered to do the evening stoves and Alexis had asked if he could squeeze into the corner of our tent and film us. Until now, most of the filming had been relatively unobtrusive, often done from a distance. It was a pure, natural and discreet way of filming that kept the experience natural and real, while I filled in the gaps with footage from within the team. As the designated video-diary cameraman of the team, my pulk contained three cameras, half a dozen tapes and eight batteries. I never let James know how much extra weight we had.

Filming was a bore but the BBC had invested a considerable amount of time and money in us. It meant I often missed a rest during our break as I was too busy filming, but I had made a promise to Alexis, the director. It did mean however that not only was I racing, I was also filming. I'm not sure Ed and James ever fully appreciated how hard it was to ski alongside them with the camera and to manage all the stock and tapes.

I regretted that we hadn't kept the documentary process this relaxed in Norway with Jonny. He would have been far more comfortable with this approach. He had called me the night before I left the UK, to wish us luck. We had shared an intense bonding experience together and I know he would have loved every minute of Antarctica. He had spoken often of a road journey across India and how it had grounded him as an individual. The South Pole Race would have changed his life.

We loved Ed though, and were incredibly lucky to share this experience with him. That he suffered a little from hypochondria rubbed James and I up the wrong way sometimes, but he was just about the most perfect team member you could ever ask for. He was good company, funny (he does a wicked Vicky Pollard impression that used to have me crying with laughter), strong, and determined. A sensitive sportsman, he also complemented our personality extremes, and we both agreed that we had made the right decision in choosing him.

I had been on stove duty dozens of times and I had a tried and tested system that had worked like clockwork. Until now.

There is a saying that 'the act of being observed affects that which is being observed'. In short, the camera distorts reality. I have spent the last ten years under the watchful eye of the camera lens. I have made a career from it and wouldn't have been in Antarctica without it, but I also have a love–hate relationship with the lens. I find it fascinating how some people will do anything to be in front of a camera. Why? I do it as a means to an end. It takes me places I never dreamed I'd reach, and I've met people I never thought I'd meet. For me, life in front of the lens is a job that allows me to follow my dreams.

Of course I'd be lying if I said there wasn't an element of vanity too. Like most presenters, I like attention and sometimes I even like showing off in front of the cameras; but the lens also has a way of stripping you naked when you least want it to.

For me, there is nothing worse than being filmed in a stressful situation. I hate it. I have no control over my speech or emotions and I loathe the nakedness of reality – but this is also what makes the best television. It has taken me ten years to learn this simple fact. Try and beat it and the audience will see right through you.

'Ignore me,' said Alexis as he jammed himself into a corner. Ed and James finished off outside and I set the stoves. I went through my little obsessive-compulsive routine and made sure everything was in the right place before pumping each bottle and turning on the little taps. There was nothing. I twisted them again. Nothing.

I unscrewed the bottles and checked there was enough fuel. Still nothing. For twenty minutes I tried to light the stoves, becoming increasingly annoyed and stressed with each minute. I could sense the lens behind me. I wanted to hit it. I wanted to put my hand over it and scream. I wanted to shout at Alexis to leave. I controlled myself as my face reddened with fury.

'Typical, fucking typical!' I muttered under my breath, I hoped out of earshot of the snooping microphone. I had lit these stoves dozens of times without a hitch, and now, the one time the camera's here, it all goes wrong.

'James,' I shouted like a sulky teenager, 'the stoves are broken!'

James was the stove master. If anyone could fix them, he could. For ten minutes he fiddled with the delicate stoves, before getting one of them working. The other, it seemed, had finally given in to the cold.

I stewed in silence while Alexis filmed tent life. No wonder I sometimes hate the camera.

32

TURN ON, TUNE IN . . .

JAMES Thankfully the whiteout was gone. Skiing in these conditions didn't bother me as much as Ben or Ed – I liked the surreal feeling of skiing into a white wall – but a day's skiing in the sunshine was of course far nicer. It wasn't a sunny day for my feet, though – they were really sore. I hadn't touched Doc Ian's taping so far, but during the first two hours skiing that day, I knew I was going to have to do something.

Upping the dose of painkillers was one option, which I was reticent to take up on principle. When I was rowing competitively I never used to take painkillers in training because of their ability to mask pain; you could end up making an injury worse without knowing it. I'd only take them if I had to do so to be able to race. I was also reluctant because I was taking so many pills already that I was starting to rattle: antibiotics, oral steroids, inhalers, anti-inflammatories, paracetamol and, since yesterday, aspirin for my frostnip/mild frostbite.

BEN 'I think we should stop early today,' said Ed.

We had both been concerned about James, who was clearly struggling, but James wasn't having any of it. Ed still didn't feel entirely comfortable telling James what to do, and I didn't have the energy for an argument.

JAMES Ed was in charge of the painkilling regime. I was deemed untrustworthy by Ben after having loaded up with Tramadol, a strong painkiller, in the last few days of our Atlantic row. At one stage I had come out of the cabin in the middle of Ben's shift and asked if I was at Freddie Flintoff's testimonial. Understandably, Ben was concerned; I might think I was a swimming champion and jump over the side when he was asleep. I thought that unlikely, as the chief side effect I struggled with, apart from the hallucinations, was drowsiness, and he'd have been more likely to have come out and found me fast asleep that anything else. In the Atlantic I'd countered the Tramadol-induced drowsiness with caffeine tablets so I could stay awake, which wasn't big or clever but did mean that I could actually sit on my bum, which was covered in sores. Like it or not, without Tramadol Ben would have spent the last five days rowing on his own, so the 'cure' had a special place in my heart. And I was glad to see Ed had got some of it in the medical kit. Well, it was in the medical kit until Ed thought it was safer in his pocket.

I hated taking it but I had no option now. We were an hour into a two-hour stint when I called us to a halt. No matter how I shifted my feet in the boot, they were killing me. I had blisters on the ball, heel and toe and couldn't get away from putting my weight on them. We sat on the pulk under the emergency shelter and had a brainstorm about what to do. Ed suggested an extra inner-sole.

'I haven't seen a shoe shop for a couple of days, where am I going to get an inner-sole from?' I asked sarcastically.

'Funny guy, get your roll mat out,' he replied.

Five minutes later I had a comedy pair of feet-shaped holes cut out of my roll mat and a new pair of inner-soles. I slipped them into the bottom of the boots and hoped that would make a difference. I also asked Ed for some Tramadol, as I knew that they would take the edge off the pain if the inner-soles didn't. He handed me a strip of the green and yellow capsules with strict instructions, and set about packing up again for the off. I took a few, and put the rest in my pocket.

*

I didn't want to think how many minutes or hours we'd wasted as a team on my feet, either in the tent or on the move. Ben was always quiet when we made an unscheduled stop; he never said he was pissed off, but I could sense his frustration. Ben's timekeeping was spot on and in a ten-minute break he managed to get everything done he wanted to and was ready to ski, whereas Eddie and especially I were a bit more hit-and-miss with our timings.

Ben didn't understand why I couldn't have a poo, eat, drink and be ready to ski again in ten minutes. I told him it was because I actually made the effort to go downwind of the pulks. Ben would instead move a few steps away, upwind, and carefully select the perfect angle to deposit his crap so the smell would be blown directly towards Ed and me.

'But if I go behind you don't have to see,' he protested when I got a noseful.

'I can look the other way or close my eyes if you do it downwind, but the first thing I know about it is the smell when you do it upwind and we're not exactly short of space. Walk a bit bloody further away,' I said, half joking, half serious, especially as my spreadsheet had shown after the acclimatization phase that Ben was a two- or three-a-day man, and that's a lot of unwanted Fogle faeces to breathe in.

To make our slack timekeeping more pronounced, Ben got colder more quickly than Ed or me, so he was the last one who should be standing around waiting. Every minute we stood still cost us nearly 60 metres, and over a three-week race that really adds up. The stop for my feet took eighteen minutes and at our average skiing speed of 3.4 kph that was 1,020 metres – unacceptable, at least to me. I was going to make sure that was the last stop for my feet from now on, and I figured my Artful Dodger move with the Tramadol would help me do that.

The new inner soles were making a difference but I was still unable to think about anything else, so I swallowed a couple more Tramadol. I knew that was more than the recommended daily amount, and I'd consumed that in just over an hour.

BEN The wind had picked up, creating a halo around the sun and a cloud of snow around our feet, rather like dry ice on a stage. It was awesomely beautiful. I was mesmerized by the wild, bleak landscape, transformed into another world by a little wind and cloud. When people talk of raw beauty, this is surely what they mean: a land unlike anything I have ever seen before, and will probably never see again. A unique snapshot of beauty that few have ever seen.

It certainly took my mind away from other things. James was still reeling from the shock of Dr Deidre's diagnosis, which seemed to have an overall negative effect on his physical and mental health as, once again, the gap to the Norwegians ahead of us began to grow.

'I need to sort my feet!' he hollered breathlessly. I resigned myself to another impromptu stop. It wasn't that it bothered me in and of itself – we were a team after all – but what started to annoy me was when I imagined how James might have reacted if I was the one struggling, if it had been me with the bad feet, the chest infection, the frostbite.

'You continue,' he said, 'I'll catch you up at the next break.'

There was an hour to go until we were due to stop. Ed and I looked at each other. 'Go on,' James repeated, 'I'll catch you up in an hour.'

One of the fundamental rules of polar travel is 'sticking together'. It is a basic strategy for safety, speed and efficiency. We were a team and we moved like a team, together, and now suddenly James was suggesting we split up.

We were puzzled. Why break from our hardened rules now?

James has always been a forceful character. I used to describe it as bullying, but I now understand it as 'railroading': his desire – and ability – to get what he wants, when he wants. I had assumed that this would be tempered by a third person. How wrong I was.

Looking back, I am amazed that James was still able to manipulate Ed and me into decisions we weren't happy with. I put this down to the 'gold factor'. I had discussed it with Ed in Switzerland, after he had admitted to sometimes feeling inferior around James, and it was something I have struggled to come to terms with for years. James is now one of my best friends and yet there is still always a voice in my head reminding me that he is one of the best athletes in the world, which is fine if you're in the pub, but in a physical challenge such as the one we were undertaking now, it can hypnotize you in a golden mist. 'James must be right!' it screams.

We were both prone to James's 'gold factor', and even here in the middle of Antarctica, we would often fall under its spell. And now, once again, he had somehow persuaded us to abandon all our rules and everything we had learned, and split up.

It wasn't long before James was out of sight. One of the main reasons for sticking together was, quite apart from relying on each other for safety and comfort, because our kit and equipment was divided up between us. Ed had the emergency satellite phone, I had the emergency EPIRB and James had the GPS with all our plots and waypoints – except that he didn't. I had it, because I was leading up at the front.

In short, James had no means of navigating apart from our tracks, and no means of summoning help. If the wind picked up and obscured our tracks, he would be instantly lost.

'Why are we doing this?' I asked Ed, genuinely perplexed by our stupidity.

'I don't know,' shrugged Ed. We were dicing with death. If we got separated now, there was no telling when, or indeed if, we would ever find one another again.

We stopped early, and fifteen minutes later James appeared through the gloom. Phew. I relaxed and swore to myself we wouldn't let it happen again, especially given that he was taking Tramadol. And then I realized: until now, Ed had been prescribing this morphine-based painkiller in conservative quantities, but James had commandeered the whole packet. Paralysed by pain and ignoring Ed's advice, James had taken seven tablets, rather than the recommended two.

JAMES   Half an hour after I took the tablets, my feet weren't feeling anywhere near as sore, and I was enjoying skiing for the first time in over a week. An hour after that and I was being awarded an honorary knighthood for services to mankind because I had married Pamela Anderson, and therefore protected the male species from her vixen ways. An hour on again and I was fighting to stay awake, couldn't focus and was dizzy and, more importantly, was struggling to keep up with Ben and Ed. The hallucinogenic side effects of Tramadol may have been taking me away to a cosy marriage with Pamela but when I snapped out of a daydream I'd fallen way behind. I was surprised I'd thought of Pamela – she wasn't my dream girl – but then again beggars couldn't be choosers out here.

*

Bearing in mind what had nearly happened at the checkpoint, I could understand why Ben and Ed were worried. Ed was determined we all looked after ourselves after my dodgy sats test, or more specifically that I looked after myself.

'You OK?' he asked as I skied up.

'Yeah, feel much better now,' I replied truthfully.

'What's been happening? You've not been skiing with us all day,' he asked more forcefully.

'I've been struggling to focus, and felt sleepy; I took too many Tramadol earlier and it's only just worn off,' I answered sheepishly, thinking it best not to bring up Pamela Anderson. He looked at me, not sure whether to believe me.

'Honestly, mate, I feel OK now,' I said. 'I'm good to go for the last couple of hours.'

He didn't look convinced, and we set off for the last two hours without saying another word.

It wasn't exactly party time in the tent that night. We hadn't covered the distance we should have done. Unscheduled stops and deeper snow had slowed us up. I got the feeling Ed was disappointed I'd taken so many painkillers; as a doctor he understands and respects the effect of drugs, but as someone with painful feet who didn't think I could ski 100 metres more, let alone another twelve hours, I felt it was better to take one too many rather than one too few – although my argument falls down slightly as I had five too many.

I decided it was best to recount my brief but eventful marriage to Pamela Anderson to lighten the atmosphere and then promise not to take more than he suggested again.

BEN   Right now, I didn't need Pamela Anderson – I needed rest, and warmth. As I lay down to sleep that night, I realized that I was shaking violently, even in my sleeping bag. It was a deep cold that came from my core. I had been disorientated and slow all day and I recognized the symptoms without the need for a rectal probe: the early signs of hypothermia.

33

TEAM QINETIQ

JAMES The next day was one of those where the place you wake up in feels totally different from the one you went to bed in. Everything about the start of the next day was grey. The cloud cover and wind totally changed the appearance of the plateau; it was as if we'd been inside the tent for a month rather than a night, or as if we'd gone to bed in summer and woken up on the edges of winter. The sky was dark, the wind was already blowing hard and the temperature had dropped 15 degrees. With wind chill, it was down to minus 41.

Even the weather wasn't as dark as our mood, though. The Americans still hadn't given us permission to cross into their restricted zone, so we were definitely going to have to circle round before coming in. Tony had played down the figures at the briefing – perhaps he was confident we'd be let across. Either way I should have checked before now.

BEN James had been in charge of navigation. We all had a GPS in case of emergency, but James held the primary device.

I had been marking our camp each morning in my GPS for back-up and on a whim I decided to type in 'the South Pole' as a final destination. My eyes struggled to digest what the GPS was telling me.

'James,' I asked, 'what does your GPS say?'

JAMES I had gone on Tony's guesstimate of the distance from the waypoint we were heading to, and the Pole. It turned out that estimate was over 50 kilometres short. I remember Tony saying 'It's about that. It might be a bit more, but with the distance you'll have covered by then, the extra kilometres won't make any difference.'

Even in the relative comfort of the checkpoint I knew that every kilometre would make a big difference, and right now 50 kilometres extra felt like a mammoth change. It was easily another day's skiing, since we had covered only 40 kilometres yesterday. By the time we got to the end of the race, every step would feel like a journey in itself. It was like working for sixteen hours on the most brutal building site in the world and then not getting paid. We would finish today with more kilometres left than we had when we went to bed last night.

BEN I was seriously annoyed. Fifty kilometres in a race as long as this might not seem like much but it was a huge psychological blow, especially since my own health was deteriorating.

JAMES We left the tent quiet and pissed off. I tried to put it out of my mind; in these freezing temperatures it was going to be a hard day's skiing without a head full of negativity. As if to remind myself that things could actually be worse, though, my ski binding broke and wouldn't stay fastened so I had to stop, get the tool bag out of my pulk and bend it back into place. I'd told the others to ski on; today was not the one to stand around getting cold. It took me forty minutes to catch them up, which I did just before the break, and then it was my turn to lead. Four hours into the day and I was already clock watching, wishing the hours to pass more quickly – they didn't.

The lower temperatures were having an effect on our pace and rhythm. If someone is cold they will ski a bit more quickly to warm up, which in turn has an effect on the person following them. Despite the cold temperature I felt good, but Ben was getting cold and complaining of mild hypothermia. I wasn't quite sure how I diagnosed that without his anal probe, but he was obviously very cold because he stopped to put his big duvet jacket on, and stepped on the accelerator for good measure. I tried to keep up, but like an old gas-guzzling car, as soon as I put the foot down I was using up too much fuel. I then got myself into a downward spiral as the extra body heat I produced steamed up my goggles. I stopped to swap them with the ones down my jacket, by which time Ben had got further ahead and I had to catch him up, which tired me out even more.

I chased after him, already planning the argument in my head about why the hell he had increased the pace when we'd still got ten hours left to ski. But I couldn't have the argument because as soon as we stopped for a break we got pulled in different directions to have a camera fitted by the crew, who had rejoined us. Ed had one put on his skis to capture a low-angle shot, Ben had one attached to a helmet and I got 'ski cam', a camera on a chest harness filming my face, a diary camera to which we could describe the situation, what we were feeling and what the others were doing. Or, it could be a 'rant cam'.

I let rip about the inconsistent pace. The cameras weren't helping the situation because they all took different times to attach, so people set off skiing as soon as they were ready. Standing around in minus 40 wasn't even worth thinking about, and typically 'ski cam' took longest to set up so I had to try to catch up the others when I was already struggling to keep pace. I realized there was no way I'd finish the day if I chased them down; I had to rely on their seeing I was behind and slowing down.

I was busy swearing at 'ski cam', firstly about my inconsiderate teammates not even checking to see where I was, and then at the 'ski cam' itself as it had become unclipped and was flapping about. Unless I'd become double-jointed there was no way I could reattach it. I thought about dumping it in the snow but realized that wasn't the nicest thing to do, as I hadn't seen a camera shop out here so far (unless it was next to the shoe shop I needed earlier).

When I caught up with Ben and Ed at our scheduled break, I'd been chasing them for two hours and skied in looking a right state, snot and ice frozen all over my face and 'ski cam' hanging off me.

'This is total bollocks,' I shouted at them, 'the pace is up and down. Why can't we just ski at one pace and stick to it? We'll cover more ground. This is crap.'

BEN I wasn't taken aback by James's rant – I'd seen them before – but I was surprised by his accusation of a fast pace. In all the years we'd done things together, he'd never complained about me going too quickly. James seemed dazed and confused. He had been rambling incoherently and he'd even demanded that he and Ed swap pulks, despite the facts that Ed's was obviously the heavier of the two. We were both worried about his frame of mind, and state of health.

JAMES 'Look,' I said, 'I'm going to ski on at my pace, you finish your break. I've no doubt you'll catch me up.' I ripped 'ski cam' off and left it with Ben to give to Alexis, who was busy filming my outburst. I skied off and within minutes realized I had made one, and possibly two, massive mistakes. I should have stopped to eat and drink something and possibly given Ed or Ben some weight out of my pulk – I was really struggling.

After an hour I stopped, leant forward on my poles and closed my eyes. Ben and Ed came up alongside. They waited for me to say something. 'Any of you guys feeling like taking some weight?' It hurt asking, but I needed to shift some.

'Yeah, I'm feeling good, I'll take some,' Ed said. I dug out the climbing harnesses and gave them to him.

'Thanks, buddy,' I muttered, head still down. I skied off, but ten minutes later I was stopping again. I was really struggling; I couldn't understand why I felt so bad. My chest had been getting better every day, so how come now I was feeling weaker? I had a brainwave; maybe my pulk was heavier than everybody else's? Yes, that must be why I couldn't keep up.

'Ed, can I have a go with your pulk? I just want to see if there's a difference,' I asked.

'Sure, but there won't be much,' he said, slightly perplexed with my behaviour. After all, my pulk had been the same for 550 kilometres, why was it an issue now?

He was right, of course. I skied off and there was no difference. After another ten minutes I stopped and we swapped back.

'I think we should call it a night,' Ed suggested. 'You're struggling, and Ben's skiing in a duvet jacket. We need to rest up, have a longer night and have a good day tomorrow.'

'I feel OK,' I protested, knowing I didn't, but desperate to start getting our mileage up again. 'I'm all right; it's the change of pace that's got me today. Let's keep it steady and I'll be good.'

'You've had pneumonia,' Ed continued, more forceful now. 'Most people would be resting up in bed, not skiing for sixteen hours a day. Stopping now will make a massive difference for tomorrow.'

'I'm fine! Fuck, will people stop telling me what's best!' I ranted and skied off. Tears of frustration were rolling down my cheeks and I was thankful for the goggles so that Ben and Ed couldn't see them.

BEN   I was shocked by James's denial, but even more surprised at Ed's new-found confidence. Where did that come from, I wondered in amazement.

JAMES   I found myself not only in a new situation, but one I had never expected to be in. I was falling so far short of my own expectations. During our training I'd been the ever-present force, tyre-pulling in Croyde Bay with Ed when Ben was tired after returning from South America, walking in the Brecon Beacons with Ed, skiing in Switzerland with Ben when Ed was injured, tyre-pulling with Ben when Ed still had his Achilles problem . . . I hadn't missed a session, I'd trained so hard at home and yet I was the one who was struggling. I wanted to come here and be a rock for Ben and Ed to lean on but it was the other way round – I was the one being a sponge and just sucking energy out of them. I couldn't understand why I was in this situation, but I had to start accepting that I was really struggling. It mustn't be about my ego, it had to be about doing the best for the team. But this was a mental step I couldn't take. I wasn't going to stop, I was going to ski on.

Ed came up alongside, then moved ahead and rammed his pole in the ground.

'We're stopping!' he stated defiantly. 'You're recovering from pneumonia, and you need to rest.'

'I'm OK; I can carry on,' I protested weakly.

'We're not carrying on. For the last three days we've done fewer kilometres each day, and for the last two days we've been all over the shop. We haven't even skied as a group. We need to rest, otherwise we'll be even weaker tomorrow.'

Suddenly all the anger and frustration came pouring out. 'I've let you down, my blisters have slowed us down throughout the race, I've got pneumonia, frostbite and now I can't pull my weight. Why has it happened? I trained so hard for this? I'm so sorry,' I said, all in a rush. Emotion had finally got the better of me; tears were streaming inside my goggles.

I felt Ben put his arm round me and hug me. He was crying as well. 'I love you,' he said. 'You haven't let us down; without you we wouldn't have been ready for this.'

Ed joined in the hug; we were all in tears now. I couldn't see it at the time, but he was right: we needed to stop. I was in pieces and the others, it seemed, weren't far behind.

This was a different Ed. He'd had a tough first week as he came to terms with the hours of skiing, the length of the race and his perceived position in the team, but two weeks later here he was, laying down the law to us both. It was brilliant to see that transformation in him. Both Ben and I had seen that quality at the selection weekend, and here he was, the man we'd picked to accompany us to the ends of the earth: the rightful third member of Team QinetiQ.

*

I don't think I'll ever look back at my collapse with any pride, but what I have learned is that sometimes admitting you're not as strong as you think is the tougher and more intelligent choice than pushing on. I could have skied on until 2 a.m. that night, but what would have happened to me and the team the next day? If I'd had any doubts that stopping was the right thing to do they were removed when I fell asleep at the stoves and was promptly banished to my sleeping bag until morning.

Whether I felt guilty in my sleep or not is impossible to tell, but it was the last emotion I remember before falling asleep, and the first one when I woke up. We had covered only 36 kilometres yesterday. I'd handed another few hours to the Norwegians, and I felt terrible.

At the time I didn't realize that my breakdown occurred on such a historic date for the British in Antarctica. 17 January was the date Scott arrived at the South Pole to see the Norwegian flag. What he, Oates, Wilson, Bowers and Evans would have made of someone not being able to cope with sore feet and a slight cold after only a few weeks on the plateau I dread to think – especially when you consider they set out on 1 November 1911 and Scott is thought to be the last to have died on 29 March 1912, still marching back to the coast 150 days later. I guess it shows how soft society has become in a hundred years; personally, I blame the PlayStation and *Big Brother*.

Meanwhile Ed was apologizing for being too forceful the previous night, saying that there wasn't a discussion and that he just made the decision.

'Ed, it was the right one,' I said. 'We all feel better this morning and I was too stubborn, egotistical and stupid to make the tough call. I'd like to think I could make it next time but someone had to step up and you did,' I said, believing every word. 'Now shut up and eat your porridge.'

34

GETTING OUR NOSES IN FRONT

JAMES 'I've got some good news, some indifferent news, some bad news and then again there might be some other news that makes all our news totally irrelevant. What do you want to hear first?' I asked, trying to keep the mood in the tent positive because no matter how I dressed it up, what I had to say wasn't going to lift our spirits.

'Just get on with it,' Ben said with an understandable mixture of impatience and tension. At the same time yesterday morning I'd worked out we had at least an extra 50 kilometres to ski in addition to what we had thought, and it sounded as if he didn't want a repeat of that.

'The good news is that the distance hasn't increased since yesterday; in fact it's decreased because of what we covered yesterday . . . But we've still got further to go than we had forty-eight hours ago. Everyone follow?' I said, meaning it as a rhetorical question.

The only response was a joint 'Hmph.'

'I've been doing the maths and here's the breakdown. We'll start nice and simple, and then it'll get more complicated.' The geography teacher was starting to come out in me. 'After the delay before the start, the race was shortened from 800 kilometres to 750 kilometres, with two halves of 375 kilometres. The first half, which we've done, was 375 kilometres, so that should leave us with a second half of 375 kilometres. You all with me?' Nods all round; the private schools of the south-east can breathe a sigh of relief.

'So far we've done 196 kilometres since the checkpoint, so in theory we should have 179 kilometres to go. Because of the exclusion zone, which we still haven't been granted permission to cross, we have another 270 kilometres to go and possibly a handful more than that. So the second "half" of the race will now be at least 421 kilometres. If the Americans let us ski through, we'll be looking at skiing 401 kilometres. So in theory it's going to be a couple of days longer than we thought. All good?' I asked and was greeted by more nods.

'I know it feels as if we've not covered much ground over the last few days and most of that is my fault, but we're only about twelve to fourteen hours' skiing behind where we were after five days in the first half when we thought we were going really well. So we need to keep it in perspective: we're not doing too badly, it just feels worse because we're tired and hungry. OK?' I asked more as a way of buying me a bit of time to deliver the bad news.

'Yeah,' came the reply. For the first time there were some positive vibes in their voices. Having the figures laid out seemed to be helping. Unfortunately, that was not going to last.

'Now, we know the maximum mileage we've got left to do is 225 kilometres; we've got enough main meals for five days, snack bags for four days and we'll be out of soup and hot chocolate in a couple of days. So we've got virtually full rations for five days. And here comes the bad news: in order to get to the Pole and keep eating well, we have to ski 45 kilometres every day for five days. In the entire race we've managed that distance only four times. So these are our options . . .' I laid it out as clearly as I could but obviously not that clearly. Ben interrupted.

'Why have we got so few meals left? We had twelve at the checkpoint,' Ben said.

'I made us a double meal at the checkpoint – one from this supply bag, and one left over from the first half,' Ed said.

'And we had a couple of double meals when we thought we were trucking along. We may not still have them to eat now, but if it helps at least you've had the benefit of the calories!' I said, attempting a cheery air. 'Look, we can say screw it, eat normally and ski 45 kilometres every day regardless of how bad we're feeling; or we can divide the meals and snack bags up, and have seven days of smaller meals – but I'm afraid we'll be out of drinks in two days whatever we do. If we make seven meals up we can still go for 45 kilometres a day, and we may be low on gas but at least we'll have a buffer for bad weather. If we stick to just the five days of food and a storm comes in, we'll be stuck in the tent not eating. What do you guys think?' I asked, knowing what I thought we should do but wanting to see what the others thought.

'I'm hungry all the time; I could eat twice as much at the moment,' Ben said.

'We all feel like that, but we've got to work out how to balance the distance and food,' I said, probably sounding slightly frustrated. 'We need to sort a strategy out, and saying "I'm hungry" doesn't really help much.'

'I don't want to start eating less, so we need to do 45 kilometres a day,' Ben said simply, and I agreed with him.

'So we leave no food reserve, and if a storm hits we're going to be tent-bound and hungry. Everyone happy with that?' I asked, wanting to make sure we all understood the consequences of our decision.

'The weather's changed and yesterday was horrible, but we were still able to ski. I'll take a risk and if we get stuck then we'll have to adjust to the situation,' Ed said.

'That's it then, target set: five days until the Pole. Let's do it!' I said, really trying to make them believe I felt better today and that they didn't have to worry about me. As convincing as positive words are though, I think they were reserving judgement until they'd seen me on the skis.

I wouldn't say I felt like a different person when I started skiing, but the extra rest, whether psychological or physiological, had definitely made a difference, and while I wasn't leading the charge I didn't have the same problems in keeping pace as I did yesterday. I was missing Pamela though, having ditched the Tramadol.

*

JAMES   We may have been only metres away from each other when we were skiing along, but there was little conversation. Everyone was tired, and a conversation involved extra energy. Occasionally we skied along listening to music, but often in silence. With the endless plateau spreading out in every direction, we were totally lost inside our own heads, which is not always a good thing. One piece of advice given to people who spend time isolated in a strange environment is not to make any life-changing decisions, such as quitting a job or leaving a partner, or if you do have an epiphany you should discuss it with someone whose opinion you trust before acting on your decision. It was easy to see why people's perspectives change in Antarctica. If I had a regular job I'd have quit it, but then I've spent my entire adult life trying to avoid one in the first place.

Rather than leaving employment, or Bev, the isolation and the pain in my feet made me think about my niece, Eva, and my sister, Louise. I'd entered the race because of the challenge of racing in these conditions but after Eva's death, raising money in her memory became a major motivation, especially because the treatment which was used to try to save her was highlighted by where I was headed. For one in six babies born with asphyxia during labour, cooling of the core body temperature can reverse the effect. Unfortunately this hadn't worked for Eva, but raising money for research in this area could stop other parents going through what my sister and brother-in-law had suffered. The link between cooling and Antarctica was easy to talk about, and so Ben, Ed and I teamed up with Sparks, the children's charity that funds medical research for kids. With their logo on our race suits I thought of Eva every time I saw it. I also had a picture of her in my pulk, wanting to make sure she got to experience the journey.

Thinking about Louise and Eva was a reminder of how lucky I am, and of what true pain is. I'd watched my sister go through a pain that at best will lie dormant for long periods, but will never go away. For eight months I'd wanted to help out, but apart from being there for her there was nothing I could really do. By getting to the Pole I would finally be doing something practical to help, but I had to actually make it to collect the money that had been pledged. So I resolved that a few blisters were not going to stop me, no matter how much they hurt. I should be for ever grateful for my healthy little boy, stop moaning and get my ass to the Pole.

*

BEN I had become increasingly frustrated by our poor timekeeping. We had been consistently late leaving and our '10-minute' breaks were becoming 30-minute theatre intervals, without the alcohol. I started to give the boys countdowns which, I hoped, would annoy them into efficiency. I think it just annoyed them.

JAMES Ben had suddenly started working for the Swiss Federal Railway, giving us a minute-by-minute countdown to when our ten minutes' rest were up. I wasn't being deliberately tardy; it's just that I'd either forgotten to do something, or left a strap on my pulk undone. That was no longer possible with Station Master Fogle shouting out 'Five minutes to go! Two minutes to go! One minute!' Annoyingly, he was, of course, totally right. After ten hours we had covered an extra kilometre just by being more efficient.

Towards the end of the day there were fewer platform announcements, and for a very good reason: Ben was convinced he'd managed to get frostbite on the end of his nose.

BEN My nose was peppered with large black marks and the front was covered in pus. I had damaged it more than I thought. I was embarrassed by my stupidity, and worried by the implications. I knew I needed to keep it warm and protected, but that was virtually impossible. Tired, cold and hungry, I became convinced I'd lose my nose.

I berated myself for my carelessness. My nose had been saved from the ravages of Leishmaniasis – only to be lost to frostbite! What would Marina think? Could I carry on presenting TV programmes with half a nose? My mind ran away in a dark fog of pessimism.

JAMES　I had to be honest, it didn't look great – and, unlike the case of my finger, if it turned out to be serious and long lasting it wasn't something that could easily be hidden away.

We may have suffered fewer reminders about how quickly our breaks were disappearing, but they were replaced by having to answer the same two questions for the rest of the race: 'Is it getting any worse?' or 'Is it covered up?' Making sure his proboscis was taken care of became his obsessive hobby for the rest of the race. As I helpfully pointed out, the horse had already left the stable and there wasn't a lot he could do to reverse the damage out here. But would you listen to me, given that I already had blisters, pneumonia and frostbite?

Looking back I don't think the injuries we were picking up at this stage were down to stupidity and neglect. We were skiing for so much longer each day than normal expeditions do and inevitably corners were being cut, important precautions neglected and risks taken.

After fifteen hours of skiing we took one of those risks.

BEN　It sounds like a cliché, but the Antarctic silence is deafening. Every noise is magnified and the ears become incredibly sensitive. The noise of the ice crunching under skis is unique and the ears become tuned to the different textures of snow.

It was 3 a.m. I was leading, and I was on my last legs.

Suddenly the noise of the snow changed. From a dull crunch, it became a hollow snap. Something was wrong. My exhaustion-addled mind failed to comprehend what was happening and I carried on. The unusual sound continued until my mind finally worked out what was happening.

'Crevasse!' I shouted, stopping dead in my tracks. We were on an ice bridge.

I gingerly moved to the side, onto an icy tussock.

'WHHHHHHHHooooooooooooooooooossssshhhhhhhh.' I could actually see the snow collapsing all around me, like sand through an egg timer.

I swore softly to myself over and over, my mouth parched as I felt the snow bridge giving way under my feet. Quite simply, I have never been so scared in my life.

I moved left, and heard the awful booming noise once again. We froze to the spot. I looked around at Ed, who was visibly shocked.

'We rope up,' I said, still trembling.

'We definitely rope up,' said Ed. 'That was the scariest thing that's ever happened to me.'

We had got safely across the crevasse field in the first half of the race, of course, but this was different – I had actually felt the snow disappearing from beneath my skis.

'We don't need to rope up,' announced James. 'I'll lead,' he said, 'and if the ice collapses, then I'll just take one for the team. Follow me and I'll lift my pole if I hit a crevasse.'

And with that, he disappeared off. Ed and I were dumbstruck. We had both just nearly died and James had marched off without listening to us. I couldn't believe his cavalier manner.

'James!' I hollered. There was no reply. He had his headphones on and had disappeared into the world of the Red Hot Chili Peppers. 'Take one for the team?' I repeated under my breath. 'Take one for the team! He's talking about falling to his death in a snowy chasm, not downing a pint in the pub.'

Ed's family had been rightly concerned about him coming to Antarctica. Ed had joked that his mother was unlikely to sleep until he was safely at the Pole. He had committed to us and in turn we had a commitment to him. We had made a promise to his family.

Somehow James had hijacked the team decision again, despite our opposition. Before we left the UK, the scientists and psychologists at QinetiQ had been concerned about our decision not to elect a leader. According to their research, having a strong leader would be mandatory to the success of any expedition. We had made a decision at an early stage that we wanted to be a team of equals, but the crevasse field had been the first time we *needed* someone with authority.

'James!' I cried again. There was no response. He was now nearly 100 metres ahead of us, skiing obliviously into the horizon.

JAMES   I wasn't being blasé, or at least I didn't think so at the time. The ground felt totally solid on the more obviously icy areas, and where there was more snow on the surface I prodded with poles and made my way steadily across. I honestly didn't feel the surface shift once and over the next 1.5 kilometres the terrain returned to the endless, icy playground we'd been skiing on all day. I turned round to give a thumbs up to Ed behind me and tell him we were back on seemingly solid ground; but I got only a half-hearted lift of the ski pole in reply.

BEN   2 a.m. came and went and there was still no sign of James letting up. We had an agreement that we would ski 45 kilometres *or* until 2 a.m. That was our witching hour and we all agreed that it was demoralizing to ski beyond that target unless we all agreed ahead of time. That 2 a.m. finish had become a sort of beacon of hope, signalling food, warmth and a little rest. To have even five minutes snatched from you felt like a mugging.

2.05 a.m., 2.10 a.m., 2.15 a.m. Ed and I stopped in our tracks. James was still tracking on and there was no sign of him stopping. Ed and I looked at each other. I was fuming.

'James!' I hollered again. My words were stolen by the Red Hot Chili Peppers once again.

Finally, at 2.20 a.m. we saw him dig his poles into the snow.

JAMES   'Forty-five kilometres guys, great job,' I said.

'Great,' Ed replied in a sulk, and Ben said nothing. They were clearly pissed off that we hadn't roped up, and the tent went up in silence. I was last inside, thinking I'd let them relax before I went in. I'm not sure whether the reverse happened and they wound each other up, but when I clambered in the atmosphere felt hostile.

'We should have roped up,' Ed said aggressively.

'I agree with Ed, it was risky,' Ben added.

'I didn't think it was as dangerous as last time, and if you two felt that strongly you should have said. It would have been a 2–1 vote in your favour,' I countered. 'Don't have a go at me if you weren't decisive enough. We got here perfectly safely.'

'Yeah, but we might not have,' Ed said.

'But we did, let's enjoy the fact we cranked off 45 kilometres and got here just after 2 a.m.,' I said, trying to sound upbeat. We should have been patting ourselves on the back and instead we were going to sleep pissed off with each other. Or to be more accurate, they were pissed off with me.

BEN I was too tired to argue with James. So I decided to get my own back by bringing back a little timekeeping to the group.

JAMES Overnight Station Master Fogle had clearly rediscovered his timetables. The other area where we'd start to get sloppy was leaving on time.

'It's 9.15!' he chirped. Then three minutes later, 'It's 9.18!' Two minutes after that, 'It's 9.20! Ten minutes until we're out of the tent!'

'Bloody hell, Ben, give it a rest!' I shouted. 'If you're trying to make a point, just say it. If not I don't need to be told the time every two minutes.'

'OK,' he said, 'I just want to leave on time today.'

There was still an unnecessarily hostile atmosphere in the tent. I'm not sure where the flash of uncharacteristic maturity came from, but I thought it would make the day pass more easily if I apologized for not entering into more of a discussion about roping up. 'Fellas,' I started, trying to sound relaxed and friendly, 'I'm sorry we didn't rope up last night. I obviously pushed you into a decision. It won't happen again.'

'It's OK. Let's have a good day – push but be sensible,' Ed said, sounding as if he meant it, which was good enough for me.

I didn't really mean it, I'm sorry to say. I still felt the ground was solid and if they'd both wanted to of course we would have

roped up. Looking back on that moment now, I'm almost embarrassed that I wasn't the one pushing to be roped up, as I had the
most to lose at home. If something had happened to me I'd have left
a wife and, come March, two children. Since having had Croyde
the sense of my own mortality is far stronger and I'm surprised and
shocked that it didn't kick in then. A tent and a warm chilli con
carne isn't a good enough excuse to take a big risk.

*

Food was very quickly becoming an issue, but in a slightly different
way from normal. Although incredibly tired I wasn't lacking
energy, and the subtle difference is important. We were now consuming about the same number of calories that our bodies could
absorb, but I was still hungry. This was purely psychological: the
comfort of being able to keep shoving food in, even if it would just
pass right through. Psychological or not, I was now savouring a
prune that I hadn't even bothered getting out of my snack bag only
a week ago. How quickly things change!

Apart from mixing our sweets and savouries we made another
mistake with our food, highlighted by the grated reindeer that the
Norwegians had taken with them: we hadn't brought enough fat.
During the race I didn't think we were losing much weight, but
shockingly, as Ben changed his top, I saw that there was no fat on
him at all, and all his ribs were bursting through.

BEN   I had been feeling much colder for days, despite skiing with
the thick duffle jacket on. I could feel my bones digging into the
ground at night and knew I was losing weight, but we were all
shocked when James pointed at me. I didn't have hypothermia – my
body was eating itself to stay warm.

JAMES   'Jesus, Ben!' I shouted.
    'W-w-what?' he stammered back, shocked by my tone.
    'Man, you've lost so much weight!' I said, still blown away by
the change in his body.

We were going to take butter to add to the main meals but we reasoned, correctly as it turned out, that the butter would melt and potentially leak while the pulks were sitting at the airport, so decided against it. Another way we could have added a similar level of calories was with peanut butter, chucking it into the porridge; inexcusably, Ben and I didn't want to do that because we don't like the taste. In the first place that's not an acceptable reason for not putting it in, and secondly, right now I'd have eaten a jar of it. The Norwegians may have hated their reindeer garnish, but they only lost around a stone each during the race.

*

At last my chest was starting to recover. My cough had all but gone, and we only had three or a maximum of four days left. Short of food we may have been, but I knew we were going to make it and personally I felt I was back on form. Better late than never, I suppose. The yin yang of Chinese philosophy was back, as it was the turn of the other two to struggle. The three days of 45 kilometres were starting to take their toll, and even though we were only a few days away from our goal, the light at the end of their respective tunnels was starting to recede. I needed to keep them both positive. Regrettably, my bag of psychological tricks had run out on about day three, so I was going to struggle to motivate them. Fortunately, though, Sarah came to the rescue during our daily safety call.

Ed was doing the honours and reporting our current position: daily distance, projected position and distance in the next twenty-four hours. At the end of the call, Sarah said, 'Can you call back when you set up camp?'

'That won't be until about 2 a.m. That OK?' Ed asked, ever the gentleman. 'Anything we need to know?'

'Just some news I think you'll like,' she said cheerily.

Cue wild speculation as to what the news was. Ben thought they might let us use the phone to call home for a few minutes, but again, why wait until 2 a.m. to tell us? We were operating on GMT so being given a free call when everyone was asleep was useless –

unless that was Tony's cunning plan: look like a nice guy without actually paying for it. The other two didn't go along with my suggestion that everybody else had dropped out of the race and we were the only ones still going. As I said, I was in a happy place that day.

That wasn't true for the other two. Ed's Achilles heel was literally his Achilles heel – it had plagued him throughout our preparation and during the afternoon I noticed he was protecting his right leg by limping slightly. We had to stop and wait while he tried to pad his boot out to make sure the heel was protected, and it took twenty minutes to bodge something together. Despite huddling in the emergency shelter Ben was feeling the cold and skied off to keep warm, while I kept Ed company to make sure his new Jimmy Choos fitted him properly.

They were better, if not brilliant. He was suffering more than he had done in Switzerland and so only utter determination could keep us moving and knock off another 45 kilometres. Having skied as a close-knit group for the last three days, we were now getting spread out over the plateau. I waited for Ed and took some weight from him to ease the pressure on his Achilles. Meanwhile, Ben had stopped a few hundred metres ahead and was bent over double. Was he being sick? Dehydration?

'Felt better?' I asked, skiing up alongside.

'I'm just feeling a bit sick and dizzy,' he replied, sounding pretty calm about it.

'Are you still cold?' I asked as he was again skiing in his down jacket, while I didn't feel particularly cold.

'I'm not really warming up, no,' he answered.

'How much have you eaten today?' I asked. It sounded as if he'd run out of energy.

'A fair bit, but I'm making sure I've got a bit more left for the next couple of days,' he replied, sounding confident in his logic.

'That's great, Ben, but there's no point running yourself into the ground. Don't hoard it, shove a load down.' He was nodding before I'd even finished speaking.

It wasn't nice seeing Ben and Ed suffer, but being able to take some weight clearly made me believe that at long last I was contributing properly to the team – just 700 kilometres too late. I broke trail for the last four hours and I was in a great place: the plateau was flatter and brighter and the horizon stretched out for miles. It may have been colder but beneath my gorilla mask and goggles I was the perfect temperature and protected from the environment. I felt the same way about being in Antarctica as Neil Armstrong and Buzz Aldrin must have done when they exited Apollo 11 – honoured to be there.

BEN   The race was really starting to take its toll on me. We were ticking off the 45 km each day but I could feel the energy draining from my weakened body. The days of careful pacing were over. We were on the home straight and I knew it would be all downhill from here, metaphorically at least. If only we had some of James's imaginary hills to ski down.

I knew my body well and had preserved it for as long as possible, but the cracks were really starting to appear. Our resolution before the race was being fulfilled: we would arrive at the finish line physically and mentally shot.

I have wondered since the race whether I'd have coped in James's condition, and the answer is probably no. I felt under such immense pressure not to fall ill during the race because everyone expected it to happen. There had been a universal assumption across the board that I would suffer the most and need rescuing.

I could almost hear the 'told you sos' and see the shaking of heads. If there was one thing that pushed me on through those final days it was a drive and determination to prove everyone wrong and reach the South Pole.

My body was taking a beating from the harsh environment, though. The final kilometre each day was agony. I was sometimes quite literally on my knees as we pitched up and clambered into the tent like zombies. My back had also started to ache and I had taken to sucking on the legendary Tramadol to alleviate the pain. Those drugs are a miracle and I would spend the latter three hours of each day in a dreamlike trance. I never met Pamela Anderson, though I did begin to see white rabbits across the plateau. I could also have sworn I heard voices, then a dog barking. I began to see people and then a phone rang.

'Hi, Marina,' I said. 'How are you?' I proceeded to have a ten-minute imaginary phone conversation with my wife. It was weird and also slightly alarming.

JAMES   For a third straight day in a row we'd clocked off the distance and, looking at Ben, head nodding as he kept drifting off with a bowl full of curry on his lap, it had taken its toll. It was time to call up the organizers and see what the much speculated about news was.

Ed called up and I had the GPS ready in case they needed our location. Annoyingly, the stoves drowned out any chance of my hearing what was being said at the other end – meaning I was forced to endure Ed's one-sided conversation and guess the gist.

'Hey, Sarah, it's Ed from Team QinetiQ.'

'Yes, all pitched up, yeah not too bad. What's the news?'

'Right, that's definite, is it? And there's no chance of it changing?'

'OK, thanks, Sarah, yeah, sleep well,' Ed finished off and his tone was hard to read but his eyes were not: life had sprung back into them.

'What did they say?' Ah, Sleeping Beauty had risen from his curried slumber.

I think Ed thought about a bluff but in the end probably didn't have the energy.

'The Americans have given us permission to ski through the restricted zone!'

'That's not going to change, is it?' I asked.

'According to Sarah, no. We're heading to the Pole!' Ed said excitedly.

'How far is it to go now?' Ben asked.

I changed the waypoint and route on the GPS, taking us directly to the South Pole. 'Holy shit!' I exclaimed.

'What?' asked Ben in a voice that half expected an extra few kilometres to have been slapped on.

'Seventy kilometres! We've got 70 kilometres left, what are the chances of that?' I said, still not really believing it. Amazingly we'd been left with exactly the same distance that we'd done in one stint before the halfway checkpoint. That was both good and bad; good because we'd done that before, but bad as it ran us into the ground and we were more tired now, and much thinner.

'Right, one skiing session left. The next time we'll be putting up the tent will be at the South Pole. Let's have another meal, we've got one spare now!' Ben said excitedly. Evidently we had all forgotten just how horrible that 70 kilometres had been last time.

35

THE LAST PUSH

JAMES Kingsley Amis once said that death has something to be said for it: you don't have to get out of bed for it.

I understood what he meant as I lay there listening to our alarm squawk above me in the Hanging Gardens of Babylon. There was the normal overriding desire to press the snooze button, but I wanted to be at the South Pole as quickly as possible. The only problem was that calling the 70 kilometres we had to cover 'a day's skiing' was like calling the banking crisis merely a 'market adjustment'.

I'm in full agreement with the famous American convenience store that a day is between seven and eleven. Out here I'd managed with the help of twenty-four-hour sunlight to stretch that out to 2 a.m., but under no circumstances can a day be considered between twenty-six and twenty-eight hours, the length of time it was going to take us to ski 70 kilometres. The French don't work that much in a whole week.

I should have felt more positive about the distance. I'd been feeling stronger every day and was storming at the end of yesterday's ski. Problems with his nose aside, Ben was being relentlessly optimistic on one side of the tent. Ed was being sentimental about the journey he'd been on and about to live up to his Tiny Tears moniker, whereas I was just being morose. The 70 kilometres to the checkpoint had left its mental scars. I needed to stop focusing on the incredibly tough four or five hours I had gone through as we approached the halfway point, or how terrible I felt when I eventually got there, and start visualizing skiing up to the Pole –

a moment I'd thought about so many times over the last eighteen months.

I needed to get out of the tent.

My mood changed as soon as I stepped out: it was the clearest day of the race, a brilliant blue sky creating a laser-sharp horizon. How could I be worried about a 70-kilometre ski when I should be down on my knees giving thanks for the privilege of being out here? No matter what the circumstances, the stunning beauty of Antarctica has the power to suspend the reality of the situation. Shackleton's ship the *Endurance* had been crushed by pack ice leaving the twenty-eight men with limited food and seemingly no way off the ice, yet Dr Alexander Macklin wrote in his diary a week after their ship had disappeared that 'It has been a lovely day, and it is hard to think that we are in a frightfully precarious situation.' Why was I moaning about a 70-kilometre ski?

Racing for the checkpoint we'd been tired, but not destroyed, when we put the tent up after 40 kilometres to make up a hot meal – but when we got skiing again we felt terrible. This time we decided to eat a hot meal under the emergency shelter and crank out the 70 kilometres in one hit. Obviously that decision was made inside our orange happy bubble where we didn't have to consider the consequences of the decisions we were making.

I reset the display on the GPS's tripometer, swapping 'distance to destination' to 'barometric pressure'. I didn't want to see exactly how far we had left every time I checked our course, and the anticipation and excitement at reaching the Pole would cause the last few kilometres to crawl by. The best way of coping, at least for the first few hours, was to try to disengage the brain, think of something else and let some of the distance just drift past.

BEN 'The South Pole, the South Pole, the South Pole,' I kept repeating in my head as we set off. The words tasted strange in my mouth as I repeated them in time to my skiing, like a mantra.

The South Pole itself is synonymous with such histrionics, and steeped in legend and lore; a place that has created heroes, confounded explorers and ended dreams. As a child I had devoured books about the great polar explorers and been seduced and enchanted by her, and now, after nearly six weeks in Antarctica there was just 70 kilometres between me and the bottom of the world.

For so long, the South Pole had been drawing me towards her with an invisible force; the pull of her remoteness and the romance and allure of her history. For eighteen long months I had thought about her day and night. She had invaded my dreams and plagued my life. She had become a part of me, as she had for countless polar adventurers before me.

It was hard to believe that we were so near to this magical place. I had become obsessed by her lure and now the dream was approaching reality, but not before we endured one last hurdle.

We still had nearly thirty hours of skiing between us and the finish. It was a huge stretch. The weather was closing in and we had stretched ourselves to the limit. We knew from bitter experience that we were in for an ordeal.

'The South Pole.' I tried the words out again under my breath as we readied the pulks, but they still felt strange. This was the place of Scott, Amundsen and Shackleton – not Fogle. I still didn't feel I deserved to be or belonged here.

JAMES Skiing behind Ed I had seen that he was reticent to put all his weight on to his right leg, and his body language showed he was in a huge amount of pain. There was a lack of rhythm to his skiing, which meant he'd lose ground on Ben, and then push on and make it up again. He'd also ski along OK for a few minutes, then stop for a few seconds and shake his head as though he was trying to clear it. We were about an hour through the first two-hour session when he stepped out of the tracks Ben was cutting and waved me through.

'Heel giving you gip?' I asked as I skied through.

'No, I've got stomach ache, I feel drowsy and I'm constipated,' he replied, sounding thoroughly pissed off with the situation.

'Bloody hell, you don't do things by halves!' I said helpfully, giving him a whack on the arse with my pole as I skied past.

For most of the second hour Ed skied with his head down. I'm no body-language expert but that didn't stop me guessing what was going through Ed's mind, and I deduced that he wasn't enjoying it. By skiing for twenty-eight hours we were all going to have periods where we would have to grapple with our minds, forcing them to stay positive.

At that moment I felt great and was determined to enjoy my last ski in Antarctica, even if the distance was going to make parts of it virtually impossible to smile through. I wanted to remind Ed how much work he had put into this trip – not just the 730 kilometres to get to this point, but the six months before we left. He should try to enjoy the day. If I was going through a tough patch would I want to be reminded of that? Probably not, but Ed had told me to tell him, when he was finding it hard, that this was his Olympics.

At the break I asked him if he was doing OK.

'I'm struggling to concentrate, and feel a bit dizzy and nauseous,' he answered. I wasn't sure if that was on top of the drowsiness, constipation and stomach ache. I shouldn't complain because earlier in the race we'd asked Ed to be more specific about how he felt; it was hard for us non-healthcare professionals to gauge what exactly was wrong when he just said 'I feel shit.'

'I think the Tramadol is affecting me,' he replied.

'Welcome to the club, big man, you'll feel OK in a few hours, just enjoy the daydreams!' I said smiling, but didn't get one back in return. He had obviously suffered the same dilemma as I had when I had really sore feet and didn't want to slow the team up or feel too much pain, so had taken some painkillers. Unlike Ed, however, I didn't know what the potential adverse effects were, and Ed seemed to be experiencing most of them. Whether they were real, perceived or exaggerated symptoms because he knew his body would probably be experiencing them in some form, didn't really matter; they were there, whatever the cause.

I didn't want Ed to go through today in a haze of negativity after he'd worked so hard, so I pressed on. 'Mate, we've got to make the most of today. How many more times are we going to arrive at the South Pole? I can tell you now, this is the only time I'm doing it, and we owe it to ourselves to enjoy it. Keep your head up and you'll be back on form soon enough,' I said breezily.

He responded to that prod like a donkey on Blackpool beach and just nodded, skiing off like Eeyore from *Winnie the Pooh* to complete the image. What Ed had shown throughout the race, though, was that he would pull himself through eventually. We just had to let him do it in his own time.

BEN   'Norwegians!' I hollered. Again, it felt as if we were in a Western.

A single track cut across the ice. It was peppered with pole marks and from our rudimentary tracking skills we established that it had been made by two people: Rune and Stian.

From the thin covering of snow over the tracks, I guessed they were more than a few hours old.

We knew they were likely to be ahead of us, but it was still disappointing to find a form of proof. We had all secretly hoped for a miracle, but the tracks seemed to put an end to that.

*

JAMES   It was my turn to join Ed in feeling down. With the Norwegians leaving the checkpoint before us and the time we'd lost – mostly due to me – I hadn't expected to be ahead of them, but there was always a chance that one or even both of them had become ill or had a problem. If that had happened, combined with the brilliant progress we'd made over the last four days, there was a possibility (admittedly remote) that we would get to the Pole first. Those hopes appeared to have been crushed just 50 kilometres from our destination.

'Shall we head off?' I asked.

'Yep, let's go,' said Ben.

'Use their tracks, or stick on the bearing we were on?' I asked. The tracks were on slightly different bearings.

'Let's stick to our route,' Ben said. I agreed. We'd cut our own trail since those first few hours of the race following the Norwegians, and none of us wanted to follow a marked path to the Pole.

Apparent confirmation that the Norwegians had beaten us was hard to take. I wondered whether it was better to know now, take time to come to terms with it and then enjoy arriving at the Pole, rather than seeing their tent and the Pole simultaneously and adjusting to coming second as we arrived. Who was I kidding: both situations were hugely disappointing.

Rather worryingly, the only comparison I had was playing in football matches where losing in the last minute felt far worse than going 2–0 down early and not being able to get back into the game. Obviously there was always a chance of winning, but in the latter situation I at least realized I might lose. Based on that analogy we were about 5–0 down going into the last 50 kilometres; it was mathematically still possible to win, but . . .

We didn't have too much time to dwell on future situations though; we had one to deal with now. The weather was starting to close in quickly, like a white curtain being lowered all around us. We had gone from skiing in a picture-perfect blue sky to a total whiteout in fifteen minutes, and it was like skiing into a white wall. The sun disappeared and the temperature plummeted – Antarctica clearly wasn't finished with us yet. Having been suckered into thinking we were going to have beautiful weather for our final ski, the rug had just been pulled from beneath us with 40 kilometres (about fourteen hours) left.

Navigating a course wasn't a problem; the wind was consistent and we could steer off that, but staring into a white wall with nothing to focus on made the lead man feel nauseous after about half an hour.

We stopped for our hot meal – well, a lukewarm meal – after 35 kilometres. Huddled together under our emergency shelter in a whiteout at minus 40 eating a tepid chicken korma, I said, 'I'm going to miss these moments!' The other two laughed.

'Antarctica's not letting us get there easily, is it?' I asked.

'Wouldn't be fun if it did,' Ed answered.

'Hmm, right now I'm not so sure. I'd take a strong following wind and beautiful sunshine,' I replied.

I felt a lot better after a hot(ish) meal. It replenished me in a way my snack bag never did, and when I found out later that the Norwegians structured their day in this way, I could see why. Not having a hot meal in the tent would have sapped my morale after a while, but as Bernie said, 'You're not going there on bloody holiday.'

We'd allowed ourselves quarter of an hour for the meal break but as I wolfed mine down in about three minutes I found I just got cold in the extra time, and I wasn't the only one. Ben skied off in his big duvet jacket and I had to stop after thirty minutes to put mine on. Once I was wrapped up in a big sleeping bag I got too hot, and suffered the nightmare of steamed up goggles. Like using a shower in an unfamiliar hotel room I was either burning myself or dousing the bathroom in freezing water, and started to become infuriated with the situation. The combination of being stuck in a nausea-inducing white room and finding it impossible to settle on a comfortable temperature was winding me up. Fifteen hours earlier, setting off in picture-postcard Antarctic conditions, I felt so lucky to be here; now I hated the place and just wanted to reach the Pole and get the hell out of here.

I was busy swearing at the whiteout and Antarctica in general when Ed stopped in front of me and lent on his poles. I thought he was stretching his Achilles, so I skied alongside.

'Still hurting? Have you taken any painkillers other than Tramadol?' I enquired.

'The heel's OK,' he said. 'I've got really bad wind.' At first I thought I'd misheard because the way he said it sounded serious, and in my experience wind is only a serious problem at a posh dinner party or in bed with a new girlfriend. Out here on the plateau it had given me some pleasurable moments. I couldn't believe Ed thought it was a problem.

'There's always something!' I snapped and skied off.

BEN I'm not sure why James reacted so angrily. In retrospect it sounds rather funny, but for James it was the culmination of weeks of pent-up frustration and annoyance. We were just a few hours from the end of our great adventure, and tensions were running high.

To be frank, I was annoyed with both of them for spoiling what should have been the best day of the whole trip. This was a moment I had been dreaming about, and I wanted to savour the feeling of achievement. Instead, my daydreaming had been shattered by childish bickering over trapped wind!

I was particularly annoyed by James for his hypocrisy. James had suffered more than any of us with his health, and his problems had affected me more than he probably imagined. I used to worry myself silly about what would happen if James couldn't go on. What if James suddenly collapsed? What if James lost his fingers? There were dozens of 'what ifs', and I never had an answer.

It seemed churlish and unfair for James to berate Ed in this final stage, especially after all the caring Ed had provided for James. Ed, too, was surprised and hurt by James's response. For my part, I suspected that James was actually just fishing for an excuse to vent his frustration.

JAMES Ed's constant ailments had been a running joke between the three of us; there was always an issue with Ed, sometimes important, often amusing or not at all serious. But for me to say what I said in that situation was wrong; it was obviously more than just wind, probably connected to the constipation he moaned about earlier. Yes, it was frustrating that Ed had spent a lot of the day mentioning different problems he was having, but who was I to judge him? He'd never taken a cheap shot at me or judged me when I was struggling five days earlier.

I skied off admonishing myself for being so insensitive, and wondered if there was an underlying reason why I had inflamed the situation like that. There was no clear-cut answer. During our six weeks in Antarctica my respect for Ed had grown enormously. He'd always been brilliant company and I had total trust in him, but found it strange that he didn't seem to totally believe in himself, despite being physically strong and mentally tough. During the last week he'd found that belief and had been a tower of strength in the team, so to see him moaning about a variety of minor problems like wind, drowsiness and feeling sick seemed to be a step back.

In the heat of the moment I had used my own frustration at the conditions to vent some anger, no more, no less. It was neither big nor clever and I had to make sure I cleared the air before we reached the Pole.

Neither of us said anything as we sat down on our pulks at the next break. I'd planned to apologize straight away but at the last minute changed my mind, somehow convincing myself that I was in the right since he'd been moaning about nothing.

BEN The two of them sat in stony silence through the break. They were both furious with one another, and neither of them was going to let this one go. You could cut the atmosphere with a knife and I was angry that they had both allowed such a petty incident to escalate to this level. We were just a few hours from the finish line and they were spoiling a moment we had spent years working towards. It was laughable.

JAMES Ben said, 'What's happened between you two? I can practically cut the atmosphere with a knife.'

'I got frustrated with Ed having done nothing but moan all day, and made a stupid comment,' I said, addressing Ed, not Ben. Ed didn't say anything so I carried on. 'You're so much better than that, Ed. You've been amazing all week and it feels as if you've taken a step back today. We're all hurting but we've just got to get on with it.'

'I know, but my insides have felt terrible all day. I've found it impossible to focus on anything,' he replied.

'I'm sorry, mate, I shouldn't have taken a cheap shot. If I had a point to make I should have made it properly, and you know what

I think of you as I told you this morning in the tent,' I explained. 'I wanted us to enjoy this day because we won't have another one like it. But the weather's turned shit and we're all tense, knackered and I'm a dickhead.'

'It's OK, we could both have handled it better. I should have got on with it and you shouldn't have been such a twat. Let's hug it out, big guy.' Taking Ed up on his offer, we shared an emotional man hug, and set off again, this time for the South Pole.

36

JOURNEY'S END

BEN   There was still no sign of the South Pole. According to our GPS, we were just 20 kilometres away and we knew that the Scott–Amundsen station ought to be visible from over 30 kilometres away. Visibility was still poor, and we skied on into the white haze.

My feet had started to blister for the first time in the whole expedition. It was as if they knew the end was in sight, and had given up. Also for the first time, I got an insight into the pain that James had had to conquer to get here, over many hundreds of kilometres.

What was the South Pole going to look like? I knew that the United States had built a large base there, and that there is a famous mirrored ceremonial ball, where explorers traditionally have their 'hero photos' taken, but apart from that I had little idea of what to expect. It seems strange, now, that I had no firm image in my mind for a place that had occupied my thoughts every day for a year and a half. My goal had no face.

Over the course of the race I had often imagined what it would be like to arrive at the South Pole. From the famous tales, I envisaged a vast white expanse, with a solitary pole at the centre, surrounded by the flags of the polar nations. I pictured the flags snapping in the wind, and a bright sun reflecting off the mirrored ceremonial ball.

As a child I had been haunted by the image of Captain Scott and his team at the South Pole, their faces weatherbeaten and etched with fatigue and the pain of defeat, blackened skin a bleak testament to the hardship of their ordeal. I still find that photograph eerie.

JAMES   We knew we'd been walking in roughly the same direction since the race started because our shadows were cast in the same direction at the same time every day, but our only indication that that was definitely south was our GPS. Not seeing the base when I had expected to made me wonder if our GPS was accurate. Had we been walking around in circles since the checkpoint?

I was snapped out of my paranoia by Ben.

'James mate, Ed's struggling.' I looked round and Ed had fallen a hundred metres behind. We stopped and waited for him.

'Having a bad time?' I asked.

'Yeah, I can't keep up with that pace,' he replied.

'We're not going fast, buddy,' I said.

'Any slower and I think I'll start getting cold,' Ben chipped in.

'Do you fancy taking something from Ed?' I asked Ben.

'I don't think I can, not at the pace we were doing,' he replied honestly.

I wanted to get going. We had about 15 kilometres left and at this pace it was going to take about five hours. I just wanted to get there. I obviously wasn't thinking clearly because I said, 'I'll attach your pulk to mine and you have a rest.' I was out on my feet but I must have wanted to make up for being the weak link earlier in the race and prove my value to the team.

I hooked up Ed's pulk to mine and set off towing a train of two pulks.

'Shit, this is bloody heavy!' I said under my breath. I couldn't stop straight away – I had to do at least a kilometre before admitting defeat; the only positive was that at least I wasn't cold. The others must have thought I'd gone mad, but why didn't they stop me? I stopped after a kilometre and admitted defeat sheepishly, giving Ed his pulk back and just taking some weight instead.

We skied off and I realized I'd either taken too much weight, or destroyed myself with that macho display as Ed skipped off ahead of me and I heaved against the harness. I couldn't stop us again to swap weight around so I'd have to suffer the consequences of trying to be the hero.

BEN On we skied in silence. The weather had started to break and though bitterly cold the wind had subsided slightly and some blue sky appeared behind the thick grey cloud.

My nose was freezing. It was colder than it had ever been, and I knew I was damaging the tissue. The cotton buff across my nose simply wasn't thick enough to keep out the biting wind. I took an emergency hand warmer out of my pocket that I had carried from the beginning of the race, and I placed it under the buff to warm my nose. It was uncomfortable and looked ridiculous, but I was terrified about losing my poor old nose.

'You can always have plastic surgery,' said James chirpily, as I fiddled with my new nose warmer.

'Yeah, great,' I replied.

*

JAMES There it was, an irregular shape on the horizon. Blind Pew Fogle didn't even bother looking, but there was no mistaking it.

BEN Every hair on my arm stood on end. I still get goose pimples even thinking about it. Tears streamed down my face and my throat ached with emotion. We were still hours from the Pole, but it finally felt as if we were going to make it.

Expeditions and adventures are about key moments, events and individual snapshots that capture the essence and define a journey. For me, this was one of those moments, captured for ever in my mind. It was a moment of sheer wonder and excitement at the prospect of fulfilling the impossible. It was the moment I realized I might just do it.

The final 6 kilometres can only be described as hell. They were the longest few hours of my life. Feet and backs ached. Our bodies cried from fatigue and hunger. Our pulks felt twice as heavy and the land felt three times as steep. It was like hauling a car up Everest, towards a summit that never appears. It was sheer agony.

I would muster every ounce of energy to haul my pulk a couple of paces before bending double with exhaustion. I closed my eyes in pain as I battled with my mind and body to continue.

I almost ran over Ed, who was laying out flat in the snow. He had stopped for a break and had actually fallen asleep on the ground. It was minus 45 degrees, but our bodies didn't care. They were screaming out for us to stop, but we had to keep going.

Slowly, the abstract silhouettes began to take shape and I thought I could make out an airport control tower. An airport control tower? Was I hallucinating? I wondered as I battled on.

We were all on our last legs and for a time it felt as if we were never going to make it. We had slowed to less than 2 kph, the slowest we'd been throughout the whole race. We would ski for a few minutes and then collapse against our pulks. I have never experienced such a painful dilemma of mind over body, and I have certainly never had to fight so hard to continue.

Ed and James were both feeling it too, and together we would make a couple of metres before collapsing. It was agonizing, and not the way I imagined we'd finish the race. I had envisaged a glorious final dash to the Pole across the vast, white plateau.

I stared down at the snow. It was too painful to look at the buildings in the distance. My eyes settled on my jacket, 'Keep going if you love me,' Marina had scrawled on my sleeve.

'Keep going if you love me, keep going if you love me, keep going if you love me,' I repeated like a broken record. I needed something to keep me going and I embraced those words like a prayer.

I thought about everything I had been through to get to this point. I thought about Marina and her miscarriage. I thought about my month of treatment. I thought about all the hard work and training we had put into this. I thought of Jonny and Bernie both willing us on.

JAMES   By now we'd totally given up skiing as a group, and with each of us going through good and bad periods our positions changing accordingly. I had Tourette's because we'd started to walk uphill. 'I can't believe it's uphill to the bottom of the world, what the fuck's that about?' I ranted. I hadn't realized Ben was skiing alongside, and he just laughed.

There was a collection of buildings in front of us and the GPS was pointing us towards a large rectangular-shaped one. We had 2.5 kilometres to go, fifty minutes, that was all. I could make that, but we were all skiing so slowly it hardly felt as if we were moving. 'One step at a time,' I kept muttering.

We were starting to get amongst the outer buildings now but were still 1,000 metres from the Pole according to the GPS, and had to climb over a mound of snow. I dragged the pulk up to the top of the mound and for the twentieth time in the last two hours regretted trying to be the hero. On the way down it capsized aggressively and the twist in the tracers knocked me over. I lay flat on the snow and shut my eyes for a second. The next thing I heard was a voice saying: 'Wakey, wakey, no time for sleeping now.' I opened my eyes and squinted at the noise. Ben and Ed were standing, looking down at me.

'We've got about 1,500 metres left I reckon. Up you get,' Ed said.

'Uh, is there another team in sight?' I asked.

'Nope,' replied Ben.

'Then let me lie here for a bit, I'm very tired,' I very sensibly reasoned, but started to push myself up before Ed did the honours with the pole and hauled me vertical. Karma.

We decided to each lead for 500 metres and then ski side by side to the Pole. We were dead on our feet; even the thought of reaching the end wasn't spurring me on any more. The rectangular building turned out to be the Scott–Amundsen South Pole Station, the two-storey stilted home to the US research centre. In front of it was a semicircle of flags at the centre of which was the ceremonial South Pole. A hundred metres away from that was a collection of tents, one of which had a small Norwegian flag fluttering outside it. We'd been skiing for just under twenty-eight hours – and it felt like it.

We skied side by side for the last few hundred metres. I could hear Ben jabbering excitedly next to me saying something about 'We've worked so hard for this, enjoy it, enjoy it.' I remember thinking I could have done with that motivation a few hours ago. Ed was quiet; he later told us that he was crying as he skied into the Pole; good old Tiny Tears.

I wasn't feeling at all emotional; there was a crowd of people standing near the semicircle of flags as we approached. I remember thinking this was a surprising number of people considering it was the South Pole, and surely they weren't all to do with the race. I wasn't really looking where I was going, my peripheral vision keeping me close to Ben and Ed as I skied along with my head down. I looked up when I heard people clapping around us; I thought, Thank God, I can stop soon. The first face I saw had a Norwegian hat on but I didn't recognize him, which must have shown on my face because the face said, 'It's Stian. Well done.' His lips were scabbed and bleeding and he had frostbite on the cheeks of a swollen face. He looked a different person.

'Well done to you, man,' I replied, stopping to give him a hug.

'Ski in together!' I heard Ben shout in my direction. I turned and shuffled in their direction.

BEN   The ice was littered with small, coloured flags marking out the pipes that criss-crossed the site. Someone was waving at us. I could make out Roly's long boom in the distance. Dr Ian was beckoning us. It was confusing. Where was the actual Pole?

'You've got to go over the wooden bridges!' barked Tony, pointing us to the right.

'Where's the goddam Pole?' I kept wondering. We diverted to a small wooden crossing and then Alexis appeared with his stills camera. He was snapping away and I watched as he tripped over backwards, the camera smacking his face leaving a bloody mark across his cheek. Onwards we skied.

Over another small bridge. More flags. More people. More buildings but no sign of the ceremonial ball. My legs were like jelly. My throat ached and my nose throbbed with pain.

'Wait for James!' I shouted again as Ed ploughed on.

Two figures in familiar orange jackets appeared alongside. Their Norwegian flag hats identified them as Rune and Stian. We'd been beaten by the Norwegains but I didn't care. None of us cared. All we wanted was to get to the Pole and end this nightmare. They walked alongside us in silence.

'What's that? what's that? what's that?' I repeated like a maniac. I could make out something fluttering in the wind. Flags! It's flags, I thought. It looked like a dozen of them, and there beneath them was a red and white stick.

'THERE IT IS!' I bellowed, overcome with emotion. I was holding back the tears. My body tingled. I was stunned. Was it a dream?

James had dropped behind again. 'Wait for James!' I hollered again. We skied on together in silence.

'Hurry up!' barked Tony. 'Everyone's waiting.'

Onwards we skied. The Pole was just 100 metres away from us. We were silent. I looked at Ed and James who were lost in their own emotional turmoil.

'Come on,' repeated Tony, 'go around the car, hurry up.'

'Fuck off, Tony!' muttered James. Tony didn't hear.

James was dropping back again. 'We go together,' I said to Ed as James caught up.

'Come on, quick as you can,' ordered Tony.

'Tony, shut up!' I screamed, 'this is our moment, let us enjoy it and don't ruin it!' I yelled. I was furious.

There was a stunned silence from the two dozen people who had gathered around for these final steps to the Pole. I wasn't about to let anyone ruin this moment. I wanted to enjoy every last step.

We were side by side. We were just a few metres from the cere-monial ball. I could barely contain my emotion. I was breathless. The small crowd had gathered on the other side.

'Are you ready, boys?' I asked. They nodded and slowly, in silence, we slid towards the Pole.

My mind was spinning with thoughts. I was confused.

Five feet. Four feet. Three feet. Two feet. One foot.

The ball was in front of us. We couldn't get any closer. It was silent except for the wind snapping the flags. I could see our reflections in the ball. What now? We hadn't planned what happened next. It wasn't something we had ever spoken about and it wasn't something we could control.

In silence we unclipped our harnesses. I didn't take my eyes off the reflection in the ball. The small crowd stared in silence.

As the harness slipped away I broke into deep uncontrollable sobbing. I fell to my knees as Ed and James did exactly the same. We were overcome with emotion. The three of us sobbed as we kneeled in front of the South Pole.

We stood and embraced one another. We held each other's heads close as tears streamed down our cheeks. 'We did it, boys, we did it!' I sobbed.

It was a moment so spontaneous and unaffected that it caught everyone off guard. I looked around and was shocked to see everyone else in tears too.

I stared into the ball at my vacant reflection. My eyes were void of feeling but my head was bursting with emotion. We'd done it.

I was lost for words. It was a feeling of pure relief and satisfaction. Contrary to all expectation I had completed the journey. I wondered whether I was dreaming, whether I was in fact still lying on a bed at University College Hospital.

I knelt in front of the ceremonial pole like a worshipper in front of some religious deity. My mind was blank. I needed time to digest the magnitude of our achievement.

Rune and Stian were in tears as they watched us wallow in our emotion.

'Congratulations,' said Stian as he hugged me.

'You need to know something,' he said, 'there was another team of Norwegian polar explorers out here trying to set the land speed record from ocean to Pole,' he explained. 'It took them twenty-eight days to cover 1,000 kilometres. You guys covered 850 kilometres in eighteen days. You do the maths,' he smiled.

'You may have beaten us, but we're proud of our achievement,' I said.

'You shouldn't be proud,' he replied, 'you should be stunned.'

I beamed with pride. Here was a member of the Norwegian army complimenting us on our polar skills.

I looked at James. I wanted to know how he felt – after all we'd come second. Was he disappointed? He was a broken man and his face was blank and expressionless. For James it had become a game of survival in the pursuit of happiness. I knew what had been driving him. He had done it for Eva. He was dazed and confused but I could tell he was content.

We had achieved our goal. We had reached the Pole having exhausted every ounce of physical and mental energy. We were spent. I had nothing more to give and I knew I had given it everything. As a team we had pushed ourselves to the very limit of our endurance and we had made it together.

We had no regrets because there were no regrets. We had raced ourselves and won. We had stuck to the strategy and together we three polar virgins had made it to the South Pole.

'The South Pole' – suddenly the words began to feel more familiar and comfortable. The place that had haunted me for so long suddenly had a face and a soul and a heart. The dream had finally become a reality.

JAMES   I'd made a conscious effort to make the most of the last day's skiing, and had been determined to absorb everything about the final run-in, but what I hadn't thought about was how I'd feel when I touched the Pole and had finished. As we skied the final few metres I looked at the silver bowling ball on top of a barber's red and white stripy pole and thought 'that looks rubbish'. More fool me: as we skied up and touched the Pole together I felt an uncontrollable wave of emotion surge through my body. I hadn't felt that emotional in the last few days; explorers we had spoken to said that after 88 degrees south funny things start happening with your mind, but I hadn't experienced anything until now. I was sobbing and had no idea why. I reached out to hug Ben and saw that he was in the same state as me. 'We did it, buddy, we did it. You're amazing,' I said, hugging him close. I then reached out for Ed, who must have felt better that Ben and I had joined him because he turned on the waterworks. 'You were brilliant; I can't believe it's over,' I half sobbed, half mumbled into his ear. Then I felt Ben hug us both.

I could hear the click of cameras and people clapping and shouting. We hadn't seen this many people since the start of the race and suddenly they were all within two metres of us. I didn't want to come out of our hug. It felt the right place to be, and I wasn't ready to be with other people. There was so much I wanted to say to Ben and Ed about what they and the journey meant to me, yet no words said it better than holding each other tight, our heads together.

'We're here, we've done it,' Ben sobbed.

'Yeah, no more bloody skiing, it's rubbish!' I cried.

EPILOGUE

JAMES   When the Norwegians and I spoke after the race, I was delighted to see they looked as though they'd been in a battle, and even more pleased to hear that they had hated every minute of the race. We had taken them by surprise by skiing so many hours straight away, forcing them to adopt a strategy they didn't enjoy. Even when they'd overtaken us, they didn't feel they could relax.

I was equally as beaten up as Stian and Rune, but unlike them I had enjoyed the experience. I wasn't happy to have come second – if there's a time when I am, I'll stop competing. What I can say is that I'm pleased with the way we performed as a team and I learned things about myself that I wouldn't have learned if we'd won. The effect of those lessons will be far more valuable to me as a person than finishing one place higher in the South Pole Race.

We spent a huge amount of time planning our aims for the race, mostly because of my overbearing personality and competitiveness. It's difficult to sit in a room and hear that people find it difficult to be relaxed with you in a competitive environment. We had to find a goal we all agreed on because Ben's fear – with good reason – was that I'd become obsessed with the competition once the race started. In the end, we signed up to arriving at the Pole with no energy left. As my rowing coach used to say, 'If you can stand on the podium to receive silver, you don't deserve gold.' We also pledged to make none of the mistakes we made during training. If we did achieve both of these things, we'd not only get the result we deserved, but the best that we could have achieved.

We got to the Pole exhausted; I don't think we could have

pushed ourselves much harder. Would we have gone faster if we had tried a different strategy? Bernie said we should have skied hard for eight hours, stopped for four and kept going with that eight on, four off routine. I'd have been up for trying that but Ben and Ed wouldn't have wanted to take such a risk. Ultimately we didn't get the most out of our strategy anyway, and that was down to me. Ben had to cope with an aggressive treatment for Leishmaniasis and not knowing whether he'd be on the trip until a week before it was due to start. Ed had to come into the team late with two guys who knew each other well and as the only one who hadn't done a long endurance race. But I was the one who had let the team down. I should have tackled problems as soon as they arose, rather than carrying on. I should have stopped to repair my blisters when I first got them. I should have dealt with the pneumonia when it was a mild chest infection, instead of pressing on until it became so bad that it was frightening to sleep because I couldn't breathe. We had to set up camp early twice in the race because of me, and on one of those occasions, according to the Norwegians themselves, they were going to throw in the towel if they couldn't see us on the horizon the next morning. They kept going only because we'd had to stop early. For me.

Have I come to terms with potentially costing us the race? Not really, especially when I think of Ben and Ed. If I was in their situation how would I feel? I think there would be more recriminations. What I have to do is learn from the experience, listen to my body more and realize that pushing too hard is not a badge of honour. The human body is something that too many of us in society abuse and underestimate, and it is not until you witness the way it copes with extreme conditions that you fully appreciate it.

The Scott–Amundsen South Pole Station is good and evil combined, it looms like a shadow over the ceremonial South Pole, and because of the reflective globe it is impossible not to get it in the picture, either in the background or as a reflection. I wished it wasn't there. At least until I went inside: all people arriving at the Pole are allowed into the centre once to see the research that goes on there, fill their faces with cookies in the canteen and visit the toilet. I'm not sure what the scientists in charge of the neutrino research make of their multi-million-dollar programme being far less exciting than a biscuit and running water.

Having escaped the scientists we could go and visit the bathroom; I couldn't wait to wash my armpits and groin – I stank. It was the first time I'd seen my face in a mirror (unless you count the back of an iPod) since we left Cape Town, and I looked as though I'd been away for months rather than weeks. The real shock came when I took my top off for the first time since the race started: my body had disappeared, veins were running over my stomach because there was no fat any more, my arms were like pipe cleaners and my legs had disappeared. I stood on the scales: I'd lost 2 stone 13 pounds since leaving South Africa. Ed and Ben had both lost over 2 stone and none of us had either noticed or felt much weaker. The human body is utterly amazing.

As is the mind. Now we'd stopped racing I suddenly began to notice the cold, though admittedly the temperature at the Pole was minus 50. I struggled to get comfortable on the roll mats now that I knew I was so skinny and there was no fat to cushion me. As I lay in the tent and got some much-needed rest I wondered how Scott and his men coped having skied and walked for seventy-eight days by the time they reached the Pole, only to find they had been beaten here; and then had to make their way back to the coast in horrendous weather. Some seventy-two days later, Scott died, 11 miles before his reaching his next food depot. We'd raced flat out for eighteen days and I couldn't be bothered to get out of my sleeping bag to turn the stoves on. Not for the first time, I marvelled at what Scott had achieved a hundred years ago.

BEN We spent five long days huddled in our smelly, cramped tent at the South Pole. One of the two Basler planes that worked Antarctica had crashed while delivering a gearbox to Tony; fortunately the air crew had walked away from the crash, but the upshot was that we would have to wait for the sole remaining plane to reach us, as the other teams made their way to the finish line.

We had finished the race in 18 days, 5 hours and 10 minutes precisely, two days ahead of Team Danske Bank and four ahead of Due South and South Pole Flag, Mark achieving his incredible goal of becoming the first blind man to ski to the Pole.

It was a strange period during which sleep was our only form of escapism, peppered with surreal radio interviews over the satellite phone. The doctor had confirmed a frostbitten nose and warned me that I could well lose the end if it refroze, so I spent five days walking around with my hand over my face. We were hungry, cold and bored.

I thought back to the day in Starbucks when we had agreed to come here. It was a distant memory, lost in a fog of preparation, planning and training. We had come a long way since that cold chamber in Oxfordshire – halfway round the world, to be precise.

The dream had become a reality.

I looked at Ed with his blackened skin and his big red beard. Soon he would be back in hospital saving lives and delivering babies while I returned to the vacuous world of televison. I was proud as punch that we had given Ed this opportunity and I knew it would change him for ever, but it was James who had gone through the most profound change. He had been forced to confront and admit his fallibility and to concede weakness for the first time in his highly competitive life.

James was slumped in his seat, his eyes sunken, his hair dishevelled. He looked like someone who had, well, skied to the South Pole. It was a very different James from the one I had rowed across the Atlantic with. He was calmer, for a start – and kinder. He had gone through an almost Zen-like transformation, caging the competitive beast within that had worried me so much before the race, and grown as a man. Where once our relationship had been dominated by physical and sporting inequality, I suddenly felt we were equals. We had been through so much together and I finally felt I knew the real James. I understood why he had become my best friend.

We were like three old men, weathered and wizened by our experience. We hadn't conquered Antarctica, but we had tamed her. I thought back to that haunting image of Scott and his team at the South Pole, and though it was difficult to imagine the hardships they had suffered, we had experienced a small taste of their bleak journey, with a far happier outcome.

What had seemed impossible cooped up in a hospital all those months ago had been achieved. Impossible really is nothing.

JAMES I didn't have a life-changing experience as people who've spent time here intimated we might; instead I had something altogether better, a life-affirming one. I realized how lucky I am to have a beautiful wife who understands me and gives me the freedom to do stupid things and is a wonderful mother to Croyde, and I can hear Bev's voice now: 'You had to go to bloody Antarctica to work that out?' Isolation gives you the opportunity to appreciate things that are normally too close to step back from. I made promises that I hope to keep now that I'm back, such as making sure as a family we see more sky than skyscrapers. It wasn't until I had the luxury of endless horizons that I realized how closed in we are in London. We went away during a terrible time for the economy, when millions of people are struggling to pay their bills, have lost their pensions or their jobs – and, having been to a place where money is irrelevant and lived in basic conditions, I promised to reassess my priorities in life.

Once you've got a family there is no decision about what comes first when it really matters. I spoke to Bev from the South Pole four days after we had finished the race, as we were waiting for the plane to take us back to Novo. Croyde had been removed from the playground at school for fighting and pushing: I know every parent thinks their child does no wrong, but he is such a sweet boy. He knew the race was over and didn't understand why his daddy wasn't home and couldn't express his frustration in any other way. Being stuck on the other side of the world from the people who rely on, need and want you is an awful feeling. It was time to get on that plane.

BEN My frostbitten nose and James's fingers had finally started to heal. At least we wouldn't lose any of our extremities to Antarctica. I sat in the tiny World War II plane as we swooped low across the icy plains just a hundred feet below us. I felt elated. I finally felt I understood James and he me. But we weren't done yet. We still had some unfinished business.

A large smile broke across my face.

'James,' I smiled.

JAMES I was staring out of the window of the Basler making the most of the view before the window iced up, looking at the Pole surrounded by the flags, and wondered what it would have been like to have got there first and imagine we were the first people to discover it. I was lost in my daydream when Ben leaned over and said,

'I've got a great idea for another trip.'

Acknowledgements

With eighteen months' preparation there are so many people to thank, but first and foremost, thanks to Dr Ed Coats for being such a brilliant team mate.

Thanks to Jonny Lee Miller for letting us turn his life upside-down for a few months, and for getting Ben turfed out of a night club.

To Shane Slater, Simon Wickes, Jon Scott, Simon Henderson, Steve Hollidge and all the staff at QinetiQ; we wouldn't have got there without you.

Special thanks to Alexis Girardet, Keith Schofield, Roland Winkler and Georg Brodegger for being the best film crew in the world; to Mel Leach, Juliette Wide, Sharon O'Connell and all at TwoFour for believing in us again; and to Lisa Edwards and the BBC for commissioning *On Thin Ice*.

Thanks to Sparks for partnering up with us for a great cause.

Thanks to Jonny Butler for being the most incredible editor and putting this book together in record time, and to Helen Guthrie and all at Macmillan.

To Mountain Equipment, Suunto, Mountain Hardware, Nokia, RAB, Patagonia, X-socks, X-bionic, Icebreaker thermals, Buff, SIS, Adidas, Adidas Sunglasses, Garmin GPS, Red Bull, Sealskinz, Trek bikes, Breitling Emergency watches – thanks for keeping us energized, warm and going in the right direction.

To Neil Jones and all at MIRA, to Professor Mike Tipton at Portsmouth University Sports and Science department, Virgin Atlantic, Crans Montana Tourism, The Royal Geographical Society, Technogym, Paramount, Eton College and Dorney Lake, Croyde Beach, KX gym and all the staff, The Hogarth Club, Kiehls, Convatec, Mumm Champagne.

Thanks to Cassandra Jardine, Will Lewis, Mark Skipworth, Jon Stock and Keith Perry at the *Daily Telegraph* for being there from the start.

Thanks to BBC *Breakfast News* for following the story.

To the school of Tropical diseases, Dr Chris Van Tulleken, Dr Chi Eziefula, Professor Vega Lopez and the staff at University College Hospital for treating Ben . . . twice.

To Suzy Pearce, Anna Bruce, Jonathan Marks and all at MTC for handling so many curveballs over the last year; to Bernie 'I wouldn't be in your team' Shrosbree; to Chris Walton, Patrick Woodhead, Ben Saunders, Joanna Hall, Hilary Murray, Alison Griffin, and to Julian Alexander at LAW.

To Emma Channon and everybody at Threshold Sports for going beyond the call – more is in you! To Alan Watson for sorting out James's sacroiliac joint. To Tony Martin and all the team at the South Pole Race for organising such a cracking race, and to Dr Ian (Weasel) Davis.

Thanks from both of us to Karina and the Coats family for lending us their son/brother/boyfriend, Ed.

JAMES To Mum and Dad Cracknell for being put through the mill again; it's been a tough year for you and I love you both so much. To Joyce and Roger for being brilliant and ever-present parents-in-law and, along with Cal, Rick and Adi, for looking after Bev, Croyde and the then-bump when I was away. To Louise and Jon for the way you've handled a year that nobody should go through, you're an inspiration.

BEN To Cosi Pole and my sister Tamara for all your sewing and stitching and for the bespoke 'Polar snack bags'. To Mum and Dad Fogle for your unwavering support and love over the years. To the Cracknells, the Turners and to Bev and Croyde for lending me James again. To Monika and Jonathan Hunt for trusting your son-in-law and to Emily, Tamara, Chiara and Olivia for being the best sisters/sister-in-laws anyone could ask for. To my nephews, Taran and Joshan, may this inspire a life of adventure. To all my friends who supported me and looked after my beautiful wife while I was gone.